Contents

Lexical and structural

Deciding which word or phrase is the right one to use in a context depends on a number of factors.

The meaning of the word may not precisely translate the equivalent word in your own language and often the range of meaning of the English word may be different. You can only learn how to choose the right English word to use in context from seeing it or hearing it used because translation is not always satisfactory. These exercises are designed to show you contexts in which commonly confused words are used so that you can distinguish between them.

1 In each of the exercises below, choose the correct word or phrase from those given. Unless more than one possibility is indicated – (*or* ....) – only **one** of the words or phrases given in the list is correct in each space, though more than one may appear in the same sentence.

In Exercises **A–C**, put the verb in the correct form. In Exercises **D–F**, use the plural form of the noun where necessary.

A *become develop get grow grow up*

1 I'm going to be a doctor when I
....
2 My uncle .... tomatoes in his garden.
3 Why did you decide to .... a member of the society?
4 She didn't hear what you said. There's no need to .... upset about it.
5 They're doing research to .... new drugs to fight cancer.

B *discover find find out get to know know meet*

1 –Do you .... Sara Brown?
–Yes, we .... at a party last week.
2 I'm not going to tell you the answer. If you don't .... , ... for yourself!
3 They .... at university, ... each other on the course, and now they're getting married.
4 Have you .... the papers you were looking for?
5 Do you know who .... Antarctica?

6 I .... it hard to believe that your grandfather was born over a hundred years before you.

C *agree fit get on with match suit*

1 You've grown so fat recently that those trousers don't .... you any more.
2 – How is Jane .... the other girls in her class?
– Very well. She's made a lot of friends.
3 – We need a light brown carpet to .... the colour of the wallpaper.
– Yes, I .... How about that one?
4 Some girls don't look very smart in trousers but they .... Anne because she has a slim figure.

D *character characteristic humour mood personality temper*

1 My grandfather was a strange .... He behaved quite differently according to the .... he was in at the time.
2 He had a very strong .... (*or* ....) and he became really frightening if he lost his ....
3 In contrast, my grandmother's most noticeable .... was her calm and her quiet sense of ....

E *couple double duet pair twin*

1 I've sent my jacket and two .... of trousers to the cleaner's.
2 The bride and groom look a very happy .... (*or* ....).
3 He sang a .... with his wife at the concert.

4 – I say. There's a boy outside who looks just like you. He could be your
....
– That's my brother Eric. We're identical
....

5 Could you lend me some money? A
.... of ten-pound notes would be enough. I want to buy my sister a
.... of earrings for her birthday and I've forgotten my cheque book.

F father neighbour parent partner relative

1 Some of her .... disapprove of her marriage – her cousins, especially – but her .... are quite happy about it. Her mother thinks John will be a wonderful husband.

2 For this photograph I'd like the
.... of the bride and groom to stand on either side. You next to your son,

sir, and you next to your daughter.

3 I invited my business .... to the wedding but otherwise we kept it within the family. My wife wanted to invite Mrs Jones from next door and several other .... but we decided that would be too many people.

G alike common likely same similar

1 My sister and I don't look much
.... but we have a lot of things in ....

2 Her hair is a .... colour to mine though it's not exactly the ....

3 It's .... to be very warm today, the .... temperature as yesterday, according to the weather forecast.

Test 1

Read the text below and decide which word or phrase **A**, **B**, **C** or **D** best fits each space. There is an example at the beginning (**0**), which has been done for you. Underline the correct answer. Only one answer is correct.

My friend Lucy

My (0) .... friend's name is Lucy. She is also a (1) .... by marriage because (2) .... brother, William, married my sister, Ruth. Lucy is (3) .... than me but we (4) .... very well because we have (5) .... tastes and interests. We are about the same (6) .... but we don't look very much (7) .... because she is (8) .... while my skin and hair are (9) .... fairer than hers.

We first (10) .... at my sister's wedding. She is the (11) .... girl in her family so I thought she would be a (12) .... spoilt. But we liked (13) .... from the (14) .... moment and I soon (15) .... friends with her.

0	A more good	B most good	C better	D <u>best</u>
1	A familiar	B parent	C partner	D relative
2	A her	B his	C their	D your
3	A elder	B elderly	C more old	D older
4	A fit	B get on	C go on	D match
5	A alike	B likely	C same	D similar
6	A height	B high	C highness	D tall
7	A alike	B common	C like	D similar
8	A dark hair	B dark-haired	C hair dark	D haired dark
9	A many	B more	C most	D much
10	A encountered	B knew	C got to know	D met
11	A alone	B lonely	C only	D single
12	A few	B girl	C little	D lot
13	A each other	B one other	C ourselves	D the other
14	A first	B one	C prime	D principal
15	A got	B grew	C made	D went

2 In each of the exercises below, choose the correct word or phrase from those given. Unless more than one possibility is indicated – (*or* ....) – only **one** of the words or phrases given in the list is correct in each space, though more than one may appear in the same sentence.

In Exercises **A**–**C**, put the verb in the correct form. In Exercises **D**–**F**, use the plural form of the noun where necessary.

A *borrow lend owe pay pay for*

1 If I .... you the money, when will you .... me back?
2 I .... the money from my aunt to .... the alterations to the house.
3 Remember you still .... me the five pounds you .... from me last week.
4 The firm .... him at the end of the month but he immediately .... most of the money to his brother.
5 The bank won't .... me the money to .... my holiday because I .... them money already.

B *close guard keep lock put away shut*

1 He's bought a dog to .... the house when they're away.
2 The shops .... (*or* ....) early on Saturdays.
3 I always .... the important papers in my desk and the desk is always .... This is the key that opens it.
4 When you do the washing-up, ... all the plates in this cupboard.
5 She's bought a farm, and now she .... ducks and chickens.
6 He .... interrupting me. Why doesn't he .... up?

C *glance look regard see watch*

1 I don't know how you can waste time .... that programme every night. I don't know what you .... in it.
2 .... ! The sun's rising. If you .... (*or* ....) carefully, you'll .... it come over that hill.
3 I .... (*or* ....) in the shop window as I was passing by but didn't .... anything worth buying.
4 – .... at this picture carefully. Is this the man that stole your handbag?

5 I've always .... her as the most efficient woman in the office.

D *address direction site situation way*

1 Would you mind giving me your name and .... , sir?
2 I'll post the letter on my .... to the office.
3 – Excuse me, I think I've lost my .... I'm looking for this ....
   – I'm afraid you're going in the wrong ....
4 The house stands on the .... of the old castle.
5 I realise that because of your financial .... you need to sell the house quickly. We must decide on the best .... of doing it.

E *field flat floor ground soil*

1 He lives in this block in a .... on the third ....
2 He dropped the keys out of the window and they fell to the .... somewhere in the long grass in the .... at the back of the house.
3 I'm going to do some work in the garden. The .... 's quite hard so I need to do some digging. But it's easy to grow things in this area. We have very good ....
4 I want to wash the kitchen .... before we go out. The children were playing in the .... and came in with their shoes covered in mud.
5 It's confusing to Americans that what they call the first floor is called the .... floor in Britain.

F *intention matter meaning mind opinion*

1 It shouldn't be difficult to find a house in this area but it depends what you have in .... In my .... you should make a list of everything you require first.
2 You haven't eaten your dinner, and you look upset. What's the .... of this? Is anything the .... ?
3 It wasn't my .... to offend the neighbours but I suppose they misunderstood what I said.

4 He is a poet who likes to use words with more than one .... and so interpreting the poem often becomes a .... of personal ....

5 It's my .... to sell the house as soon as possible, but if I change my .... I'll let you know.

G *alone lonely only single unique*

1 I can assure you, Madam, that this house is .... You won't find anything like it anywhere else.

2 He lives .... in a .... cottage, miles from anywhere.

3 They liked the house very much. They hadn't a(n) .... complaint to make. The .... problem is that they can't really afford it.

4 I've stayed .... because the .... person I wanted to marry was already married to someone else but that doesn't mean I prefer to live .... It's .... if you have no one to talk to.

H *actually currently immediately presently suddenly*

1 I stood there wondering why there were so many flowers in the house and then I .... remembered it was her birthday.

2 If you'll just wait here for a few minutes, the doctor will see you ....

3 She's in a film that's .... on show in London. ...., it's the first time she's ever acted in a film.

4 I'll ring you .... I have any news for you.

Test 2

Read the text below and decide which word or phrase, **A**, **B**, **C** or **D** best fits each space. Underline the correct answer. Only one answer is correct.

Our neighbours

When you make up your (1) .... to buy a house, (2) .... of the things you are concerned with are practical, (3) .... deciding whether you can (4) .... it or the house is too far from the station. You do not usually get the chance to (5) .... about the neighbours before moving (6) ....

Flats are on the whole (7) .... houses from this point of view, but we have been lucky. When the old lady in the flat above saw we had a little boy, she was worried. 'I hope he won't make (8) .... noise,' she said. Fortunately, the man underneath us has a full-time (9) .... in the city, so he doesn't hear Tom running up and down all day. His main interest is (10) .... the communal garden. He told us when we moved in that we were (11) .... for mowing the (12) .... once a month. The young couple who live on the same (13) .... as us are very friendly; their only (14) .... is that they are very forgetful. The day we arrived, Betty came to ask us if she could (15) .... a phone call to Steve at work. She had come out without her keys and couldn't get back into her flat.

1	A decision	B intention	C mind	D opinion
2	A more	B most	C the more	D the most
3	A as	B such	C like	D example
4	A afford	B cost	C pay	D spend
5	A discover	B look up	C find	D find out
6	A address	B direction	C home	D house
7	A worse than	B worse that	C worst than	D worst that
8	A so many	B so much	C too many	D too much
9	A business	B employment	C job	D work
10	A attending	B assisting	C caring	D looking after
11	A careful	B expected	C interested	D responsible
12	A field	B green	C ground	D lawn
13	A flat	B floor	C ground	D level
14	A fault	B blame	C mistake	D guilt
15	A make	B do	C give	D put

3 In each of the exercises below, choose the correct word or phrase from those given. Unless more than one possibility is indicated – (*or* ....) – only **one** of the words or phrases given in the list is correct in each space, though more than one may appear in the same sentence.

In Exercises **A–C**, put the verb in the correct form. In Exercises **D–F**, use the plural form of the noun where necessary.

A *arrive get reach*

1 – What time does her flight ....?
   – It .... in at 7.30.
2 We .... the station just as the train was leaving.
3 When we .... at the cinema, the film had already started.
4 I don't think I'll have time to .... to the shops today.
5 Can you .... that packet on the top shelf?
6 – They took a long time to .... a decision.
   – Oh, and what decision did they finally .... at?
7 I tried to .... (*or* ....) you on the phone yesterday but you were out.
8 It was a very interesting book. I couldn't put it down until I .... to the end.

B *charge cost pay*

1 – How much did they ....you for that dress?
   – Oh, it didn't .... very much. It was a bargain. But they wouldn't accept my credit card. I had to .... cash.
2 I've .... the bill. They .... us extra for the wine and it .... ten pounds a bottle.
3 – The rooms .... a hundred pounds a night but they .... a hundred and fifty for a suite.
   – That's too expensive. I'm not going to .... that much.
4 I .... a visit to the bank the other day. Do you know they .... you these days if they write you a letter?
5 If you don't .... attention when they're adding up your bill they may .... you too much and it could .... you a lot of money.

C *enjoy matter mind prefer would like would rather*

1 I .... shopping in the High Street. I .... shop there than in the big supermarket.
2 .... you .... keeping an eye on the dog while I go into the shop?
3 In general I .... to eat at home but I .... to go out to dinner this evening.
4 – .... you .... to have steak for dinner?
   – I .... have fish, if you don't .... But if you've already bought steak, it doesn't .... I'll have that.
5 I .... shopping in the market to taking the car to the new shopping centre. For one thing, I .... talking to the people on the stalls. They probably charge a bit more but I don't .... that. I .... do that than have to wait for half an hour to park the car. Time .... as well as money.

D *advertisement advice announcement notice publicity*

1 I see Mary's got engaged. There was a(n) .... about it in the newspaper.
2 I'm sorry but we can't let you bring your trolley into the supermarket. There's a .... about it over the door.
3 I don't care how beautiful their jumpers are. I would never buy anything from a company that uses disgusting .... like that to give .... to its products.
4 Take my .... and look at the sell-by date on the packet before you buy any of these products at reduced prices.

E *count level limit number rate*

1 I never remember my passport ....
2 Fortunately, the crime .... is falling. Fewer crimes were committed in the city last year.
3 He was driving at 50 miles an hour, well over the speed .... in a built-up area.
4 We've had so many requests for the book that I've lost .... The total .... must be well over a thousand.
5 The .... of the water is rising fast. At this .... there is serious danger of flooding.

F *bill fare fee fine tip*

1 Can you tell me what the bus .... is to the High Street?
2 He had to pay a .... because he parked his car outside the supermarket entrance.
3 Taxi drivers around here expect a .... as well as the .... for the journey.
4 I've got to pay the children's school .... this week, as well as the gas and electricity ....

G *crowded full plenty plentiful*

1 The shop's .... of people. I'll come back later.
2 The store is always .... with people when the annual sales are on.
3 There's no need to hurry. There's .... of time before the shops open.

4 You'll find a .... variety of fruit at the greengrocer's.

H *ago during for since while*

1 Oh, look, strawberries! I haven't had any .... ages, ... I was on holiday last year, in fact.
2a They opened the supermarket about a year ....
 b It's been open .... about a year.
 c It's been open .... last summer.
3a .... we're in town, we can do the shopping.
 b We can do the shopping ....our visit to town.
4 That baker's has been here .... a long time, ... I first came here. .... that time, one or two rival bakers have opened and closed – the last one closed only a little while ....

Test 3

Read the text below and decide which word or phrase, **A**, **B**, **C** or **D** best fits each space. Underline the correct answer. Only one answer is correct.

Two American cities

I (1) .... to the United States (2) .... a few years now but I (3) .... remember my first visit (4) .... clearly. Most Europeans (5) .... hundreds of American films and so everything seems familiar as soon as you arrive (6) .... Kennedy airport. I spent a few days in two cities, New York and Boston. New York, of course, is very lively and (7) .... of activity, but I don't think I would (8) .... to live there. The worst thing about it were the taxidrivers. Apart from (9) .... a lot of money, none of them seemed (10) .... English and they pretended they did not know how to (11) .... to places everyone has heard of, like the Empire State Building. I preferred Boston (12) .... New York, partly because I felt (13) .... walking around the streets at night – I am sure the crime (14) .... is much lower – but also because I got on better with the people there. Perhaps it was just that I could (15) .... what they were saying.

1	A	don't go	B	am not going	C	haven't been	D	haven't gone
2	A	for	B	since	C	during	D	it's
3	A	already	B	ever	C	still	D	yet
4	A	as	B	enough	C	too	D	very
5	A	have seen	B	saw	C	were seeing	D	have been seeing
6	A	at	B	on	C	through	D	to
7	A	plenty	B	plentiful	C	full	D	crowded
8	A	like	B	mind	C	rather	D	enjoy
9	A	asking	B	charging	C	costing	D	insisting
10	A	speak	B	speaking	C	to speak	D	they spoke
11	A	arrive	B	get	C	make	D	reach
12	A	as	B	than	C	that	D	to
13	A	safer	B	safely	C	more safe	D	more safely
14	A	count	B	limit	C	number	D	rate
15	A	know	B	realise	C	discriminate	D	understand

4 In each of the exercises below, choose the correct word or phrase from those given. Unless more than **one** possibility is indicated – (*or ....*) – only one of the words or phrases given in the list is correct in each space, though more than one may appear in the same sentence.

In Exercises **A–C**, put the verb in the correct form. In Exercises **D–G**, use the plural form of the noun where necessary. Before completing Exercise **H**, study the Appendix on Connectors on page 116.

A *appoint choose elect nominate pick*

In this exercise, only use *choose* if it is the **only** possible answer.

1 He's been .... as the Liberal candidate in the elections and this time we hope he will get enough votes to be .... to Parliament.

2 Before .... her to be head teacher, we made a short list, ... out the three best qualified candidates from those who applied for the post.

3 I'd like a volunteer from the audience to .... the winning number out of this hat.

4 Everyone plays football at this school except those who .... to play hockey.

B *bring up educate instruct learn study teach*

1 – He's been very well ....! He went to one of the most expensive private schools in the country.
– Well, it's a pity they didn't .... him manners there. He behaves very badly.
– Oh, well, they think it's the parents' job to .... children.

2 – Where did you .... to play tennis?
– Well, my parents .... me how to play, and then I had a coach to .... me in the finer points of the game.

3 She's at the university, ... to be a doctor. They .... the theory there but of course it's the practical experience in a hospital that .... them most of what they need.

C *lay (laid, laid (laying)) lie (lay, lain (lying))*

1 Don't just .... on the floor, doing nothing! You can help me by .... the table, ready for dinner.

2 – I found this box outside the door on the ground. The caretaker just left it .... there, I suppose.
– I know what it is. Just .... it down in the corner over there, will you?

3 The old city .... at the foot of the mountain. The Romans .... the foundations for it two thousand years ago.

4 I've .... awake since I woke up listening to the birds singing and the hens, too, clucking every time one of them has .... an egg.

D *file procession queue rank row*

1 When the teacher turned round, all the children in the back .... started laughing.

2 Every year there is a .... to the village church and the children walk in single .... behind the priest.

3 He has been promoted to the .... of Captain.

4 Look at that woman going to the front of the .... when the rest of us have been waiting here for half an hour. Hey!

E *certificate degree experience licence qualification*

Apart from possessing the necessary academic ...., a university .... in economics, the successful candidate will also need to demonstrate previous .... in a similar field of work. Candidates should possess a current driving .... and should attach a photocopy of their birth .... to their application.

F *game hobby move play practice sport*

1 He's not interested in playing .... or doing any outdoor .... like cycling or skiing. But he should have some kind of .... to keep him occupied, collecting stamps or something like that.

2 It's one thing to pass the ball well in ....; it's another to do it on the field of .... at a vital moment.

3 The surprise of today's .... at Wimbledon was the defeat of Smith. He has not played very much this year and looked out of ....

G *damage harm injury pain wound*

1 She's cut her knee and it's quite a deep .... so it will take some time to heal.

2 He's had an accident. Fortunately, no one suffered any serious .... but there was quite a lot of .... to the car.

3 If you are still in .... tonight, take an aspirin. It won't do you any ....

4 Plenty of children play games like rugby without coming to any .... but there's no doubt that .... on the field are quite frequent.

5 People say that you don't feel any .... immediately after you are shot, but I noticed it as soon as I saw the bullet .... in my leg.

H One word is missing from each of the phrases in **bold** type. Complete the phrases with the correct word.

.... **the whole**, students at private schools achieve better examination results than those at state schools, but to argue from this that they provide better education is only true **up to a** .... Students at private schools have many advantages. **As a** .... classes are smaller, and .... **general** the students live in homes with better conditions for study. You may think that as private school teachers are better paid, ... **speaking**, they should teach better, but that is only true **to a certain** .... **the main**, teachers are motivated by vocation, not by how much they earn.

Test 4

Read the text below and decide which word or phrase, **A**, **B**, **C** or **D** best fits each space. Underline the correct answer. Only one answer is correct.

First day at a new school

On the whole I (1) .... a good time at school. Of course I (2) .... into trouble sometimes but I don't think it did me any (3) .... For instance, I remember my first day at a new school near my home when I was about eight (4) ....; up till then I (5) .... going to one that had involved a long bus (6) .... every day. I already knew some children at the school and I supposed that I would (7) .... reasonable progress in class because I had always (8) .... attention and had very seldom been (9) .... from school because of illness.

On the first day I joined in a (10) .... with a hard ball before school started, and unfortunately broke our classroom window. Then I reached through the window to get the ball back and cut (11) .... hand. When we went into class the teacher asked who had broken the window. (12) .... said anything. Then the teacher came to the back (13) ...., where I was sitting, and said: 'How (14) .... that?', pointing to my hand. I looked down as a little (15) .... of blood fell on the floor beside me.

1	A got	B had	C passed	D spent
2	A fell	B got	C was	D went
3	A harm	B hurt	C pain	D wrong
4	A year	B years	C year old	D years old
5	A was	B would be	C had been	D have been
6	A drive	B journey	C travel	D voyage
7	A do	B get	C obtain	D make
8	A cared	B looked	C paid	D showed
9	A absent	B missed	C out	D truant
10	A game	B joke	C play	D sport
11	A me	B my	C myself	D the
12	A Anyone	B No one	C None	D Someone
13	A file	B line	C range	D row
14	A did you	B did you do	C did you make	D you did
15	A drip	B drop	C piece	D spill

5 In each of the exercises below, choose the correct word or phrase from those given. Unless more than one possibility is indicated – (*or* ....) – only **one** of the words or phrases given in the list is correct in each space, though more than one may appear in the same sentence.

In Exercises **A**–**C**, put the verb in the correct form. In Exercises **D**–**F**, use the plural form of the noun where necessary.

A *achieve cope manage reach succeed*

1a If the company .... to make a profit this year, its problems will be solved.

 b If the company .... in making a profit this year, its problems will be solved.

2 She was determined to .... her ambition, to .... the top in the company.

3 We have an enormous number of problems to .... with but I have no doubt we will .... in the end.

4 You needn't bother to help me. I can .... (*or* ....) on my own.

5 We have .... (*or* ....) the export targets for the year.

B *attend expect hope look forward to wait*

1a We .... to increase our sales this year. The market prospects are very good.

 b We .... to increase our sales this year, even though the prospects are not very good.

2a I wrote to them last week so I'm .... an answer quite soon.

 b I wrote to them last week but I'm still .... for an answer.

3 We .... hearing from you soon. Our kindest regards to your parents.

4 I was .... being present at the conference, but now I'm not sure if I'll be able to .... I .... (*or* ....) so but something may come up at the last minute.

5 We've been .... here for half an hour. I .... there's a lot of traffic on the road and the bus is delayed.

C *can't stand put up with resist support tolerate*

1 I .... the sight of rats. They make me feel sick.

2 The firm want the workers to work longer hours. A few of us are in favour. We'll .... the idea if they pay us extra. But the union is against it on principle. They're certain to .... it.

3 I don't mind staff arriving late occasionally but I'm not prepared to .... (*or* ....) rudeness.

4 He doesn't earn enough in this job to .... his family.

5 I .... Mr Evans. He makes such unpleasant remarks. I don't know why the rest of you .... it, either.

D *career course duty employment job work*

1 If you plan to make a .... as an engineer, this .... of study at the university is the most suitable one for you.

2 Police are not supposed to drink when they're on .... and I don't to drink when I'm at .... , either.

3 He's got a wonderful new .... in Scotland. It will be very hard .... at first but I'm sure he'll enjoy it.

4 The Government is committed to a policy of full .... but that doesn't mean we can find a .... for everyone who is out of ....

E *company enterprise factory industry manufacture product*

1 The .... has built several .... in the area to make its ....

2 These days the chemical .... is subject to a number of controls regulating the .... of its ....

3 If you want to build up a .... into a serious competitor with others in the .... , you need a spirit of .... and the willingness to take risks.

4 The old argument between the supporters of private .... and state ownership still goes on.

F *aspect attitude opinion respect view*

1 In my .... (*or* ....) you have to have the right .... to work to succeed in this job.

2 From some points of .... the idea is a good one but there's one .... of the

problem that it doesn't deal with.

3   Out of .... for public .... ,
    we will not make a decision until all
    .... of the matter have been studied.

4   He's a good worker in some .... but
    I don't like his .... towards his
    colleagues. Still, in .... of his youth,
    we'll take no notice.

G   able   capable   reliable   responsible

1   I don't think I'll be .... to finish the
    job on time.

2   She's .... of doing any job you give
    her in the office.

3   – Who's .... for typing the letters?
    – Joan, but she's not very .... , I'm
    afraid. She's .... of making ten
    careless mistakes in a paragraph.

4   Acting on .... information received,
    the police have been .... to arrest the
    men .... for circulating false
    banknotes. An expert commented that the
    forged notes were .... of deceiving
    almost anyone.

**H   at present   at this moment
    in those days   nowadays**

1   They used to set the type by hand ....
    .... it's done by machine, of course.

2a We have no vacancies for new employees
    .... but if you leave your telephone
    number, we'll get in touch with you.

 b I'm not sure where she is .... but if
    you leave your telephone number, I'll get her
    to ring you.

Test 5

Read the text below and decide which word or phrase, **A**, **B**, **C** or **D** best fits each space. Underline the correct
answer. Only one answer is correct.

Temps

Temps are people (1) .... to work when (2) .... is ill or (3) .... Most of them are temporary
secretaries, so they must be (4) .... to go into a different office every time they are employed. Twenty
years ago all (5) .... was required of a temp was shorthand and typing but (6) .... a secretary needs
(7) .... a number of computer programs.
Penny Andrews has been a temp for over 40 years. 'I'd rather (8) .... have a permanent job,' she says.
'At my age I want to be free to take a week (9) .... when I feel like it; (10) .... that, I like the
(11) .... of going somewhere different all the time. The worst thing about temping,' she says, 'is
finding out where everything is. The boss (12) .... you to know where all his files are, (13) ....
you've only just arrived. Other secretaries aren't very (14) .... on helping you, because they know you
won't be there for long. You have to have the right (15) ...., be charming and persistent.'

1	A	which come	B	which comes	C	who come	D	who comes
2	A	anyone else	B	anyone other	C	someone else	D	someone other
3	A	in holiday	B	on holiday	C	in holidays	D	on holidays
4	A	able	B	capable	C	reliable	D	responsible
5	A	that	B	what	C	which	D	work
6	A	actually	B	instantly	C	this time	D	these days
7	A	know	B	knowing	C	known	D	to know
8	A	temp to	B	temp than	C	to temp to	D	to temp than
9	A	off	B	holiday	C	out	D	leave
10	A	apart from	B	as well as	C	beside	D	nevertheless
11	A	aim	B	challenge	C	intention	D	success
12	A	demands	B	expects	C	hopes	D	supposes
13	A	although	B	whether	C	even	D	however
14	A	eager	B	enthusiastic	C	keen	D	willing
15	A	aspect	B	attitude	C	point	D	view

6 In each of the exercises below, choose the correct word or phrase from those given. Unless more than one possibility is indicated – (*or* ....) – only **one** of the words or phrases given in the list is correct in each space, though more than one may appear in the same sentence.

In Exercises **A**–**D**, put the verb in the correct form. In Exercises **E**–**G**, use the plural form of the noun where necessary.

A *ask ask for claim demand insist*

1 This is a first-class ticket. I .... second-class.
2 .... him if the train goes to London.
3 At the border, they .... me my name, and also .... (*or* ....) evidence of my identity.
4 When the inspector .... to see his ticket, he .... he had lost it.
5 I .... an explanation for this treatment. I .... on seeing the station manager.
6 You .... this seat is yours. I didn't see you sitting here but we can talk to the inspector about it if you ....

B *climb drive get in(to) get on(to) mount ride*

1a He .... (*or* ....) his horse and .... away.
 b She .... her car and .... away.
2 She has .... most of the highest mountains in the Alps.
3a ....! There's room for you in the back seat.
 b ....! You can sit behind me on the scooter.
4 I learnt to .... a bicycle when I was six but I have never learnt to .... a car.

C *bend fold wind wrap*

1 You must slow down. There's a sign showing that the road .... sharply there.
2 The road .... through the forest, following the course of the river.
3 I've .... your clothes up carefully and put them in your suitcase.
4 .... the present up in this pretty paper.

5 Don't .... this envelope. There's a photograph inside.
6 .... up warmly because it's cold outside.
7 He .... down and picked up the envelope from the floor.
8 My watch is slow. I forgot to .... it up.

D *insist persist persuade suggest urge*

1 I've tried to .... him to come skiing with us this weekend but he won't agree. I .... that you should talk to him but if he .... in his attitude, we'll have to go without him.
2 I .... them not to go by car because it would be tiring for the children, but they .... on the advantages. However, I finally managed to .... them.
3 His companions .... taking the east route up the mountain but he .... in the idea of climbing by the west.

E *audience onlookers sightseers spectators viewers*

1 There were 50,000 .... at the football match.
2 The programme was watched by several million ....
3 The .... applauded at the end of the concert.
4 The beautiful city square is a great attraction to ....
5 There were several .... when the fight started but they just stood there, doing nothing.

F *band crew gang group party staff team*

1 He formed part of a ....(*or* ....) of criminals who robbed banks.
2 My wife and I belong to the same blood ....
3 A search .... are out looking for the lost climbers.
4 Johnny plays the trumpet in the school ....
5 When the ship sank, all the .... were drowned.
6 There are lots of pictures of wedding .... in the photographer's window.

7 I think they're the best .... in the football league.

8 I've never wanted to join a political ....

9 All the .... of the firm came to her goodbye ....

10 You get the best results in a company if all the .... work together as a ....

G *award cost expense price prize reward*

1 He had the hospital built at his own ....

2 The .... of living goes up every year. The .... in the shops are terribly high.

3 The police have offered a thousand pounds .... to anyone who can give them information about the robbery.

4 The court has made a(n) .... of several thousand pounds to the people who were injured.

5 I'll pay for the meal. I'll put it on my .... account.

6 She won first .... in the competition.

7 What .... are they asking for apples today?

8 The .... of the Nobel .... to Professor Smith is a just .... for his contribution to science.

Test 6

Read the text below and decide which word or phrase, **A**, **B**, **C** or **D** best fits each space. Underline the correct answer. Only one answer is correct.

The paper chase

Last weekend the kids (1) .... us to join a (2) .... to take part in a paper chase. In this kind of race you have to solve clues to find check-points (3) .... the way. The first people to reach the finish after (4) .... in at all the points win the (5) ....

We (6) .... up warmly because it was cold, and met the other competitors at the start. There were a lot of (7) .... to see us set out. (8) .... we made good time; while others (9) .... and wandered around, not knowing (10) .... way to go, we guessed the answers to the clues very quickly.

All went well (11) .... we decided that the quickest way to the final checkpoint in the village was to climb a steep hill. I can't (12) .... heights but the kids (13) .... on it. When we reached the top, we (14) .... see the village below us but there was no way down. We had to retrace our steps and by the time we got to the village, everyone else was there (15) .... for us.

		A		B		C		D	
1	A	persuaded	B	suggested	C	proposed	D	insisted
2	A	band	B	crew	C	group	D	team
3	A	on	B	in	C	at	D	through
4	A	check	B	checking	C	checked	D	to check
5	A	award	B	price	C	prize	D	reward
6	A	clothed	B	dressed	C	folded	D	wrapped
7	A	audience	B	sightseers	C	spectators	D	watchers
8	A	At first	B	Beginning	C	Firstly	D	Principally
9	A	lost	B	loosed	C	got lost	D	missed
10	A	best	B	how	C	what	D	which
11	A	as far as	B	unless	C	until	D	while
12	A	stand	B	put up	C	suffer	D	support
13	A	persisted	B	insisted	C	demanded	D	urged
14	A	can	B	could	C	may	D	might
15	A	attending	B	expecting	C	hoping	D	waiting

7 In each of the exercises below, choose the correct word or phrase from those given. Unless more than one possibility is indicated – (or ....) – only **one** of the words or phrases given in the list is correct in each space, though more than one may appear in the same sentence.

In Exercise **A–C**, put the verb in the correct form. In Exercises **D–F**, use the plural form of the noun where necessary.

A *arise get up lift raise (raised, raised (raising)) rise (rose, risen (rising))*

1 The company have .... their prices considerably this year, but after all, prices are .... everywhere.

2 I always .... when the sun .... in the morning.

3 I booked my holiday last month but a number of difficulties have .... since then.

4 The baby's getting too heavy for her to ....

5 I haven't .... the question before because it wasn't appropriate but now these difficulties have ...., I've decided to .... at the meeting and speak my mind.

B *carry dress put on wear*

1 She .... very well, in my opinion. She always .... something that looks smart.

2 I got ...., ... my shoes and went out.

3 She was .... gloves and .... an umbrella.

4 The bride .... white and .... a bouquet of flowers, while her sisters were .... in blue.

5 She .... the children very well, though it must cost a lot of money.

6 Have you .... weight since I last saw you?

C *drip drop fall pour sink spill*

1 She .... the milk jug and .... the milk on the floor.

2 Would you mind .... the tea?

3 The heavy box .... to the bottom of the river.

4 Careful! The floor is slippery and you might ....

5 The water was slowly .... from the ceiling and onto the kitchen floor.

6 It's raining heavily outside. It's .... down!

7 I was so tired that I .... asleep immediately.

8 Oh dear, I've .... coffee on my new dress!

D *excursion flight journey travel voyage*

In this exercise, only use *journey* if it is the **only** possible answer.

1a You're going by train. Is it a long ....?

b You're going by sea. Is it a long ....?

c You're going by air. Is it a long ....?

2 I went to the .... agent's to book a full-day .... to the mountains tomorrow.

3 We announce the departure of .... 169 to Athens.

4 He wrote a book about his .... round the world in a boat.

5 I'm very fond of foreign .... but I always make sure I have something interesting to read on the ....

E *outbreak outcome outdoor outfit outlet outlook output outskirts*

1 She's an .... girl. She loves being out in the open air.

2 They've built a house on the .... of the city.

3 There has been an .... of disease among the sheep.

4 The water flows down under the rock here, looking for an ....

5 The .... of the factory last year amounted to a million tons.

6 They were discussing the topic when I left, but I don't know what the .... of the discussion was.

7 That's a smart skiing .... you're wearing!

8 The weather has been rather disappointing today but the .... for tomorrow is fine and dry.

F *protection refuge shade shadow*

1 We took shelter from the storm in a mountain ....

2 It's very cool here in the ...., under the trees, and they give you a degree of .... from the sun.

3 The sun does not reach that part of the garden. It remains in ....

4 Wherever you go your .... will follow you.

5 His paintings are a wonderful contrast of light and ....

G *common ordinary popular vulgar*

1 It's a(n) .... fishing village – there's nothing very special about it – but it's become a(n) .... holiday resort in recent years.

2 Goats are quite .... in the mountains round here.

3 I think it's a(n) .... form of entertainment, in very bad taste, but it seems to be .... with young people.

H *beside besides except nearby next to*

1 We sheltered from the rain under some trees ...., ... a mountain stream.

2 He sat .... (*or* ....) me on the flight from Madrid.

3 I enjoyed the holiday, ... for the weather, which was very bad.

4 She lives ...., in that house over there.

5 I don't think I'll have time to go on holiday this year. ...., I can't afford it.

Test 7

Read the text below and decide which word or phrase, **A**, **B**, **C** or **D** best fits each space. Underline the correct answer. Only one answer is correct.

A storm in the mountains

We spent a few days last summer in the mountains. We (1) .... leave the car in the village and go for long walks. In general we had (2) .... weather but it can change very quickly, (3) .... we discovered one morning. It is also important to be properly equipped. As we climbed up a muddy path I (4) .... twice because I wasn't (5) .... the right sort of boots.

We were heading (6) .... a shelter where people can take (7) .... if they are (8) .... in a snowstorm in winter. (9) .... it, there is a café, open in the summer months. Suddenly a dark cloud came towards us and it started to rain quite (10) .... Soon it was (11) .... down and we were soaked to the skin. The storm passed as we struggled on up the slope, but (12) .... this time our clothes were steaming in the warm sunshine, and we were beginning to regret having come on our (13) .... When we reached the café the people there (14) .... out laughing as they saw us come in with the steam (15) .... from our clothes.

		A	B	C	D
1		usually	used	used to	were used to
2		good	a good	the good	so good
3		as	like	so	when
4		dropped	sank	swung	slipped
5		carrying	dressed in	putting on	wearing
6		at	for	there	to
7		protection	refuge	retreat	shade
8		caught	held	overtaken	surprised
9		Along	Next	Beside	Besides
10		hard	hardly	heavily	strong
11		dripping	dropping	pouring	throwing
12		at	by	for	in
13		outcome	outing	outdoors	outbreak
14		burst	rang	shouted	threw
15		lifting	putting up	raising	rising

8 In each of the exercises below, choose the correct word or phrase from those given. Unless more than one possibility is indicated – (*or* ....) – only **one** of the words or phrases given in the list is correct in each space, though more than one may appear in the same sentence.

In Exercises **A**–**C**, put the verb in the correct form. In Exercises **D**–**F**, use the plural form of the noun where necessary.

A *remark say speak talk tell*

1a 'Hello,' she ...., 'my name's Sally.'
 b She .... 'hello' and .... me her name was Sally.
2a 'It's the first time I've been here,' she .... (*or* ....).
 b 'It's the first time I've been here,' she .... me.
3a No one .... when I came in.
 b No one .... anything when I came in.
4a If you have any problems, you should ....(*or* ....) to the manager about it.
 b If you have any problems, you should .... the manager.
5 How many foreign languages can you ....?
6 Can you .... me where she lives?
7 Pay attention and don't start .... while I'm writing on the blackboard.
8 I don't know if the story he .... us was true.
9 While I was .... (*or* ....) to Jane at the party, she.................. me her daughter was getting married. She .... (*or* ....) that it had come as a surprise to her.
10 When Mr Jones arrives, ... him to come in, please.

B *indicate nod shake sign wave*

1 The old man .... his head. 'I don't know where she lives,' he said.
2 We .... hands and he got into the train. As it was leaving he .... goodbye to me.
3 They all .... their heads to .... their agreement.
4a She .... her umbrella to attract the taxi driver's attention.

 b She .... her wet umbrella to get the water out.
5 This parcel is for you. Would you mind .... for it?

C *intend mean plan pretend try*

1 I don't know what this word ....
2 You have to .... for the future if you want to succeed.
3 He .... he was in love with her but she knew he was lying.
4 You see all these travel brochures? I'm .... my holiday. I'm .... to find the cheapest way of going round the world. I could fly to Japan via the North Pole but that .... missing out America.
5a I .... (*or* ....) to warn him of the risk but I forgot.
 b I .... to warn him of the risk but he wouldn't listen.

D *blow crash knock shock stroke*

1 What was that? It sounded like a .... at the door.
2 He was badly injured in a car ....
3 The old lady wasn't hurt but the experience had frightened her. She was suffering from ....
4 He knocked the burglar down with one ....
5 Motor cyclists have to wear .... helmets because a .... on the head could kill them.
6 At the third .... the time will be exactly ten o'clock.
7 Don't touch that! You could get an electric ....
8 The people in the boat saw me fall into the water and rescued me. What a .... of luck!

E *accident chance luck occasion opportunity*

1 If you have the ....(*or* ....) of going round the world, you should take it.
2 He has .... to travel quite a lot in the course of his work.
3 Good ....! I hope you win.
4 We met in the street, quite by ....(*or* ....).

F *attempt intention process proof trial*

1   He climbed the mountain at his first
....

2   Before you can get a work permit you have to
get a certificate of good conduct as
.... of good behaviour. It can be
quite a long .... because the papers
have to go to the capital.

3   Our .... is to submit the ....
to extensive .... to see if it works as
well as they say.

4   At his .... the prosecution made a
(an) .... to show that it was his
.... to kill his brother but they could
provide no ....

G *at the same time during meanwhile while*

1a   The accident occurred .... the
voyage.

 b   The accident occurred .... they were
on a voyage.

2a   .... he was climbing the mountain,
the rest of the team were waiting patiently in
the camp.

 b   We saw him slowly climbing the mountain;
....................., we waited patiently in the camp.

3   The accident occurred because he was trying
to do two things ....

4a   I lived in New York .... the 1970s
.... as Jack.

 b   Jack lived in New York .... I was there.

Test 8

Read the text below and decide which word or phrase, **A**, **B**, **C** or **D** best fits each space. Underline the correct
answer. Only one answer is correct.

Arctic encounter

In his memoirs, the Norwegian polar explorer, Fridtjof Nansen, (1) .... an interesting story of survival.
Nansen and a companion, Johansen, had (2) .... out to reach the North Pole (3) ...., but had had
to abandon their (4) .... when they were 400 kilometres from their destination. They (5) .... to
survive the winter in a hut, living on bear meat. (6) ...., though they were unaware of it, (7) ....
expedition, led by an Englishman, Frederick Jackson, was camped about 150 kilometres away.
(8) .... the following summer, Nansen saw a dog's tracks in the snow, and heard a man shouting. He
was so (9) .... that he wondered if he was dreaming. Then he saw the man in the distance and
(10) .... to him. The man came towards him and they (11) .... hands. Nansen recognised Jackson
because they had been (12) .... on a previous (13) .... but Jackson did not recognise him at first
because his face was black with the (14) .... from his camp fire. Then he suddenly said: 'Good
heavens! You're Nansen, aren't you?' He (15) .... to take him back to Europe in his ship.

1	A	says	B	tells	C	gives	D	remarks
2	A	set	B	put	C	gone	D	left
3	A	by foot	B	on foot	C	with foot	D	walking
4	A	attempt	B	essay	C	intent	D	trial
5	A	could	B	might	C	managed	D	succeeded
6	A	Currently	B	During	C	Meanwhile	D	While
7	A	another	B	other	C	some other	D	one other
8	A	A day	B	One day	C	A time	D	One time
9	A	exciting	B	excited	C	emotional	D	moving
10	A	indicated	B	signed	C	talked	D	waved
11	A	gave	B	offered	C	shook	D	showed
12	A	introduced	B	made known	C	met	D	presented
13	A	happening	B	opportunity	C	time	D	occasion
14	A	cloud	B	flame	C	fog	D	smoke
15	A	claimed	B	delighted	C	offered	D	would

9 In each of the exercises below, choose the correct word or phrase from those given. Unless more than one possibility is indicated – (*or ....*) – only **one** of the words or phrases given in the list is correct in each space, though more than one may appear in the same sentence.

In Exercises **A**–**D**, put the verb in the correct form. In Exercises **E**–**F**, use the plural form of the noun where necessary.

A *approve lose miss pass spend waste*

1 Hurry up, or you'll .... the bus!
2 Oh, dear! I think I've .... my watch!
3 He didn't .... the exam because he .... (*or* ....) most of his time playing football.
4 She doesn't .... of students .... lectures without a reasonable excuse.
5 He had .... his way and so he .... by her house without realising it.
6 I don't see any harm in you .... the weekends climbing as long as your parents ....
7 She was my best friend at school and I .... her now that she's gone abroad.

B *prove test try try on try out*

1a I'd like to .... that dress to see if it fits me.
 b I'd like to .... the new model of the car.
2 I hope your tea is sweet enough. .... it and see if you like it.
3 If the door doesn't open, ... using this key.
4 All our products are .... before they leave the factory, and if any of them .... to be faulty, we will replace them free of charge.
5 We .... the paint used in the picture and .... that it was a fake.
6 I .... (*or* ....) the recipe you gave me and the meal .... a great success.

C *memorise remember remind*

1 I don't .... when I last had my eyes tested. .... me to make an appointment with the optician.

2 When I was at school we had to .... whole poems and recite them in class. I could never .... all the lines so I used to make notes on the back of my hand to .... me.
3 That girl .... me of my sister Alice.
4 I must .... to ask the teacher what that word meant.

D *consider realise regard think of*

1a That painting is .... to be his masterpiece.
 b That painting is .... as his masterpiece.
2 What do you .... this picture? Isn't it wonderful?
3 I .... (*or* ....) buying that picture for my living room but when I saw the price I .... I couldn't afford it.
4 I was so interested in the objects in the museum that I didn't .... what time it was until I noticed the caretaker beside me, ... me with an impatient expression.

E *appearance aspect complexion expression outline*

1 The Mona Lisa is famous for the mysterious .... on her face.
2 We expect our employees to present a smart, attractive .... to the public.
3 Now Doris uses our revolutionary skin cream, all her friends envy her fresh ....
4 At first sight, it has the .... of being a Roman camp but if you study these aerial photographs you can see the .... of a much older settlement underneath.
5 The book is interesting as an .... of deep personal feeling and it gives a brief .... of the history of the country at the beginning, but the only .... that really concerns me is the effect it may have politically.

F *autograph firm mark sign signature subject*

1 Is this where we turn left? What does that .... say?
2 The black horse is the trade .... of the .... he works for.
3 You've got a black .... on your nose. Here's a handkerchief to rub it off.

4 On the entrance form for the exam you must indicate all the .... you are taking; it is not valid without your .... at the bottom.

5 – That's the lead singer of the Idiots. My brother's got his ....
– Really? I'm surprised he can write. I'd imagine he'd just put a .... on the paper.

G *foreign odd rare scarce strange*

1 Seven is a(n) .... number.

2 Have you visited many .... countries?

3 I've never seen a wild cat. They're very .... in this area.

4 The bad weather spoilt the harvest this year so apples are rather .... at present.

5 I never feel comfortable in a .... house where I've never stayed before.

6 I'm not going shopping yet. I've got a few .... jobs to do around the house.

H *at one time at once one day*
once upon a time once and for all

1 .... there was an old woman who lived in the middle of a forest. .... she saw two children coming towards her cottage.

2 .... it was believed that these stones dated from prehistoric times but now they are thought to be more recent.

3a You must do something about it .... It's urgent.

b You must do something about it .... but there's no hurry.

4 I've warned you for the last time. ...., if you don't work harder, you'll lose your job.

Test 9

Read the text below and decide which word or phrase, **A**, **B**, **C** or **D** best fits each space. Underline the correct answer. Only one answer is correct.

The First Lady of crime

Agatha Christie's novels were (1) .... into over 100 languages so she (2) .... the most popular writer of crime stories who ever lived. Yet it is (3) .... a mystery to some people that her books (4) .... so attractive to readers. She did not write very well. She invented a detective, Hercule Poirot, who is (5) .... to be Belgian and can hardly speak English unless the author (6) .... it necessary to (7) .... the reader of a vital clue; then Poirot suddenly becomes fluent and explains (8) .... how only the murderer (9) .... known where to get the poison used and why the (10) .... on the vital document is not the victim's. The police solve almost all crimes in real life but Poirot needs no (11) .... from them. The reasons for Agatha Christie's success are really quite simple. Her stories are a puzzle we can do just to (12) .... the time, like a crossword. (13) .... likeable is ever killed and we are never (14) .... of how horrible murder really is or left to wonder whether the wrong person has been (15) .... of the crime.

1	A revised	B transposed	C translated	D transferred
2	A had to be	B can have been	C was to be	D must have been
3	A already	B long	C still	D yet
4	A proved	B happened	C showed	D resulted
5	A expressed	B imagined	C meant	D signified
6	A realises	B finds	C requires	D sees
7	A inform	B notice	C provide	D remark
8	A us	B it is	C to us	D us of
9	A can be	B could be	C can have	D could have
10	A firm	B mark	C sign	D signature
11	A assistance	B attendance	C auxiliary	D presence
12	A pass	B spend	C use	D waste
13	A Anyone	B No one	C None	D Someone
14	A reminded	B remembered	C recalled	D memorised
15	A condemned	B convicted	C charged	D blamed

10 In each of the exercises below, choose the correct word or phrase from those given. Unless more than one possibility is indicated – (*or* ....) – only **one** of the words or phrases given in the list is correct in each space, though more than one may appear in the same sentence.
In Exercises **A–C**, put the verb in the correct form.
In Exercises **D–F**, use the plural form of the noun where necessary.

A *accept admit agree approve*

1 It was a terrible thing to do. I .... I was wrong.
2 I knew you wouldn't .... of my behaviour.
3 I suppose I made the wrong decision. I thought you wouldn't .... with me about it.
4 I .... to write an introduction to his book.
5 They won't .... you to the restaurant if you're not wearing a jacket.
6 I've .... the commission to write the book but I don't know if my agent and I will .... on the terms.

B *explain notice remark report*

1 The teacher .... the meaning of the word to us.
2a She had had her hair cut, but he didn't .... the difference.
 b 'You've had your hair cut!' he ....
3 He's won a prize for his latest novel. They .... it in the newspapers.
4 I can't .... how the mistake occurred. It's a good thing you .... it before the book was published.
5 'Have you .... a strange man hanging around here recently? One of the neighbours has .... it to the police.'

C *continue follow keep remain rest stay*

1 If you .... his example, you can't go wrong.
2 .... going in the same direction and you'll soon see it.
3 The argument .... long after the guests had gone home.
4 Which hotel are you .... at?

5 I'm too tired to go any farther. I need somewhere where I can lie down and ....
6 He's spent all his money. This is all that ....
7 I'll .... (*or* ....) here, ... comfortably in this armchair, while the rest of you go for a walk.
8 'If you .... the line of my argument,' he ...., 'it is pointless for you to .... (*or* ....) here any longer.'

D *agenda article diary paper sheet text*

1 He wrote the .... for the magazine on a single .... of .... and posted it immediately.
2 It seems strange to pick someone's personal .... for a set .... in the exam but this one is particularly interesting.
3 I wrote down the date of the next meeting in my .... but they haven't sent me the .... listing topics for discussion.
4 For the reading comprehension .... you have to read the .... and then write the answers on a separate ....
5 The .... of the speech he gave has been included in the .... about him published in today's ....

E *absence fault lack loss shortage*

1 The firm has closed down with heavy financial ....
2 There's a (an) .... (*or* ....) of trained workers here.
3 She'll be doing my work during my .... on holiday.
4 His worst .... is his .... of consideration for others.
5 His dog died and the .... affected him deeply.
6 If there's a food ...., it's the people's own .... It shows the .... (*or* ....) of any system of planning.

F *choice election selection taste variety*

1 They have a good .... of crime novels in the shop.
2 Who are you going to vote for in the ....?

3   The illustration on the front cover is in bad ....

4   People read books for a (an) .... of reasons and some like serious novels, others romances. It's a matter of ....

5   She doesn't like her job because it lacks ...., but there's not much .... open to young people in this town.

G   as as though like such as though

1a He speaks .... an expert in the subject; he knows what he's talking about.

  b He's only been studying for a few weeks but he already speaks .... an expert.

2   When Charlie talks .... that, he sounds .... he thinks he is the Prime Minister.

3a He went to Cambridge University, ... me.

  b He went to Cambridge University, ... I did.

4   He worked .... a librarian for some time .... he really wanted to be a writer.

5   .... you know, I did odd jobs .... (*or* ....) washing up in a café before I became a writer.

6   You look .... you've been running, even .... you're still late, ... usual.

Test 10

Read the text below and decide which word or phrase, **A**, **B**, **C** or **D** best fits each space. Underline the correct answer. Only one answer is correct.

A book review

Victoria Glendinning's novel, *Electricity*, (1) .... in the 1880s, uses the notebooks of the heroine, a girl (2) .... Charlotte, to tell the story. Charlotte is determined to escape from her (3) .... suburban background and overcome her (4) .... of education. Under the circumstances she is bound to (5) .... in love with a lodger who is (6) .... in the house, Peter Fisher. (7) .... Peter allows her to escape to the country, where Peter has been engaged to (8) .... the installation of electricity in a big house. (9) .... the title suggests, there are not only electric (10) .... but social tensions, too, running through it. There were many who did not (11) .... of electricity, especially those whose (12) .... of life was (13) .... and being replaced. The novel (14) .... because of its accurate reconstruction of a historical period; but above all it (15) .... attention to the difficulties that faced women in society a hundred years ago.

1	A	located	B	put	C	seated	D	set
2	A	called	B	entitled	C	titled	D	numbered
3	A	alone	B	lonely	C	single	D	sole
4	A	fall	B	fault	C	lack	D	missing
5	A	become	B	fall	C	get	D	grow
6	A	keeping	B	inhabiting	C	staying	D	remaining
7	A	Marrying	B	Marrying to	C	Getting married	D	The marrying
8	A	carry out	B	put up	C	realise	D	turn on
9	A	As	B	Like	C	Though	D	While
10	A	crashes	B	impacts	C	shakes	D	shocks
11	A	accept	B	agree	C	approve	D	favour
12	A	conduct	B	custom	C	habit	D	way
13	A	destroying	B	dying out	C	passing out	D	reducing
14	A	distinguishes	B	shows up	C	materialises	D	stands out
15	A	brings	B	draws	C	makes	D	pays

11 In each of the exercises below, choose the correct word or phrase from those given. Unless more than one possibility is indicated – (*or* ....) – only **one** of the words or phrases given in the list is correct in each space, though more than one may appear in the same sentence.

In Exercises **A–B**, put the verb in the correct form. In Exercises **C–E**, use the plural form of the noun where necessary.

A *check control review revise*

1 I'm sure we answered their letter, but would you mind ....?

2 They .... the book very favourably in the newspapers.

3 There are a number of errors of fact in the manuscript so you'll have to .... it before sending it for publication.

4 They no longer .... your passport when you come into the country so it's more difficult for them to .... immigration. If the problems increase, they may have to .... the situation and possibly .... the regulations.

5 I used to think he was a pleasant man but when I saw he could not .... his temper and started shouting like that, I .... my opinion of him.

B *deny refuse reject resist*

In this exercise the speeches in inverted commas ('...') indicate what the person might say. The sentences with the spaces define the statement.

1 'No, you can't go to your aunt's funeral!' He .... permission.

2 'I didn't do it, honestly!' He .... the accusation.

3 'We don't accept this as evidence.' The court .... the evidence the prisoner put forward.

4 'Take your hands off me.' The man .... the attempt to arrest him.

5 'I'm not going to help you.' He .... to help me.

C *attention care notice remark signal*

1 You should take .... of what your mother says.

2 You should pay .... to the teacher.

3 Take .... of the children while I'm out.

4 How could she make such an unkind ....?

5 The drivers are waiting for the .... to start the race.

6 They've put up a .... giving information about the course.

7 The train crashed because the driver didn't see the .... in the fog.

8 This letter is for the personal .... of the manager.

9 This substance is dangerous and must be handled with ....

10 He's a child with problems so he needs personal .... in class.

D *brand breed model pattern race recipe*

1 The Yorkshire terrier is an aggressive .... of dog.

2 It's hard to believe that someone who behaves like that is a member of the human ....

3 Persil is a well-known .... of detergent.

4 He's made an exact scale .... of the aircraft.

5 I'm going to make a dress, using this .... in the magazine.

6 My aunt's given me a .... for an Indonesian meal.

E *advantage behalf benefit profit sake*

1 He has sold his house for a very good ...., much more than he paid for it.

2 It's a wonderful opportunity and you should take .... of it.

3 They say that if you suffer from stress, keeping a cat is a (an) .... to your health.

4 On .... of all animal lovers, I'd like to thank you for the efforts you have made.

5 He's retired to the country for the .... of his health.

F *sensational sensible sensitive sentimental*

1 She reads those .... love stories where the hero and heroine kiss on the last page and live happily ever after.

2 The article in the newspaper contradicted the .... exaggerations of the popular press.

3 She has a .... skin and cannot spend much time in the sun.

4 There's no need to be so .... to criticism and take offence. The .... attitude is to take no notice.

G *although despite however in spite of*

1a .... it was cold, we enjoyed our holiday.

b We enjoyed our holiday, ... (*or* ....) feeling cold.

c We enjoyed our holiday, ... (*or* ....) the cold.

2a .... they are usually friendly dogs, they can be vicious.

b They are usually friendly dogs. ...., they can be vicious.

3 We climbed the mountain .... (*or* ....) the bad weather. When we got near the top, ..., we had to turn back.

Test 11

Read the text below and decide which word or phrase, **A**, **B**, **C** or **D** best fits each space. Underline the correct answer. Only one answer is correct.

Which are the dumb animals?

Most dog owners are so (1) .... about their pets that they (2) .... them by letting them have their own (3) .... all the time. They make absurd claims about their intelligence, and (4) .... to believe that they could ever do any harm. It is no (5) .... them, either, that city life does not (6) .... the (7) .... they have chosen and it would have been better if they (8) .... picked something smaller. There are other animal lovers, however, who argue that large dogs should be banned from cities for the (9) .... of their health.

A Dalmatian I read about recently, however, had the good (10) .... to live near a big park, and the vet that it was taken to when it was ill had a house not (11) .... off. One day, the dog woke up with a bad leg; when its owner took it for a walk, it (12) .... painfully beside him (13) .... the park but then pulled its owner across the road. The owner followed it along several streets until it (14) .... the vet's house, where it (15) .... up its injured foot and waited patiently for attention.

1	A	sensible	B	sensuous	C	sentimental	D	sensational
2	A	impair	B	damage	C	spoil	D	tolerate
3	A	desire	B	want	C	will	D	way
4	A	deny	B	refuse	C	reject	D	resist
5	A	use saying	B	use telling	C	use to say	D	use to tell
6	A	agree	B	fit	C	match	D	suit
7	A	breed	B	grade	C	race	D	variety
8	A	should have	B	would have	C	have	D	had
9	A	aid	B	behalf	C	profit	D	sake
10	A	chance	B	fate	C	luck	D	success
11	A	far	B	long	C	much	D	away
12	A	hurried	B	limped	C	ran	D	strolled
13	A	as far as	B	as long as	C	as much as	D	until
14	A	arrived	B	got	C	reached	D	went
15	A	held	B	got	C	took	D	rose

12 In each of the exercises below, choose the correct word or phrase from those given. Unless more than one possibility is indicated – (*or* ....) – only **one** of the words or phrases given in the list is correct in each space, though more than one may appear in the same sentence.

In Exercises **A–E**, put the verb in the correct form.

A *advertise advise announce threaten warn*

1   The man .... to hit her if she told anyone about it.
2   I .... you to wait here until they .... your flight on the loudspeaker.
3   They've .... for a qualified accountant in today's paper.
4   We've .... those children a hundred times not to play in the road.
5   I .... you that people might protest if you used those disgusting pictures to .... your products.

B *bring carry fetch take*

In this exercise, only use **carry** if it is the only possible answer.

1   Don't .... it over there! .... it here to me!
2   It's upstairs. I'll go up and .... it.
3   She was .... a heavy case so I offered to help her.
4   Mum! I've .... some friends home to tea!
5   Don't call a taxi! I'll .... you to the airport.
6a Let's go, then! I'll .... the baby if you .... the luggage.
 b Come on, then! I'll .... the baby if you .... the luggage.
7   Wait here while I .... my car.
8   It .... her over an hour to get to work every day.

C *dismiss give up resign retire withdraw*

1   I can breathe better now I've .... smoking.
2   He'll get a good pension when he .... at 65.
3   She was .... for consistently bad work.

4   I .... my objection to her appointment.
5   If she doesn't get promotion, she'll ....
6   When the prosecution .... the charges against her, the judge .... the case.

D *do and make (1)*

Before attempting this exercise, study Appendix 3 on page 119.
Note that the same verb may appear more than once in these sentences.

1   If you continue to .... your best, you'll .... good progress.
2   When you .... an exercise like this, ... sure that you haven't .... a lot of mistakes before you hand it in.
3   I don't mind .... the job if we .... money out of it but I'm not going to .... the effort just to .... him a favour.
4   I don't like her .... such a long journey to school every day even though I don't suppose it will .... her any harm. But it would .... a difference if she .... friends with another girl who would travel with her.
5   I don't see what you're .... such a fuss about. I said I'd .... the repairs as soon as I could and I will. I'm not .... excuses but if you want to .... a complaint to the manager, you're free to .... so.

E *do and make (2)*

In this exercise you must complete sentences with the correct form of one of the verbs in the list. Note the verbs we use in each context, where the equivalent of **do** or **make** may be used in other languages.

ask be drive give pack pay take write

1   Stand still! I want to .... your photograph.
2   I can't stand the noise. It's .... me mad.
3   I'll .... my case and then I'll be ready to leave.
4   It .... a long time since I saw her last.
5   She .... me a strange look.
6   She's .... a poem about it.

7   I'll .... them a visit on my way home.
8   If I .... you a question, will you answer?

**F   *cabinet   cupboard   dresser
      dressing table   shelf   wardrobe***

1   Could you get me the frying pan, please? It's on the bottom .... in the .... in the kitchen.
2   Hang your jacket up in the .... Don't just leave it there on the bed for me to do it.
3   In Britain you'd find a .... in the living room. It's a piece of furniture with open .... on top and a .... below for plates and glasses. But in the USA it would be in the bedroom, with drawers for clothes. We call that a ....

**G   *for the time being   from time to time
      in time   on time   time after time***

1   He still comes to see us .... but not as often as he used to.
2a She's very punctual. She always arrives at the office ...., at exactly nine o'clock.
 b She had to run all the way from the station to arrive .... for work.
3   I've told you .... that I will not tolerate rudeness to customers. This is your last warning.
4   They're staying with her parents ...., until they find a flat of their own.
5   The bus usually arrives .... but it's late this morning. I hope it gets here .... for me to get to work.
6   You should bring the car in for servicing .... but there's nothing wrong at the moment so you needn't worry ....

Test 12

Read the text below and decide which word or phrase, **A**, **B**, **C** or **D** best fits each space. Underline the correct answer. Only one answer is correct.

A woman farmer
(1) .... the number of women who manage their own farms is still only (2) .... two per cent of the total, most farms would not function without the farmer's wife. Yet the farming community is still prejudiced against having a woman in (3) ....
Susan Wilson, who (4) .... a farm in Kent, explained the fight she had with her father to prevent him (5) .... it because he had no sons. '"What about me?" I said to my father. "I wish you'd give me the (6) ....!" Dad was astonished: "What are you making such a(n) (7) .... about?" he said. "When you (8) .... married, you'll be too busy thinking about new clothes for your (9) .... to take farming seriously." It wasn't until I (10) .... him that Mum had been (11) .... the accounts and paying the (12) .... for years that he had second (13) .... At the time I was angry but I was very proud when he (14) .... to the whole family that I would be taking over when he (15) ....'

1	A	Although	B	Despite	C	Even	D	In spite
2	A	a	B	about	C	the	D	one
3	A	charge	B	direction	C	head	D	boss
4	A	conducts	B	leads	C	runs	D	undertakes
5	A	sell	B	to sell	C	selling	D	sold
6	A	chance	B	challenge	C	occasion	D	possibility
7	A	excitement	B	fuss	C	nuisance	D	trouble
8	A	become	B	get	C	will become	D	will get
9	A	cupboard	B	dresser	C	shelf	D	wardrobe
10	A	recalled	B	remarked	C	remembered	D	reminded
11	A	counting	B	doing	C	making	D	costing
12	A	bills	B	additions	C	prices	D	recipes
13	A	ideas	B	opinions	C	thoughts	D	views
14	A	advertised	B	advised	C	announced	D	informed
15	A	dismissed	B	retired	C	resigned	D	retreated

13 In each of the exercises below, choose the correct word or phrase from those given. Unless more than one possibility is indicated – (*or* ....) – only **one** of the words or phrases given in the list is correct in each space, though more than one may appear in the same sentence.

In Exercises **A**–**C**, put the verb in the correct form. In Exercises **D**–**F**, use the plural form of the noun where necessary. Before attempting Exercise **H**, study the Appendix on Connectors on page 116.

A accept allow let

1a She didn't .... the children stay up late.
 b The children weren't .... to stay up late.
2a Thanks, but I can't .... you pay for my lunch.
 b Thanks, but I can't .... you to pay for my lunch.
3 We don't .... smoking in this part of the restaurant.
4 We don't .... cheques in the restaurant.
5 I'm glad you've been .... as a member of the club.
6 He refused to .... my apology.

B cure heal mend recover repair solve

1a They say that this new drug will .... cancer.
 b They say that this new drug will .... the problem of cancer.
2a I'm glad to see your wound has ....
 b I'm glad to see you've .... from your illness.
3 I'm glad they were able to .... him of his disease.
4a The workmen have come to .... (*or* ....) the fence.
 b The technician has come to .... the TV.

C ache damage harm hurt injure wound

In this exercise, only use *hurt* if it is the **only** possible answer.

1a Ow! That ....! Let go of my arm!
 b My head's been .... all morning.
2a The house was badly .... by the explosion.

 b He was badly .... in the car accident.
 c He was badly .... in the battle.
3 The dog's very friendly. It won't .... you.
4 She's very sensitive and the remarks you made .... her feelings.

D energy force power strength

1a It's too heavy for me. I haven't the .... to lift it.
 b I'm too tired. I haven't enough .... left to lift it.
2 This building belongs to the armed ....
3 You've been working too hard. You need to go on holiday to get your .... (*or* ....) back.
4 The electrical .... is supplied from this central .... station.
5 I'm sorry. I did it by .... of habit. I just wasn't thinking.

E extension extent limit point scope

1a Up to a(n) .... I agree with you.
 b To some .... I think you're right.
2 He's building a(n) .... onto his house to make a separate flat for his mother.
3 They're selling their business because there's no .... for developing it further.
4 Miss Wilson? Yes, she's on .... 286. I'll put you through.
5 If you stretch your arm to its full ...., you'll be able to reach it.
6 If you push your body to the ...., you'll break the record.
7 People visiting the wildlife park are allowed to bring their cars as far as this ...., and no further.
8 There's no .... in giving them the contract unless you can set a .... on how much they spend.

F disease illness infection sickness

1 She's been away from the office for some time, recovering from a long ....
2 The main cause of death in this country is heart ....
3 We must do something to control the .... and not allow the .... to spread to other parts of the body.

4 – What were the symptoms of the ....?
– .... – she vomited twice – and a high temperature.

5 You can claim .... benefit while you are away from work.

G *ill infectious sick unfit unhealthy*

In this exercise use *sick* only if it is the **only** possible answer.

1a She rang to say she was .... and couldn't come to work.
b Oh, dear! I think I'm going to be ....! It must be those cakes I ate.

2 This is a hospital for patients suffering from .... diseases.

3 His face had a rather .... look, as if he never took any exercise.

4 He can't play in the match tomorrow. He's hurt his ankle, and the club medical officer has declared him ....

H One word is missing from each of the phrases in **bold** type. Complete the phrases with the correct word.

.... **my opinion** this emphasis on keeping fit is exaggerated. **As I** .... **it**, jogging will probably give you a heart attack. But **as far as I'm** ...., you're free to do as you like. .... **the same**, I've no intention of getting up at six in the morning to go with you. **To my** ...., it's a waste of time and energy.

Test 13

Read the text below and decide which word or phrase, **A**, **B**, **C** or **D** best fits each space. Underline the correct answer. Only one answer is correct.

Storm in a teacup

Foreigners entertaining people from Britain to tea often wonder how to make tea to their (1) .... Among the British themselves the question usually (2) .... is (3) .... put the milk into the cup before or after the tea. Essentially, the contrasting points of (4) .... relate to bitterness. (5) .... you leave the tea in the pot the more bitter it becomes; you add milk (6) .... the bitter taste. 'Milk first' supporters claim that pouring the milk on the tea will not achieve this to the same (7) .... ; 'milk second' people say it is the only way of making sure it is the right (8) ....
When the Tea Council were (9) .... their advice, they said people should take no (10) .... of the debate and do what (11) .... them best. Personally, I (12) .... to put the milk in first because I know (13) .... strong I like it to be, but my advice to foreigners is to pour the tea first and (14) .... guests add their own milk. Still, most of you will probably think the whole question is not worth (15) .... about, just 'a storm in a teacup'.

	A	B	C	D
1	choice	enjoyment	inclination	taste
2	made	raised	risen	roused
3	if one	whether one	if to	whether to
4	attitude	opinion	view	sight
5	The longer	The long	How longer	How long
6	for lowering	for reducing	to lower	to reduce
7	extent	level	quantity	rate
8	force	power	strength	weakness
9	demanded	asked for	inquired	inquired for
10	attention	notice	remark	thought
11	fitted	matched	suited	tasted
12	favour	like better	prefer	would rather
13	how	the	what	which
14	allow	let	make	may
15	arguing	to argue	discussing	to discuss

14 In each of the exercises below, choose the correct word or phrase from those given. Unless more than one possibility is indicated – (*or* ....) – only **one** of the words or phrases given in the list is correct in each space, though more than one may appear in the same sentence.

In Exercises **A–B**, put the verbs in the correct form. In Exercises **C–E**, use the plural form of the noun where necessary. Before attempting Exercise **H**, study the Appendix on Connectors on page 116.

A ***accuse blame complain criticise protest***

1 You can't .... what happened on me.
2 You shouldn't .... her work in front of others.
3 If you're not satisfied with the service, you should .... to the management about it.
4 The demonstrators are .... against the war.
5 I ....! You are .... an innocent man of a crime without any evidence.

B ***abandon forget ignore leave let***

1 When it grew dark they decided to .... the search for the lost climbers.
2 Up to now I've been willing to .... his bad behaviour but I'm not prepared to .... him get away with this.
3 Oh dear! I've .... my books at home.
4 I'll never .... how kind she was to me when I was a child.
5 You should be more careful. When you .... your sister in, you .... the front door open.
6a Don't get upset about losing the book! .... it!
 b Don't get upset when he makes nasty remarks. .... them!

C ***action effect event fact success***

1 They've arranged a number of .... to entertain the children.
2 The operation was a (an) .... but he's still weak and feeling the .... of the anaesthetic.
3 We may be convinced by what people say but the .... is that we judge them by ...., not words.

4 At the time their meeting was considered the most important political .... of the year but it was not a(n) .... and had very little .... on what happened later.
5 The book has been a great .... and I'll put the order to reprint it into .... immediately.

D ***blame error fault guilt mistake***

1 I don't see why I should take the .... for their .... (*or* ....). It wasn't my .... that the goods weren't delivered on time.
2 His worst .... is that he doesn't listen to advice.
3 The accident took place a year ago but he cannot overcome his feeling of .... At first they thought it was due to a mechanical .... but in fact it was a simple case of human .... He pressed the wrong button by ....
4 If he does something wrong he never admits he was at .... He just shifts the .... onto someone else and never shows a sign of .... at having done so.

E ***charge complaint demand trouble***

1 The bank will honour your cheque on .... and will make no extra ....
2 The .... with him is that he doesn't take any notice of what people tell him.
3 He's in .... with the police because they received .... from the neighbours about his aggressive behaviour.
4 I decided not to make a .... to the manager because I didn't want to get the assistant into ....
5 The Ruritanian embassy has sent a formal .... to the Government, together with a .... for a full apology, following the arrest of the ambassador's son on a .... of drunken driving.

F ***ashamed confused disappointed disgusted embarrassed***

Describe how you would feel in the different situations indicated below, choosing from the list above.

1   I had been looking forward to seeing the show but in the end we couldn't get tickets. I was ....

2   I asked the teacher a question but I didn't understand her explanation. I was ....

3   At the party, this attractive man asked me if I knew the man who was behaving so badly. It was my brother. I was ....

4   I knew I shouldn't have made those unkind remarks to her. I was ....

5   Instead of offering to help clear up after the party, they just left the flat in a terrible state. I was ....

G   *elder elderly former older prior*

1   That's my .... brother, Thomas. He's two years .... than me.

2   The .... man over there – he must be over 60 – is her .... husband, before she married Ron.

3   He had to refuse her invitation because he had a .... engagement somewhere else.

4   Ms Juliet Branston is the newly appointed head teacher at Coverdale School. Her .... appointment was at New Mill school, and .... to that she taught in Canada.

H   One word is missing from each of the phrases in **bold** type. Complete the phrase with the correct word.

1   In theory the ambulance should be there in five minutes but **in** .... it often takes longer.

2   **At first** .... it looked as if many people were injured, but **in** .... no one was hurt.

3   – Who's that funny looking man over there?
– **As a** .... **of fact**, that's my father.

4   **On the** .... **of it**, there's nothing much to worry about, but I'm not happy with the situation.

Test 14

Read the text below and decide which word or phrase, **A**, **B**, **C** or **D** best fits each space. Underline the correct answer. Only one answer is correct.

Old champions

There is (1) .... that pleases the sporting public more than seeing an old champion they once (2) .... adore coming back after (3) .... and reviving memories of (4) .... victories. But (5) .... the other hand, seeing a once great player (6) .... easily to a beginner is an embarrassing experience. The secret of growing old gracefully is knowing when to (7) .... Unfortunately, few sports stars are willing to face up to the (8) .... that they have got slower and can (9) .... compete on equal (10) .... with the (11) .... This is not always their own (12) .... Without meaning any (13) .... , their managers and supporters have never (14) .... telling them that they will always be the best and so they cannot (15) .... believing it.

1	A	anything	B	everything	C	nothing	D	something
2	A	used to	B	were used to	C	have used to	D	would
3	A	resignation	B	retirement	C	retreat	D	withdrawal
4	A	elder	B	former	C	latter	D	prior
5	A	at	B	by	C	in	D	on
6	A	defeating	B	failing	C	losing	D	missing
7	A	abandon	B	fall out	C	give up	D	vacate
8	A	effect	B	event	C	fact	D	happening
9	A	no longer	B	no more	C	still not	D	not yet
10	A	relations	B	rules	C	scores	D	terms
11	A	young	B	youngs	C	youngers	D	youth
12	A	blame	B	fail	C	fault	D	guilt
13	A	bad	B	damage	C	harm	D	hurt
14	A	ended	B	left	C	rested	D	stopped
15	A	help	B	refuse	C	resist	D	stand

15 In each of the exercises below, choose the correct word or phrase from those given. Unless more than one possibility is indicated – (*or* ....) – only **one** of the words or phrases given in the list is correct in each space, though more than one may appear in the same sentence.

In exercises **A–C**, put the verb in the correct form. In Exercises **D–F**, use the plural form of the noun where necessary.

A *achieve beat earn gain win*

1 You have to work hard to .... your living here.
2 He took the job to .... experience, hoping that it would help him to .... his ambition of becoming the managing director and .... a lot of money.
3a They .... the match by three goals to one.
 b They .... the other team by three goals to one.
4 In .... the race, they also .... the world record time.
5 If you .... your aims in life, you should be happy. You don't need to .... the Nobel Prize to be a success.

B *avoid escape prevent stop*

1 The bad weather .... us from completing the match.
2 The rain's .... We can go home now.
3 He's a peaceful man. He would rather keep out of the way and .... trouble than get involved.
4 A dangerous criminal has .... from prison this afternoon.
5 Now .... talking and listen to me!

C *rob* and *steal*

1a A group of people .... him.
 b A group of people .... his money.
2a He was .... within ten minutes of his arrival.
 b His money was .... within ten minutes of his arrival.
3a They've .... us of everything we possessed.
 b They've .... everything we possessed from us.

4a They've .... the bank and .... all the money in the safe.
 b The bank's been .... and all the money in the safe has been ....

D *behaviour custom fashion habit manner way*

1 You should always adapt your .... in public to the .... of the country. That's the only .... to avoid giving offence.
2 Her hair style is out of .... now.
3 He has a very odd .... and a peculiar .... of speaking but what annoys me most about him is his .... of turning away from you when you say something to him.
4 It may no longer be the .... to take a present to the host when you go to a party but it's still bad .... to leave without saying goodbye.
5 These tribes have forgotten their traditional .... in their attempt to adapt to our .... of life.

E *cloth clothes costume dress material*

1 Actors often wear their own .... in modern plays but in classical drama they may have to have a .... specially made.
2 What a pretty ....! What .... is it made of?
3 She got the table .... out of the cupboard, ready for dinner.
4 You can't wear a lovely .... like that to work in the garden! Why don't you put on some old ....?
5 The tribesmen were wearing their traditional .... (*or* ....) of loose shirts and long trousers.

F *conference lecture meeting performance reunion*

1 He's giving a .... at the international .... on Latin American history.
2 Her former students organise an annual .... at the end of the academic year.
3 I'd like a few words with you after the business ....
4 At the end of the .... the audience applauded the actors.

5 After his ...., Professor Schmidt will take part in the press ...., answering reporters' questions.

G even except provided unless whether

1a I'm going, ... you like it or not.
 b I'm going, ... you object.
 c I'm going, ... if you object.
 d I'm going, ... you don't object.
2a He does everything in the house .... the cooking.
 b He does everything in the house – he .... cooks the meals.
 c He does everything in the house, ... you give him time.

3a I'm going to play tennis later, ... it doesn't rain.
 b I'm going to play tennis later .... it rains.
4a I'll be there on Sunday, ... I ring you or not.
 b I'll be there on Sunday .... I ring you beforehand.
5a They all came to the party .... Angela. She stayed at home.
 b They all came to the party – .... Angela, though she doesn't usually like going out.

Test 15

Read the text below and decide which word or phrase, **A**, **B**, **C** or **D** best fits each space. Underline the correct answer. Only one answer is correct.

Going to live in the country

I have lived in cities (1) .... my life and so I can't imagine myself living in the country, (2) .... from almost all forms of entertainment (3) .... from television. The country people I have come into (4) .... with have never (5) .... me the impression that I would be welcome there, either. Instead of (6) .... you with a cheerful 'hello', (7) .... you might expect from watching TV serials, they ignore you (8) .... they know you are related to someone in the village. (9) .... I don't blame them for that. I can see why they don't like townspeople (10) .... them to change their ways. Newcomers from the towns like the country but usually don't (11) .... their living there. They regard sheep (12) .... sweet, harmless animals but for country people sheep (13) .... a practical purpose, providing meat and wool. As an old countryman said to me: 'If some townsman interferes with my work but he can't (14) .... one kind of tree from another, I tell him to mind his own (15) ....'

1	A all	B for all	C the whole	D for the whole
2	A avoided	B cut off	C separate	D turned away
3	A apart	B besides	C except	D only
4	A contact	B junction	C meeting	D touch
5	A given	B made	C produced	D shown
6	A greeting	B nodding	C signalling	D waving
7	A that	B what	C as	D like
8	A except	B provided	C unless	D whether
9	A Above all	B By all accounts	C All the same	D At any rate
10	A demanding	B expecting	C insisting	D suggesting
11	A do	B earn	C gain	D win
12	A as	B for	C like	D to be
13	A comply	B follow	C respect	D serve
14	A decide	B describe	C say	D tell
15	A affair	B business	C job	D living

In one section of the First Certificate examination students are asked to complete a passage. There are a number of spaces and you must put **one** word in each space. When you attempt this kind of exercise, there are three rules you **must** always obey:

1 **Always** read the passage at least **twice** and try to understand its meaning as a whole before you write any words in the spaces.

2 **Never** write a word in a space until you have studied the rest of the sentence carefully and also the sentences before and after it.

3 The right word to write in the space must be **grammatically correct** and must also **make sense in the context**. You must always consider two questions:

a **What kind of word is missing?**

b **How does it relate to the rest of the sentence?**

Before you attempt the exercises in the section that are like those in the First Certificate examination, do the preliminary exercises. These are intended to help you to follow the rules given above and show why they are necessary.

Preliminary exercises

A What kind of word is missing?

The missing word in a sentence may be a noun, a verb form, an adjective, a preposition etc. Can you see what kind of word is missing in these sentences? Complete each of the sentences with one word that seems logical to you before you read on.

1 He has built a big .... here.
2 He .... in the village.
3 She is a very .... girl.
4 She plays the piano very ....
5 She is reading .... letter.
6 They have brought .... books.
7 They live .... me.
8 .... they arrive, we must do some work.

Compare your answers with other students. How many of you have written the same word?

There is generally a correct grammatical form for each space, but note that there is **not** a single correct answer. In sentence 1, the missing word is almost certainly a noun, but it could be **house**, **factory** or even **cinema**. In sentence 3 an adjective is needed but almost any adjective is possible if we do not know any more about the girl. We need information from other sentences to

know if she is **good**, **bad**, **pretty**, **ugly** etc. In sentence 5 the missing word could be **a**, but it could also be a personal pronoun, **her**, and in sentence 6, the word could be a personal pronoun, **their**, but it could also be **some**, and without more information we do not know if **their** is more likely to be correct than **your** or **my**. In sentence 8, most of you have probably chosen **When** but the word could be **Before** or **After**. Nevertheless, the missing word is clearly a time conjunction. It cannot be a noun or a verb or an adjective. It is always important to decide what kind of word is missing.

B Looking at the context

Simple sentences in English can be linked by **and**, **but**, **so** or **because** without any punctuation between them. Choosing which one should fill a space is therefore not a matter of grammar. You must decide by the sense in the context. Choose **one** of these words to complete each of the sentences below and then compare with other students to see if they have chosen the same one. Why did you choose the word?

1 There was no food in the house .... the children were hungry.
2 There was a lot of food in the house .... the children weren't hungry.
3 There was no food in the house .... my mother had not been to the shops.

4 There was no food in the house .... I went out to buy some.

5 I went out to buy some food .... there wasn't any in the house .... when I got home the children were busy playing a game .... I put it in the fridge .... waited until they said they were hungry.

Did you choose the same word as other students? There may be a case for putting **so** instead of **and** for question 1 but in all the others only one word makes sense in the context of the whole sentence. It is always important to read the sentence **after** you have written your word in the space to make sure that it makes sense.

C The form of the verb

Students sometimes make careless mistakes with verb forms in this kind of exercise because:
– they do not check whether the form should be infinitive (**play**), present participle/gerund (**playing**), past participle (**played**);
– they do not check whether the tense is present (**play**, **plays**) or past (**played**);
– they forget the **s** on the third person singular in the present (**he/she/it plays**).

Complete the passage below, using one verb only. Use the context to decide which verb is needed, and take care to put the verb in the correct form.

James (1) .... football for the town team. He has been (2) .... for them for several years. At school he (3) .... football quite well but he didn't think he would be good enough to (4) .... professionally. But one day a man came to the park where the school matches were always (5) .... The school team were (6) .... against another school and James (7) .... very well. The man said: 'If you can (8) .... as well as that I've got a job for you.' (9) .... football for a living is not a very safe career but James enjoys it, partly because he (10) .... for his home town and feels happy there.

D Pronouns and possessive forms in context

Another careless mistake is not to read the whole context carefully enough and so to put the wrong pronoun or possessive form or to confuse the singular or plural form of the verb that follows. Complete the passage below with one suitable word in each space.

Dickens died over a hundred years ago but (1) .... books (2) .... still popular with children today. Every year (3) .... visit (4) .... house at Broadstairs in Kent in large numbers and many of (5) .... leave messages for (6) .... to read, like this: 'Dear Charles, I love (7) .... books. It (8) .... been a wonderful experience to come here and know that (9) .... lived here and wrote some of (10) .... at this desk.'

E Negative forms

If students do not read the whole context carefully they may not notice that in some cases only a negative form makes sense. They must use the context to decide whether the missing word is affirmative (**some, somebody, always**) or negative (**no, nobody, never**) or whether the sense of the context indicates **more** or **less, most** or **least, many** or **few** etc. Before you attempt this exercise, study Reference Section **45, 46** and **66**.

There is (1) .... doubt that Annie Oakley, who worked in Buffalo Bill's Wild West Show, was one of the (2) .... famous women shots in history and until now (3) .... has ever questioned her ability. But now a scientific examination of (4) .... of the bullets she used suggests they were specially made and this made it (5) .... difficult for her to hit balls thrown in the air. (6) .... of the bullets had been examined until an old man who had worked in the circus a hundred years ago gave them to a dealer without asking for (7) .... money for them. But Annie's niece, Mrs Edwards, says she has (8) .... heard of strange bullets being used, and the curator of the Buffalo Bill Centre says he knows circus performers used a (9) .... tricks like that but a woman who could shoot a cigarette from a man's mouth, like Annie Oakley, did not need to employ (10) .... of them.

F Confusing *there, it, they*

Students sometimes confuse **it/they** with **there** and this leads to error when one of these words is the correct one to write in the space. Before you attempt this exercise, study Reference Section **37** and **71–73**.

(1) .... are few cities more beautiful than Budapest. (2) .... lies on the banks of the River Danube and (3) .... is nothing quite like (4) .... anywhere else. Our guide said: 'If (5) .... is the first time you have visited the city, (6) .... is a good idea to go down to the river at night and look across. (7) .... is a wonderful view of Castle Hill on the opposite side.'

She told us that Budapest is not expensive for tourists and (8) .... are plenty of interesting shops. (9) .... are mainly found near the city centre and (10) .... is especially worthwhile to look at the record shops. '(11) .... is not time for dinner yet so (12) .... may be time to visit one before we go back to the hotel,' she said.

G Confusing *a, an, the, this, that*

It is very often possible to put any of these in a space for purely grammatical reasons but because of the context only one will be correct. Remember that **a** (**an**) is used in general, when something is first mentioned, **the** when we already know which thing we are talking about or when a phrase that follows it defines it. In the same way **this** is associated with **here** in time and place, **that** with **there**. Before you attempt this exercise, study Reference Section **1, 70a** and **70c3**.

(1) .... article in today's newspaper refers to (2) .... interest tourists show in visiting places where TV series are made. As (3) .... example it mentions (4) .... series (5) .... BBC is making of George Eliot's classic novel, *Middlemarch*. (6) .... town George Eliot really had in mind when she wrote (7) .... novel was Coventry, but at (8) .... time, over (9) .... hundred years ago, it was much smaller. (10) .... was (11) .... reason

why (12) .... producers of (13) .... series decided to look for (14) .... town that still looked like (15) .... one described in (16) .... book. (17) .... series is being made in Stamford, and in (18) .... last few days there have been hundreds of enquiries at (19) .... town tourist office. Information is available if you ring (20) .... telephone number: 01780 55611.

H Choosing the right preposition: *at, in, on*

A large number of spaces in this kind of exercise are filled by prepositions. As preparation for dealing with such cases, you should gradually become familiar with Appendix 4 , which tells you which prepositions generally follow different verbs. You should also learn common collocations, like **at work**, **on business**, etc. The most important uses of prepositions to learn, however, are the common ones used for time and place. Before attempting this exercise, study Reference Section **52** and **53**.

I was born (1) .... home – children were not born (2) .... hospital so often (3) .... those days – (4) .... my parents' house. It was (5) .... spring, (6) .... the month of April. The birth took place (7) .... night, (8) .... three o'clock (9) .... the morning. My parents lived (10) .... the outskirts of London (11) .... a quiet road (12) .... number 47. There was a park (13) .... the other side of the road, a grocer's shop (14) .... the corner and (15) .... the far end of the road the railway line.

We moved away when I was two years old but my aunt and uncle lived (16) .... the road next to it and I often went to see them (17) .... Christmas Day or (18) .... weekends or when I was (19) .... holiday from school. (20) .... a few days' time, I have to go to visit that part of London again (21) .... business. I am curious to have another look at the house where I was born.

Tests

Test 1

Read the text below and think of the word which best fits each space. Use only **one** word in each space. There is an example at the beginning (**0**). Write your words in the spaces provided.

My Family and Other Animals
The (0) ....most...... amusing book I have read about a family is Gerald Durrell's *My Family and Other Animals*. Gerald was the (1) .... of four children; he had two elder brothers and a sister, all of them already (2) .... up and much older (3) .... he was. While his father was (4) .... the family lived in India, but when he died they returned to England. They did not have (5) .... money because Mrs Durrell only had her pension as the (6) .... of a Government servant. When Gerald was about ten his brother Lawrence (7) .... married and the family went to live on the Greek island of Corcyra (Corfu in English); the cost of living (8) .... was not as expensive (9) .... in England.
In the book Gerald tells us about the animals, birds and insects he collected as a child; years later he became famous (10) .... a zoo collector. But the funniest incidents concern his family. Lawrence is very selfish but always blames everyone (11) .... when things go wrong. Leslie (12) .... all his time outdoors; he is very keen on sports (13) .... shooting. Margot, Gerald's sister, is (14) .... worrying about her health. Mrs Durrell tries to control the family but always ends up by (15) .... what they want her to do.

Test 2

Read the text below and think of the word which best fits each space. Use only **one** word in each space. Write your words in the spaces provided.

Making space for the TV
Many people cannot imagine (1) .... happily in a house without a television, video and hi-fi system but they sometimes don't want visitors to (2) .... them in the living room. If the house is big (3) .... for them to spare the space they can put the equipment in a special room (4) .... most of us have to buy a (5) .... of furniture for it, (6) .... a cabinet, so that it stays out of sight.
A friend of mine found (7) .... ingenious solution. Instead of (8) .... a cabinet in a shop she (9) .... use of an old cupboard. The first time I went to see her, she happened to (10) .... me alone for a few minutes in her living room and I had a terrible shock; suddenly (11) .... was a scream of pain; (12) .... came from the cupboard and at first I was (13) .... frightened to open it because I half expected to find (14) .... hiding inside. When I did, I realised that my friend had forgotten to turn the TV (15) ....

Test 3

Read the text below and think of the word which best fits each space. Use only **one** word in each space. Write your words in the spaces provided.

Back to the High Street
(1) .... several years now the big supermarket chains (2) .... competed with (3) .... other throughout the country by following the (4) .... policy. They have all moved their stores (5) .... of the High Street and built new ones outside. But (6) .... now most people in Britain live near a supermarket so there is no more room for expansion (7) .... that direction. Consequently, the chains have been (8) .... for different ways of attracting customers. One has just opened a store (9) .... the centre of London (10) .... you can buy a bottle of good wine and a packet of smoked salmon (11) .... the way home (12) .... work; in contrast, another has a shop in Manchester where everything is sold (13) .... the lowest possible (14) .... In both cases, however, people will spend money in the High Street again (15) .... of going out of town.

Test 4

Read the text below and think of the word which best fits each space. Use only **one** word in each space. Write your words in the spaces provided.

A new kind of school

Vera is the head teacher at a new kind of school that opened a few years ago. She applied (1) .... the job when someone told her that only a man (2) .... be able to (3) .... a success of it. The school is called a city technology college. (4) .... concentrates on subjects students will need in business later in life and (5) .... been very successful since it opened. Vera told me she had never had such an interesting job (6) .... For the first time in her life, she (7) .... had the opportunity to (8) .... her ideas into practice. Her main aim was that (9) .... of leaving school (10) .... early, (11) .... their parents, the students would (12) .... the course (13) .... interesting that they would want to stay on (14) .... they were 18. The secret of the school's success was that everyone enjoyed (15) .... together as a team.

Test 5

Read the text below and think of the word which best fits each space. Use only **one** word in each space. Write your words in the spaces provided.

Businesswoman of the Year

(1) .... Friday Joan Wingfield was named Businesswoman of the Year. In her restaurant they served champagne, a gesture typical of a woman (2) .... aggressive approach to business has brought her success. Most of it has been achieved in car dealing, supposed to be a field in (3) .... women have no place, but Joan has always (4) .... determined to (5) .... to the top. She did well (6) .... school but left early to become an accountant (7) .... of going to university. When one of her clients went bankrupt, she (8) .... a risk and bought the company with (9) .... the money she had. A year later she saw a restaurant was for (10) .... in her neighbourhood but before (11) .... it she worked there (12) .... three nights. 'I wanted to know (13) .... it was like,'

she told me. She starts work early every morning. Her husband (14) .... the shopping. 'I hate shopping,' says this woman (15) .... can't stand doing nothing.

Test 6

Read the text below and think of the word which best fits each space. Use only **one** word in each space. Write your words in the spaces provided.

Armchair sport

These days people have more spare time for leisure activities and there are more to (1) .... from. When I was a child, most people worked (2) ....Saturday mornings, if (3) .... all day, and in the afternoon the choice was between going to a football match (4) .... a cinema, or staying at home and (5) .... to the radio, though even then there were people who climbed mountains (6) .... weekends or got on their bicycles and (7) .... away somewhere. Nowadays it is more difficult to decide (8) .... to do. Yet there is still a division between those who would (9) .... play than watch and those who are more passive. Occasionally, you can mistake one for the other. A friend of (10) .... said one Friday afternoon: 'I'm playing St Andrews with my son tomorrow. The (11) .... time we played I went round in 65.' I was so surprised that he (12) .... scored so well on the world's (13) .... famous golf course that I did not ask how they were (14) .... to travel up to Scotland. It wasn't (15) .... the following week, when he talked about playing in California, that I realised he was playing on a computer.

Test 7

Read the text below and think of the word which best fits each space. Use only **one** word in each space. Write your words in the spaces provided.

Tower Bridge

Tower Bridge is (1) .... of London's most famous landmarks and many visitors (2) .... holiday in the city think it is the original London Bridge. In (3) .... that bridge, the only one that crossed (4) .... Thames in the Middle Ages, is further up the river. Tower Bridge was not built until 1894. In

(5) .... days London was (6) .... a busy port so the bridge (7) .... to be opened whenever a ship approached. Nowadays the rule is that ships (8) .... give twenty four hours' notice (9) .... the bridge to be opened. For many years pedestrians were not (10) .... on the walkways 50 metres above the water, but now visitors can cross the bridge on them and there are all (11) .... of devices describing the view. Over half (12) .... million visitors come every year and there is an exhibition for children showing (13) .... the bridge works. The story of the bridge is (14) .... through animated figures seen at different moments in (15) .... history.

Test 8

Read the text below and think of the word which best fits each space. Use only **one** word in each space. Write your words in the spaces provided.

Rescued at sea

It was a fine morning for sailing, and I was (1) .... my own in my boat, enjoying the fine weather. But my enjoyment turned to alarm when I went below and suddenly found (2) .... up to my ankles in water. I began pumping it out immediately but after half (3) .... hour's hard work I (4) .... made no progress. The water was still (5) .... fast, so that (6) .... now it was (7) .... to my knees.

I radioed the coastguards for help. I told them my position, and (8) .... my boat looked like. They advised me to keep pumping and said the lifeboat was already (9) .... its way, but (10) .... was another half hour before it reached me. Two men came (11) .... board. They brought a much bigger pump than (12) .... and soon cleared the (13) .... out of the boat. I wasn't (14) .... to see what had happened until we had finished. A locker that holds the anchor had come open. While it was open, water was coming in (15) .... fast as I was pumping it out.

Test 9

Read the text below and think of the word which best fits each space. Use only **one** word in each space. Write your words in the spaces provided.

The mystery of Prospero's Island

Shakespeare's play, *The Tempest*, is (1) .... Prospero, who was abandoned at sea but eventually reached a desert island. Years later he attracts his enemies' ship to the island by (2) .... of his magic skill. (3) .... of the many mysteries related to this play is whether Shakespeare had a real island (4) .... mind and if so, (5) .... it was. Different critics have suggested that Shakespeare was thinking (6) .... Corfu or even Tierra del Fuego.

Prospero's enemies are apparently (7) .... their way from Tunis to Italy and (8) .... the island should be in the Mediterranean. But someone Shakespeare knew had been wrecked on the Bermuda Islands and this may have influenced him. Even (9) .... the seventeenth century these islands had (10) .... bad reputation. In our own times, ships and aircraft have disappeared mysteriously in (11) .... is now known (12) .... the Bermuda Triangle.

According (13) .... some modern interpretations of the play, the real hero is Caliban, a savage who lives (14) .... the island. This seems improbable. Shakespeare's genius helped him to portray the mind of a savage, but this does not mean he preferred a savage life (15) .... civilisation.

Test 10

Read the text below and think of the word which best fits each space. Use only **one** word in each space. Write your words in the spaces provided.

My first real book

The first real book I remember reading, and by that I mean (1) .... of about a hundred pages (2) .... any pictures at all, was a children's edition of *Robinson Crusoe*. All I (3) .... remember about it now is the cover, (4) .... was light blue; I don't know (5) .... much of the story is familiar from that reading because almost (6) .... child in Britain has heard of Robinson Crusoe,

(7) .... was abandoned on a desert island and lived there (8) .... nearly thirty years. I suspect, however, that not very (9) .... people have read the original book by Daniel Defoe, (10) .... in 1719 and one of the earliest novels in English. Those (11) .... have must surely have been surprised to (12) .... out that Crusoe does not have much (13) .... common with the hero of the children's story. Defoe was a typical colonialist; so is Crusoe, (14) .... tells us proudly (15) .... the end of the book how he became rich and conventionally successful.

Test 11

Read the text below and think of the word which best fits each space. Use only **one** word in each space. Write your words in the spaces provided.

Interfering with nature
(1) .... the whole our attempts to control other species in the world have been a failure. If we (2) .... left things alone, the threat posed by pests like rats would probably (3) .... have been so serious. (4) .... thousands of years we have been moving species about (5) .... one reason (6) .... another but we have seldom achieved our objectives and have often (7) .... more harm than good. Rabbits were introduced into Australia, for example, (8) .... the first place (9) .... a source of food but they multiplied at (10) .... a tremendous rate that they (11) .... to be destroyed. Toads were introduced into Pacific islands to provide food (12) .... lizards, themselves introduced (13) .... kill rats, but the poison in the toads' bodies killed the lizards instead. In Britain American grey squirrels were originally introduced just to look pretty, and (14) .... a result our native species, (15) .... red squirrel, is now threatened with extinction.

Test 12

Read the text below and think of the word which best fits each space. Use only **one** word in each space. Write your words in the spaces provided.

A woman climber
Mountain climbing was not thought of (1) .... a sport until the nineteenth century. It was only then that people (2) .... climbing in the Alps for pleasure, and it was not (3) .... some time later that women became (4) .... keen to participate as men. (5) .... then, however, the popularity of mountain climbing among women has grown (6) .... much that (7) .... of them, Rebecca Stephens, has recently climbed the highest peaks in seven continents. A friend of (8) .... suggested climbing the first, Kilimanjaro in Africa, for fun, and this (9) .... her the idea of attempting the rest. The highest, Everest, did not prove the (10) .... difficult; seven climbers died while she was on Mount McKinley; she was almost at the top of Carstensz in New Guinea before she realised that she might have (11) .... a mistake and taken the (12) .... route. Her worst experience, however, was on Aconcagua in the Andes. The wind was so strong near the summit that it (13) .... her an hour to cover the (14) .... thirty metres. The view was wonderful but she couldn't enjoy it because she was sick as (15) .... as she reached the top.

Test 13

Read the text below and think of the word which best fits each space. Use only **one** word in each space. Write your words in the spaces provided.

Dressing up for the wedding
Deciding (1) .... to wear at a wedding nowadays can be as much a problem for the guests (2) .... for the bride. Years ago, you just wore your best clothes. The members of the bride or groom's family were the (3) .... ones who felt obliged to buy (4) .... special for the occasion and even they normally chose clothes they could wear somewhere else so (5) .... not to spend money unnecessarily. Now, however, dress is optional, so (6) .... happens is that people often wear their everyday clothes and look (7) .... if they haven't bothered to

(8) .... any effort at (9) ....
In the United States, weddings can be held
anywhere so guests (10) .... complete
freedom to choose (11) .... they dress.
The (12) .... typical feature of a New
York wedding is that the more expensive the
wedding, the (13) .... the female guests
will try to dress better than the bride. The men
dress (14) .... formally than in Britain and
can wear reasonably colourful clothes
(15) .... causing offence to their hosts.

Test 14

Read the text below and think of the word which best
fits each space. Use only **one** word in each space. Write
your words in the spaces provided.

Identity cards

There must be times when the Prime Minister feels
(1) .... one ever understands him
(2) .... listens to anything he says. As
(3) .... as he makes a suggestion about
what ought to be a harmless topic, everyone starts
(4) .... him why his idea is no good. Take
identity cards, (5) .... instance. He
suggested giving them to everyone claiming social
security to prevent fraud, but now even his
supporters say he (6) .... have kept quiet.

British objections to identity cards surprise people
in most European countries. The (7) ....
of the members of the European Union use them
and they (8) .... be used (9) .... of
passports to cross frontiers. But although they may
have advantages – (10) .... is said that
(11) .... they were in existence
(12) .... would be fewer illegal immigrants
and football hooligans could be prevented
(13) .... going abroad – the British still
associate them with the Second World War and
rationing. There is (14) .... doubt that
they would save money but for many people
reintroducing them sounds (15) .... the
first step towards a police state.

Test 15

Read the text below and think of the word which best
fits each space. Use only **one** word in each space. Write
your words in the spaces provided.

Oslo

People (1) .... impression of Norway is
formed as a result of (2) .... Ibsen's plays
in the theatre must be surprised the plays are
(3) .... dark and depressing, when they
visit the lovely city of Oslo. In contrast to many
capitals, it is beautifully clean. There are
(4) .... empty packets and cans lying
around in the streets; Norwegians are
(5) .... tidy to (6) .... their lovely
city get dirty. There are no ticket collectors on the
buses or trams (7) ...., so perhaps they are
more honest than the rest of us, too. (8) ....
are there any signs of (9) .... is thought by
some to be the Scandinavian vice, drinking too
much to cure melancholy, though this may simply
be a sign of no one (10) .... able to afford
alcohol (11) .... local prices.
A Norwegian friend, however, commented on this
by saying: 'We are certainly proud (12) ....
our city and try to (13) .... it clean, but we
do get depressed in winter. The winters are very
long and then you wish you (14) .... get
away somewhere where the sun is (15) ....'

Rewriting

In one part of the Use of English paper in the Cambridge First Certificate examination you are asked to rewrite sentences in a different way, using a word given, so that each one means the same as a sentence provided. This tests your knowledge of alternative structures and in some cases of phrasal verbs.

The 15 units in this section each consist of four preparatory exercises, of which one or two of them usually deal with phrasal verbs. There is a

fifth exercise, which is in the format of the examination question. The four preparatory exercises do not follow the examination format but provide the necessary practice to deal with the fifth exercise and with questions of the same kind. Before you answer the preparatory exercises, you will find it helpful to look at relevant entries in the Reference Section; the Reference Section number is given in brackets beside the exercise heading, like this: (RS3).

1 **A Comparison of adjectives and adverbs** (RS3, 4)

Compare these sentences:

She's **taller/more intelligent than** her brother.
Her brother is **not as/so tall/intelligent as** she is.

She plays tennis **better/more aggressively than** her brother.
Her brother doesn't play tennis **as/so well/aggressively as** she does.

Rewrite the sentences below without changing the meaning, beginning with the word in brackets.

1 I don't work as hard as she does. (She ...)
2 He's more interested in sport than I am. (I ...)
3 They're not as well off as their cousins. (Their cousins ...)
4 She doesn't write as beautifully as Anne. (Anne ...)
5 I can run faster than all my friends. (None of ...)

B *The same, as ... as* (RS3, 4, 61)

Compare these sentences:

She **weighs as much as** her elder sister.
She **is the same weight as** her elder sister.

Rewrite the sentences below without changing the meaning, using the words given in brackets.

1 I paid as much for my car as he did. (price)
2 Mary's room is the same size as mine. (big)
3 She earns as much as her father. (gets, salary)
4 The baby's eyes are as blue as his mother's. (are, colour blue)
5 I was born on the same day as she was. (am, old)

C *the only ... who/that, everyone/no one else ... except/but* (RS19)

The only one who/that came to her wedding **was** Ruth.
No one else came to her wedding **but/except** Ruth.

The only one (whom/that) you **don't** know is John.
You know **everyone else but/except** John.

Rewrite the sentences below without changing the meaning, using a construction with the word(s) in (brackets).

1 The only one who ever loved her was James. (else)
2 No one else brought a present except Charles. (only)
3 The only one who didn't accept the invitation was Alan. (else)
4 I've introduced you to everyone else but my cousin. (only)
5 Everyone else has gone home except Sarah. (only, still here)

D Phrasal verbs (*make*)

We can use phrasal verbs (a common verb with one or more prepositions, like **make up for**) as alternatives with the same meaning as other verbs or phrases. In this exercise, replace the phrase in *italic* type with the correct phrasal verb in the correct form, as in this example.

The children were so disappointed that they couldn't go out to play that I took them to the cinema to *compensate for* (..make up for..) it.

1   He spoke English so badly that we couldn't *understand* (.................) what he was saying.
2   He *invented* (.................) a story to tell the children when they went to bed.
3   She *pretended* (.................) that she didn't know where it was but I knew she wasn't telling the truth.
4   I'm collecting these pictures of film stars and I only need two more to *complete* (.................) the set.
5   The name painted on the front door was so faint that I couldn't *read* (.................) what it said.

Test 1

Complete the second sentence so that it has a similar meaning to the first sentence. Use the word given and other words to complete each sentence. You must use between two and five words. **Do not change the word given**. There is an example at the beginning (**0**).

0   Her eyes are a different colour from mine.
same
Her eyes are **not the same colour as** mine.
1   My sister is younger than me.
old
I'm not .... as my sister.
2   I don't think Jane and I are much alike.
like
I don't think .... Jane.
3   Johnny's almost as tall as Bob now.
height
Johnny and Bob are almost the .... now.

4   Helen is slim and has fair hair.
fair-haired
Helen is a .... girl.
5   The only person I still keep in touch with is Teresa.
else
I've lost touch with .... but Teresa.
6   I know my sister will always write better than me.
well
I know I will never .... my sister.
7   Our good points compensate for our weaknesses.
make
Our good points .... our weaknesses.
8   She has too much common sense to marry a man like that.
sensible
She .... to marry a man like that.
9   Her parents have a lot of money.
well
Her parents .... off.
10 I'm not nearly as good looking as she is.
much
She's .... I am.

2 A *enough* and *too* (RS20)

Compare these sentences:
They are**n't rich enough** to buy a house like that.
They're **too poor** to buy a house like that.

Rewrite the sentences below without changing the meaning, using the word given in brackets.

1   He wasn't well enough to go to the party. (ill)
2   The house is too small for their needs. (big)
3   We arrived too late to have dinner at the restaurant. (early)
4   It isn't warm enough for you to go out. (cold)
5   Fortunately, the car was travelling too slowly for anyone to be badly hurt in the accident. (fast)

B *almost (never, nothing, no one, none)* and *hardly (ever, any, anything, anyone)* (RS21, 27)

Compare these sentences:
He **almost never** comes into town these days.
He **hardly ever** comes into town these days.

Rewrite the sentences below without changing the meaning, using the word in brackets.

1 He's very quiet. He almost never says a word. (ever)
2 Almost no one works in the village now. (anyone)
3 He spent nearly all his money on the house and now he has hardly anything left. (nothing)
4 I hardly ever watch TV these days. (never)
5 Almost none of her friends have come to see her in hospital. (any)

C *ever* and *never* (RS3, 21)

Compare these sentences:

I've **never** seen **such a beautiful** house.
It's **the most beautiful** house I've **ever** seen.
I've **never** seen **such lovely** flowers.
They're **the loveliest** flowers I've **ever** seen.

Rewrite the sentences below without changing the meaning, using the word given in brackets.

1 I've never had such a good meal. (best)
2 They're the nicest people I've ever met. (such)
3 It's the prettiest village I've ever visited. (pretty)
4 The country has never experienced such unpredictable weather. (most)
5 She says she's never had to look after such badly behaved children. (worst)

D **Phrasal verbs (*look*)**

Replace the phrase in *italic* type, using a phrasal verb with **look** in the correct form.

1 I'll *take care of* (..................) the children while you're out.
2 Can you help us? We're *trying to find* (..................) the road to Fairton.
3 *Be careful!* (..................) There's a car coming!

4 We'd like to *visit* (..................) the house *to see if we want to buy it* before we make up our minds.
5 I'll *investigate* (..................) the matter and see if we can find something to suit you.

Test 2

Complete the second sentence so that it has a similar meaning to the first sentence. Use the word given and other words to complete each sentence. You must use between two and five words. **Do not change the word given**.

1 I can't get all those clothes into my case.
room
There .... for all those clothes in my case.

2 It's no problem for me to get up early.
Getting
....
no problem for me.

3 The house was too expensive for us.
enough
We ....
to buy the house.

4 He complained because the neighbours made so much noise.
objected
He ....
making so much noise.

5 Being on good terms with your neighbours is sensible.
makes
It ....
on good terms with your neighbours.

6 The children aren't allowed to go out on their own.
let
She doesn't ....
go out on their own.

7 The price includes the house and the garage, too.
well
The price includes the garage ....
.... the house.

8 There wasn't enough light in the room for me to study.
dark
It ....
in the room for me to study.

9 We're trying to find a house in the country.
looking
We're ....
a house in the country.

10 It's his job to look after the garden.
responsible
He's ....
after the garden.

3 **A** *for, since* and *ago* (RS5, 24)

Compare these sentences:

I **haven't been** to the High Street **for** a long time.
It's a long time **since** I (last) **went** to the High Street.
The last time I went to the High Street **was** a long time **ago** (*or* I **last went** to the High Street a long time **ago**.)

Rewrite the sentences below without changing the meaning, using the word in brackets.

1 The shop hasn't opened for several weeks. (since)
2 It's at least a year since she last wrote to me. (for)
3 I haven't had steak for lunch for ages. (ago)
4 The last time I went to the hairdresser's was two months ago. (for)
5 It's some time since I last saw her. (for)
6 They last came to see us several days ago. (since)
7 It's over a year since they were living in the district. (for)
8 I've haven't bought anything there for quite a while. (since)

B *the first time* and *never before* (RS73)

Compare these sentences:

It's **the first time** I've **ever** shopped here.
I've **never** shopped here **before**.

It **was the first time** she had **ever** driven a car.
She had never driven a car **before**.

Rewrite the sentences below without changing the meaning, using the word in brackets.

1 It's the first time she's ever said anything to me. (before)
2 He'd never had a meal in an Indian restaurant before. (time)

3 She's never invited me to her house before. (time)
4 It was the first time he had ever travelled abroad. (before)
5 They'd never thought of attracting tourists to the town before. (time)

C *prefer* and *would rather* (RS83)

Compare these sentences:

I **prefer shopping** in the High Street **to going** to the Supermarket.
I'd **rather shop** in the High Street **than go** to the Supermarket.

I'd **prefer not to go** out this afternoon.
I'd **rather not go** out this afternoon.

Rewrite the sentences below without changing the meaning, using the word(s) in brackets.

1 I'd rather cook for myself than go out for a meal. (cooking)
2 I prefer staying in and watching the TV to going out at night in winter. ('d rather)
3 I don't feel very well. I'd rather not have anything to eat. ('d prefer)
4 Which would you prefer to do? Go to the football match or go to the zoo? (rather)
5 He likes the sound of his own voice. He'd rather talk than listen to other people. (talking)

D Phrasal verbs *(work)*

Replace the phrase in *italic* type, using a phrasal verb with **work** in the correct form.

1 I'm trying to *calculate* (..................) how we spent so much money at the supermarket.
2 They didn't want to move the supermarket out of town at first but in the end the move *resulted* (..................) for the best.
3 I just couldn't *produce in myself* (..................) the energy to walk all the way to the High Street.
4 If you bought a dozen of them for one pound twenty that *amounts to* (.................. at) ten pence each.
5 We're trying to decide on the best way to attract shoppers back into the town but so far we have very little data to *use as a basis for action* (..................).

Test 3

Complete the second sentence so that it has a similar meaning to the first sentence. Use the word given and other words to complete each sentence. You must use between two and five words. **Do not change the word given**.

1   I haven't bought any new clothes for a long time.
    since
    It's a long time ....
    .... any new clothes.

2   I last visited Glasgow twenty years ago.
    for
    I ....
    twenty years.

3   I like living in the city better than in the country.
    rather
    I ....
    in the city than in the country.

4   'Would you like to spend the weekend with me?' she said to Jane.
    invited
    She ....
    the weekend with her.

5   I've only been working here for a few days.
    started
    I ....
    here a few days ago.

6   She has lived here since she was born.
    life
    She has lived here ....

7   I'd be quite willing to go with you.
    mind
    I ....
    with you.

8   I think what she says is right.
    agree
    I ....
    what she says.

9   I'm trying to calculate the cost of the journey.
    work
    I'm trying to ....
    .... the journey cost.

10 The town centre is full of shops.
    plenty
    There ....
    the town centre.

4   A   *either, neither, nor* (RS45)

Compare these sentences:

Neither of us knew the answer.
I didn't know the answer, **and she** didn't, either.

Neither of the girls was a neighbour **of hers.**
She **wasn't** a neighbour of **either** of the girls.

I don't like him, and **neither/nor does** she.
I don't like him, and she **doesn't, either.**

Neither Paul nor Peter **knows** anything about it.
Paul **doesn't know** anything about it, and Peter **doesn't, either** (and **neither/nor does** Peter).

Rewrite the sentences below without changing the meaning, using the word(s) in (brackets).

1   I didn't go to school yesterday, and she didn't, either. (Neither of us)
2   Neither of the girls was in the same class as Susan. (Susan wasn't)
3   Frank hasn't done his homework and Bob hasn't done it, either. (Neither, Frank)
4   Barbara hasn't arrived, and Pauline hasn't, either. (nor)
5   Neither Jack nor Jill can come to the party. (Jack can't)

B   *it seems that, seems to be, to have been*

Study these sentences. With verbs like **seem, appear** we can either use an impersonal construction with **that** or a construction that can have a personal subject with the infinitive or perfect infinitive. Compare these sentences:

It seems that they're winning.
They **seem to be winning.**

It appears that she **doesn't attend** classes regularly.
She **appears not to attend** classes regularly.

It seems that they've gone out.
They **seem to have gone out.**

It appears that they **didn't do** much work last year.
They **appear not to have done** much work last year.

It seemed that he had left school quite young.
He **seemed to have left** school quite young.

Rewrite the sentences below without changing the meaning, beginning with the word(s) in (brackets).

1 It seems that they're having a party. (They ...)
2 It seems that we've arrived at the wrong time. (We ...)
3 It appears that the shops don't open here on Sundays. (The shops...)
4 It seems that he ran away from school. (He ...)
5 It seemed that she had lost her way. (She ...)

C Phrasal verbs (*put*)

Replace the phrase in *italic* type, using a phrasal verb with **put** in the correct form.

1 I'm not going to *tolerate* (...............) any more interruptions in class.
2 It's too late for Sarah's school friend to go home, so we're going to *give her a bed* (......... her ....) for the night.
3 The noise outside *prevents me from concentrating on* (.............. me ....) my work.
4 We've had to *postpone* (...............) the meeting with the parents because the Head Teacher is ill.
5 When the teacher asked him what he was doing, he *assumed* (...............) an innocent expression.

D Phrasal verbs (*stand*)

Replace the phrase in *italic* type, using a phrasal verb with **stand** in the correct form.

1 She's easily the best student in the class. She *is easily distinguished* (..............) from the rest.
2 What do the letters EU *represent* (...............)?
3 I'm not prepared to *put up with* (.............) that sort of behaviour.
4 You can be unhappy at school if you don't *defend* (...............) yourself.
5 I'll *keep* (...............) my promise to help you.

Test 4

Complete the second sentence so that it has a similar meaning to the first sentence.

1 I had never been to school before.
first
It ....
I had been to school.
2 Please send me your brochure.
grateful
I ....
if you would send me your brochure.
3 Neither of the students was familiar to her.
either
She didn't ....
.... of the students.
4 When he said 'hello', I recognised him.
until
I .... he said 'hello'.
5 It seemed that she had forgotten everything she had learnt.
have
She ....
forgotten everything she had learnt.
6 I was the one who marked her exam paper, as it happens.
happened
I ....
who marked her exam paper.
7 Her parents expected her to get a good mark in the exam.
well
Her parents expected her ....
.... in the exam.
8 She was not aware that she had fallen asleep.
realising
She had fallen asleep ....
.... it.
9 I lost interest in the subject when the teacher didn't answer my questions.
put
When the teacher didn't answer my questions it .... the subject.
10 He was so tall that he was easily visible in a crowd.
stood
He was so tall that he ....
.... in a crowd.

5 **A** **Relative adverb,** *where* (RS58)

Compare these sentences:

A baker's is a shop **that sells** bread.
A baker's is a shop **where you can buy** bread.

My father works **at** that factory over there.
That factory over there **is where** my father works.

Rewrite the sentences below without changing the meaning, using **where**.

1 An ironmonger's is a shop that sells tools and household articles.
2 I went to school at that school over there.
3 A stationer's is a shop that sells pens and writing materials.
4 I was born in that little village near the railway line.
5 They made the TV serial of *Middlemarch* in that town.

B *have, get something done* (RS28)

Compare these sentences:

That's where **they cut** my hair.
That's where **I had** my hair cut.

I went to the hairdresser's **because I wanted them** to cut my hair.

I went to the hairdresser's **to get** my hair cut.

Rewrite the sentences below without changing the meaning, using the word(s) given in brackets.

1 That's the hospital where they took my appendix out. (had)
2 I'm going to the garage because I want them to service my car. (get)
3 I've come to see you because I'd like you to paint my house. (have)
4 I went to the passport office because I wanted them to renew my passport. (get)
5 I'm looking for a shop where they'll mend my glasses. (can get)

C **Phrasal verbs** *(come)*

Replace the phrase in *italic* type, using a phrasal verb with **come** in the correct form.

1 I *met her by chance* (................ her) in the street the other day.

2 I'm waiting for his new book to *be published* (................).
3 This question *arose* (................) some time ago but we haven't found a solution yet.
4 They were interested in buying the house but when they went to see it, it didn't *reach the level of* (................) their expectations.
5 She *inherited* (................) a lot of money when her parents died.

D **Phrasal verbs** *(take)*

Replace the phrase in *italic* type, using a phrasal verb with **take** in the correct form.

1 You can see from his eyes that he *resembles* (................) his grandmother.
2 What time does your flight *depart* (................)?
3 They have bought some shares and *gained control of* (................) the rival company.
4 When I retire from this job, I'm going to *start playing* (................) golf.
5 You must be busy, so I don't want to *occupy* (................) too much of your time.

Test 5

Complete the second sentence so that it has a similar meaning to the first sentence.

1 A dairy is a shop that sells milk.
   where
   A dairy is a shop .... milk.
2 Mark's the only one who doesn't arrive on time.
   except
   Everyone .... Mark.
3 That's the shop where they took my photograph.
   had
   I .... in that shop.
4 He doesn't care about anything but work.
   only
   Work is .... about.

5   When I first came here, I only expected to stay for a month.
    longer
    I didn't ....
    a month when I first came here.

6   She seems to be interested in becoming a lawyer.
    keen
    She seems to be ....
    a career as a lawyer.

7   When the police are working, they are not supposed to drink.
    duty
    When they're ....
    the police are not supposed to drink.

8   He succeeded his father as manager when his father retired.
    took
    He ....
    as manager when his father retired.

9   I found these old photographs by chance the other day.
    came
    I ....
    these old photographs the other day.

10 We're looking for a properly qualified, experienced guide.
    proper
    We're looking for a guide ....
    .... and experience.

6 **A** *may, might* **and possibility** (RS42)

Compare the sentences with **possible** with the forms using **may** or **might** that follow them:

It's **possible that** they are out.
They **may be** out.

It's **just possible that** they **are playing** tennis.
They **might be playing** tennis.

It's **possible that** she **will arrive** late.
She **may arrive** late.

It's **just possible that** they **won't be expecting** her.
They **might not be expecting** her.

Rewrite the sentences without changing the meaning, using the word given in brackets.

1   It's possible that they don't know we're here. (may)

2   It's just possible that she will catch a later flight. (might)
3   It's possible that they will meet her at the airport. (may)
4   It's just possible that they aren't working today. (might)
5   It's possible that she's going away for the weekend. (may)

B *if not, unless* (RS75)

Compare these sentences:

I can't help you **if** you **don't tell** me what's wrong.
I can't help you **unless** you **tell** me what's wrong.

Rewrite the sentences without changing the meaning, using the word given in brackets.

1   If we don't hurry, we'll miss the train. (Unless)
2   Unless you pay the fare, you'll have to get off. (If)
3   I don't suppose she'll want to come unless John does. (if)
4   I'll see you next Sunday at the station, if you don't ring me before then. (unless)
5   If there's nothing else for us to discuss, we'll end the meeting. (Unless)

C **Phrasal verbs** *(go)*

Replace the phrase in *italic* type, using a phrasal verb with **go** in the correct form.

1   What's *happening* (.................) this weekend? What are you planning to do?
2   I'm *entering* (.................) for the First Certificate examination soon.
3   I'm sorry I interrupted you. Please *continue* (.................).
4   If you're going on a picnic, make sure there's enough food to *provide for everyone* (.................).
5   I was a bit frightened when I first started climbing but as time *passed* (.................) I overcame my fears.

D Phrasal verbs (set)

Replace the phrase in *italic* type, using a phrasal verb with **set** in the correct form.

1 We *started our journey* (.................)
(*or* ....) early the next morning.
2 They've *established* (.................) an
information bureau for tourists.
3 If someone gets into the house and stands
in front of this light it *makes the alarm
ring* (................. the alarm).
4 All the brochures for the different holidays
were *displayed* (.................) on her desk
at the travel agency.
5 I'd like to go on holiday before winter
establishes itself (.................).

Test 6

Complete the second sentence so that it has a similar meaning to the first sentence. Use the word given and other words to complete each sentence. You must use between two and five words. **Do not change the words given.**

1 It's possible that they'll come with us this
weekend.
may
They ....
.... with us this weekend.
2 'I'd make an early start, if I were you,' she
told us.
advised
She ....
an early start.
3 If it doesn't rain later on, we'll go for a picnic.
unless
We'll go for a picnic ....
.... later on.
4 She has a small chance of winning but I don't
expect her to.
might
She ....
though I don't expect her to.
5 She owns the company and she's the
managing director, too.
well
She owns the company, ...
.... the managing director.

6 The first thing I'm going to do when I arrive
home is to ring her.
soon
I'm going to ring her ....
.... home.
7 They're going to hold the festival next
weekend.
place
The festival ....
.... next weekend.
8 It's cold throughout the year in the north of
Norway.
round
It's cold ....
.... in the north of Norway.
9 We must start our journey at six o'clock
tomorrow morning.
set
We must ....
.... at six o'clock tomorrow
morning.
10 The facilities are not very well looked after.
condition
The facilities are not ....
....

7 A Active and passive (RS49)

Study the examples in Reference Section 49, and then rewrite the sentences below without changing the meaning, beginning with the words given in brackets. There is no need to use an agent (**by ...**) when converting to a passive construction.

1 They take the tourists up the river from
here. (The tourists ...)
2 We'll inform you of any changes in the
programme. (You ...)
3 They've reserved these rooms for the
Queen's party. (These rooms ...)
4 We are posting the brochure to your
address. (The brochure ...)
5 You can obtain further information at the
counter. (Further information ...)
6 They're going to offer their customers
cheap flights to New York. (Their
customers...)
7 They didn't make offers like that last year.
(Offers like that ...)
8 They shouldn't expect you to pay for the
tickets in advance. (You ...)

9 If you haven't paid for the tickets, the booking will be cancelled.
(If the tickets …)

10 They're putting through your call to Reception now.
(Your call …)

B Past tenses, *whenever, used to, would* (RS76)

Compare these sentences:

I **lived** in London before I moved here.
I **used to live** in London (before I moved here).

Whenever (**Every time**) I went to my grandmother's, she **made** a cake.
When I went to my grandmother's she **would make** a cake.

Rewrite the sentences below without changing the meaning, using the word in brackets and leaving out the phrase in *italic* type.

1 I had a dog when I was little *but it died a long time ago*. (used)

2 I worked in an office in the city *in those days*. (used)

3 Every time I arrived at the office the old caretaker looked at his watch to see if I was late. (would)

4 I caught the same train every morning *then*. (used)

5 Whenever it was late all the passengers complained. (would)

C Phrasal verbs *(get)*

Replace the phrase in *italic* type, using a phrasal verb with **get** in the correct form.

1 I'm glad to see she has *recovered from* (………………) her illness.

2 It *depresses me* (………. me ……….) when it rains like this on holiday.

3 She works hard and is very intelligent, so she's sure to *make progress* in life (………………).

4 We ran after the thief but he *escaped* (………………).

5 He's *becoming rather old* (………………) and doesn't hear you very well.

D Phrasal verbs *(give)*

Replace the phrase in *italic* type, using a phrasal verb with **give** in the correct form.

1 They got near the top of the mountain but in the end they had to *abandon* (………………) the attempt to climb it.

2 They could not go any further because their food had *been used up* (………………)

3 They have just *announced* (………………) on the loudspeaker that the flight has been cancelled.

4 He pretended he was someone else when he rang but his voice *told me who he was* (………. him ……….).

5 He's *resigned from* (………………) his job and gone to live abroad.

Test 7

Complete the second sentence so that it has a similar meaning to the first sentence. Use the word given and other words to complete each sentence. You must use between two and five words. **Do not change the words given**.

1 We'll give you more information later.
given
You …………………………………………… more information later.

2 Nobody has consulted me about the holiday plans.
I
…………………………………………… about the holiday plans.

3 They're opening new hotels all over the island.
opened
New hotels …………………………………… ……………… all over the island.

4 When I was a child, we spent our summer holiday by the sea.
used
We …………………………………………… our summer holiday by the sea when I was a child.

5 Whenever I visited my aunt Sarah, she gave me sweets.
would
My aunt Sarah ………………………………… ……………… sweets when I visited her.

6 Can you see the sea from your hotel?
view
Is ....
the sea from your hotel?

7 How much would it cost us to stay there for a fortnight?
charged
How much ....
.... there for a fortnight's stay?

8 She got very angry and started to shout at me.
temper
She ....
and started to shout at me.

9 By the time we reached the hostel, I was exhausted.
worn
I ....
by the time we reached the hostel.

10 How much does it cost to join the club?
member
How much does it cost ....
.... the club?

8 A Reported speech (statement) (RS59a)

Study the examples in Reference Section 59a and then rewrite the sentences below without changing the meaning, beginning with the phrase in brackets.

1 'I'm feeling rather tired,' she said. (She said she ...)
2 'I took up climbing two years ago,' she told me. (She told me she ...)
3 'I always wear strong boots when I go climbing,' she said. (She said she ...)
4 'I've never been in a more dangerous situation,' he told me. (He told me he ...)
5 'I didn't understand the problem at first,' he said. (He said he ...)
6 'I'm going to go down the mountain to see if I can find someone to help,' she told me. (She told me she ...)
7 'I think I can still make the effort to get to the top,' she said. (She said she ...)
8 'I expect there will be a lot of people here tomorrow,' she said. (She said she ...)
9 'I may need to take a few days off in view of what the doctor told me yesterday,' he said. (He said he ...)
10 'I hope we'll still be alive when the rescuers get here,' I said. (I said I ...)

B Reported speech (orders and requests) (RS59c)

Study the examples in Reference Section 59c and then rewrite the sentences below without changing the meaning, beginning with the phrase in brackets.

1 'Call an ambulance!' she said. (She told me ...)
2 'Don't stand there doing nothing!' he said. (He told me ...)
3 'Please don't smoke here,' she said. (She asked him ...)
4 'Give me a hand with the luggage, will you?' she said. (She asked me ...)
5 'Please don't move me from here,' he said. (He begged us ...)

C Indirect speech, Paraphrase 1 (RS34)

Study the examples in Reference Section 34 and then rewrite the sentences below without changing the meaning, beginning with the phrase in brackets.

1 'You left your companion alone on the mountain,' the team leader said to him. (The team leader accused ...)
2 'I'm sorry I didn't tell you I was coming,' she said to me. (She apologised ...)
3 'I didn't take the money,' he said. (He denied ...)
4 'I'll go with you,' she said to him. (She offered ...)
5 'I'm not going out in weather like this,' he said. (He refused ...)
6 'You shouldn't spend so much time indoors,' the doctor told her. (The doctor advised ...)
7 'Be careful not to go too close to the edge of the river,' she told Charlie. (She warned Charlie ...)
8 'Don't forget to pack your climbing boots,' my mother said to me. (My mother reminded ...)
9 'I'll punish you if you do that again,' he told the boy. (He threatened ...)
10 'Let's try to get to the top before it gets dark,' she said to them. (She suggested ...)

D Phrasal verbs (*run*)

Replace the phrase in *italic* type, using a phrasal verb with **run** in the correct form.

1 They *used up all their supplies* (................) of food when they were only half way up the mountain.
2 She's upset because her cat has been *knocked down* (................) by a car.
3 The doctor said she was *tired and overworked* (................) and needed a rest.
4 I just want to *check quickly* (................) the main points of the speech again.
5 I met him *by chance* (................ *him*) in Oxford Street last week.

Test 8

Complete the second sentence so that it has a similar meaning to the first sentence. Use the word given and other words to complete each sentence. You must use between two and five words. **Do not change the words given**.

1 He succeeded in escaping from the burning house.
managed
He ....
from the burning house.
2 'I haven't had anything to eat since yesterday,' she said.
she
She said that ....
anything to eat since the day before.
3 'If the missing climbers don't appear we'll have to send out a search party,' he said.
they
He said that if the missing climbers .... have to send out a search party.
4 'I can hardly believe we've been saved,' he said.
they
He said he ....
.... been saved.
5 The first thing I did when I entered the house was to turn off the gas.
soon
As ....
the house, I turned off the gas.

6 'Don't worry about me if I'm late!' she told her husband.
her
She told her husband ....
.... if she was late.
7 He was foolish to go climbing alone in this weather.
own
He was foolish to go climbing ....
.... in this weather.
8 They had no petrol left.
ran
They had ....
petrol.
9 She started skiing last year.
took
She .... ago.
10 She couldn't see her companions any more because of the fog.
sight
She ....
her companions in the fog.

9 A Reported speech (questions) (RS59b)

Study the examples in Reference Section 59b and then rewrite the sentences below without changing the meaning, beginning with the phrase in brackets.

1 'Do you know how old it is?' she asked him. (She asked him if …)
2 'Did you go on the visit to Stonehenge last week?' I asked her. (I asked her if …)
3 'Are you planning to go on the excursion next weekend?' he asked me. (He asked me whether …)
4 'How long have the stones been there?' they said. (They wanted to know how …)
5 'Why did they carve this figure in the chalk?' I asked. (I asked why …)
6 'Is the article you are writing going to provide the answer to the mystery when it appears?' they asked her. (They asked her if …)
7 'Do you know where I can get information about these strange monuments?' she asked me. (She asked me if …)
8 'What will people say when they realise I've solved the mystery?' she wondered. (She wondered what …)

9 'Do you believe the police are right in thinking a burglar got into the house?' she asked him. (She asked him if …)

10 'May someone who works here have been responsible?' she wondered. (She wondered if …)

B Indirect speech, Paraphrase 2 (RS34)

Study the examples in Reference Section 34 and then rewrite the sentences below without changing the meaning, beginning with the phrase in brackets.

1 'Will I ever be rich?' she asked herself. (She wondered …)

2 'Why didn't you answer the door bell?' she complained. (She complained because …)

3 'Would you like to spend the weekend with us?' she asked me. (She invited …)

4 'Would you like me to carry your case for you?' I asked her. (I offered …)

5 'Why don't we make a thorough search of the house to see if we can find it?' he said to us. (He suggested …)

C Possibility and deduction in the past (*may have*, *might have* and *must have* + past participle) (RS43)

Compare these sentences:

It's possible that they **were not involved** in the crime.
They **may not have been involved** in the crime.

It's just possible that they **knew** nothing about it.
They **might have known** nothing about it.

But **I'm sure** they **helped** the thief to escape.
But they **must have helped** the thief to escape.

I'm certain he **didn't get away** by himself.
He **could not have got away** by himself.

Rewrite the sentences below without changing the meaning, using the word given in brackets.

1 It's possible that his death was an accident. (may)

2 It's just possible that he fell and hit his head on the stone floor. (might)

3 But, judging from the state of the room, I'm sure someone else came in. (must)

4 I'm certain he didn't throw all these papers on the floor himself. (couldn't)

5 It's possible that the thief did not mean to kill him. (may)

6 It's just possible he had got in and was looking for something. (might)

7 It's logical that the owner heard a noise and came downstairs and surprised him. (must)

8 I suppose the thief didn't have time to get away without being seen. (couldn't)

9 I expect he knocked him down, trying to escape. (must)

10 But of course it's possible that it didn't happen like that at all. (may)

D Phrasal verbs (*break*)

Replace the phrase in *italic* type, using a phrasal verb with **break** in the correct form.

1 The thieves must have *entered the house by force* (................. the house) and stolen the papers.

2 I was late for the meeting because my car *came to a stop* (..................) and I had to walk the rest of the way.

3 They are afraid that war will *start* (.................) between the two countries.

4 The end of term is on December 21st. That's when school *ends for the holidays* (..................).

5 When she saw him lying dead she *collapsed and burst into tears* (.................).

Test 9

Complete the second sentence so that it has a similar meaning to the first sentence.

1 'Do you know his name?' I asked her.
if
I asked her .... his name.

2 'Have you had time to read the book?' she asked me.
wondered
She .... time to read the book.

3 'Where did you find the ticket?' he asked her.
   she
   He asked her ....
   .... the ticket.

4 He wondered if he would ever solve the mystery.
   I
   He said to himself: '.......................................
   .... ever solve the mystery?'

5 Perhaps the postman hasn't come yet.
   may
   The postman .... yet.

6 I'm sure the thieves broke the window.
   must
   The thieves .... the window.

7 I'm sure Jane wasn't the one who answered the phone.
   couldn't
   It .... Jane who answered the phone.

8 He wasn't involved in the crime.
   nothing
   The crime had .... him.

9 'Are you in charge of the investigation?' she asked him.
   responsible
   She asked him if ....
   .... the investigation.

10 'I'm sure there was a logical explanation for what had happened,' she said.
   must
   She said there ....
   a logical explanation for what had happened.

10 A Linking sentences (non-defining relative clauses) (RS58b, 79)

Study the examples and the table of relative pronouns used in non-defining relative clauses in Reference Sections 58b and 79. Then rewrite the sentences below, linking them with the word given in brackets, following a comma.

1 Sir Arthur Conan Doyle invented Sherlock Holmes, but he was a doctor by profession. (, who …)

2 The first book he wrote about Holmes was *A Study in Scarlet*; this came out in 1888. (, which …)

3 The book also features Dr Watson, as Conan Doyle invented him at the same time. (, whom …)

4 A few years later Conan Doyle 'killed' Holmes; his adventures had begun to bore him. (, whose …)

5 But when someone gave him the idea for *The Hound of the Baskervilles* he had to revive Holmes. Without him the story would lose its interest. (, without …)

6 The story takes place on Dartmoor. The most famous prison in England was there. (, where …)

B Linking sentences (sentence-relative clauses) (RS58c)

Study the examples of sentence-relative clauses in Reference Section 58c. Then rewrite the sentences below, linking them together with **which**, following a comma.

1 Sherlock Holmes is still very popular and that's rather surprising.

2 The stories are set in a world quite different from ours, and you'd imagine that would put young people off.

3 They often involve people who had made a fortune in the 'colonies'; that was quite common in those days.

4 But of course they have been dramatised so often in films and TV, and that has made the characters familiar.

5 Perhaps far more people know who Sherlock Holmes was than have read the stories; that would make sense.

C *needn't, it isn't necessary to* (RS44)

Compare these sentences:

It isn't necessary for you to wait for me.
You needn't wait for me.

Is it necessary for us to buy the book?
Need we/Do we need to buy the book?

It isn't necessary to pay for the books in cash.
You needn't pay for the books in cash.
The books needn't be paid for in cash.

It wasn't necessary for me to borrow the video; I've already seen it.
I didn't need to borrow the video; I've already seen it.

It wasn't necessary for you to buy the video; you could have borrowed my copy.
You needn't have bought the video; you could have borrowed my copy.

Rewrite the sentences below without changing the meaning, beginning with the word(s) given in brackets.

1   It isn't necessary for you to write a synopsis of the whole book. (You …)
2   Is it necessary for us to include all the characters in the synopsis? (Need …)
3   It isn't necessary to hand in the synopsis until the next lesson. (The synopsis …)
4   It wasn't necessary for you to read the whole book by today but if you've already finished it, it will save time. (You …)
5   It wasn't necessary for us to read the whole book by today because the teacher only said we had to do the first chapter. (We …)

D   Phrasal verbs (*bring*)

Replace the phrase in *italic* type, using a phrasal verb with **bring** in the correct form.

1   When her parents died, she was *taken care of and taught how to behave* (………………) by her aunt and uncle.
2   They're *publishing* (………………) her new book in the spring.
3   I hope he doesn't *raise* (………………) that question at the meeting.
4   I haven't written a word of any of my books by hand since they *introduced* (………………) word processors.
5   She seems to have fainted. What can we do to *make her conscious again* (……… her ………)?

Test 10

Complete the second sentence so that it has a similar meaning to the first sentence. Use the word given and other words to complete each sentence. You must use between two and five words. **Do not change the words given**.

1   She wrote several books but most of them are out of print now.
    which
    She wrote several books, ……………………………… ………………………………… out of print now.
2   I'm going back to Farley, the town I grew up in.
    where
    I'm going back to Farley, ……………………………… ………………………………… grew up.
3   I lost the book I borrowed from her and so she was annoyed.
    which
    I lost the book I borrowed, ……………………………… ………………………………… annoyed her.
4   It doesn't matter what you say; they won't be satisfied.
    whatever
    They won't ……………………………………………… ………………………… you say.
5   'I'm afraid I haven't had time to read it,' he said.
    admitted
    He ……………………………………………………………… had time to read it.
6   'Come with me to France!' he said to her.
    begged
    He ……………………………………………………………… him to France.
7   In the next chapter, Jane meets Mr Rochester, the hero.
    whose
    In the next chapter, Jane meets the hero, …………………………………………………………… Mr Rochester.
8   It's the most interesting book I've ever read.
    never
    I've ……………………………………………………………… interesting book.
9   Now that the book has been published, we can all read it.
    come
    Now that the book ……………………………………… ………………………… we can all read it.
10 It isn't necessary to answer the questions in ink.
    needn't
    The questions ……………………………………………… ………………………… in ink.

11 A *although, even though, despite, in spite of* (RS7)

Compare these sentences:

Although/Even though the dog was angry, it didn't bite me.
Despite/In spite of being angry, the dog didn't bite me.
Despite/In spite of its anger, the dog didn't bite me.
Although/Even though I had been kind to it, the cat never showed any gratitude.
Despite/In spite of my having been/being kind to it, the cat never showed any gratitude.
Despite/In spite of my kindness to it, the cat never showed any gratitude.

Rewrite the sentences below without changing the meaning, using the word(s) given in brackets.

1　In spite of having very little room to move, the animals seem quite happy. (Although)
2　The animal was shivering with cold although the weather was fine. (in spite of)
3　Despite its bad temper, we were fond of the dog. (Although)
4　The dog broke away from her despite being on the lead. (even though)
5　Although I had been away for so long, the dog still remembered me. (Despite)
6　In spite of the children's screams, he went into the lion's cage. (Although)
7　The animal refused to eat anything even though it felt hungry. (despite)
8　Even though it's such a lovely dog, I wouldn't want to keep it in the city. (In spite of)

B *so and such* (RS60)

Compare these sentences:

That dog is **so noisy** that it keeps me awake.
It's **such a noisy dog** that it keeps me awake.

The weather has been **so bad** that we couldn't take the dog out for a walk.
It's been **such bad weather** that we couldn't take the dog out for a walk.

Those dogs are **so affectionate** that they can't bear to be left alone.
They're **such affectionate dogs** that they can't bear to be left alone.

Rewrite the sentences below without changing the meaning, using the word(s) given in brackets.

1　The cat is so beautiful that it knows everyone admires it. (such)
2　It has such soft fur that I love to stroke it. (so)
3　But it's so independent that we never know where it is. (such ... cat)
4　The dogs are so large that they eat pounds of meat every day. (such ... dogs)
5　But they have such a healthy look that I don't mind paying for it. (look so)
6　Its teeth were so sharp that I was frightened of it. (had such)
7　The horse is so strong that it can run for miles. (such)
8　It has such a sweet look that it seems to be smiling. (looks)

C Conditional sentences and alternatives (RS16c–f)

Study the examples given in Reference Section 16c–f and compare these sentences:

I **don't know** the answer to your question **or I'd tell you/so I can't tell you.**
If I knew the answer to your question, I'd tell you.

I **didn't see** the accident **or I'd have reported it/ so I didn't** report it.
If I'd seen the accident, I'd have reported it.

It would be nice to have a lot of money; **then** I'd buy a house in the country.
If I **had** a lot of money, I'd buy a house in the country.
It's a pity I didn't study more last year; **then** I'd have passed the exam.
If I'd **studied** more last year, I'd have passed the exam.

Rewrite the sentences below without changing the meaning, beginning with the word(s) in brackets.

1　It would be nice to go away this weekend; then we could have a good long rest from work. (If we ...)

2 It's a pity they didn't come by car; then they could have given us a lift home. (If they …)

3 I can't remember her phone number or I'd ring her. (If I …)

4 They weren't at home so we couldn't carry out the repairs. (If they …)

5 I made her sit down or she'd have fainted. (If I …)

6 I haven't got her address so I can't give it to you. (If I …)

7 I should have made a note of it; then I'd have it in my diary. (If I …)

8 If you should happen to find it, please let me know. (Should …)

9 If I'd known you were coming, I'd have made adequate preparations for your visit. (Had …)

10 If we were to lend you the money, what terms could you offer us for repayment? (Were …)

D Impersonal construction (*It is said that* …) and alternatives

Compare these sentences. Note the differences in form and tense:

It is thought that the fire **is spreading** fast.
The fire **is thought to be spreading** fast.

It is expected that the situation **will get** worse tomorrow.
The situation **is expected to get** worse tomorrow.

It is said that the Government **has taken** special measures to deal with it.
The Government **is said to have taken** special measures to deal with it.

It is believed that someone **set** the forest on fire deliberately.
Someone **is believed to have set** the forest on fire deliberately.

Rewrite these sentences without changing the meaning, beginning with the word(s) in brackets.

1 It's thought that this species of monkey is dying out. (This species …)

2 It's expected that conservationists will take action to protect it. (Conservationists …)

3 It's said that these monkeys were very common a few years ago. (These monkeys …)

4 It's believed that changes in the environment have affected their food supply. (Changes …)

5 It's reported that a team of experts set out for the jungle last week to investigate. (A team …)

6 It's understood that the team are exploring the jungle at present to estimate how serious the problem is. (The team …)

Test 11

Complete the second sentence so that it has a similar meaning to the first sentence.

1 Although he felt sorry for the animal, he couldn't afford to keep it.
despite
He couldn't afford to keep the animal, ………
…………………………………………… sorry for it.

2 It was such a friendly cat that we all liked it.
so
The cat ………………………… that we all liked it.

3 In spite of his fear, he approached the dog.
although
He approached the dog …………………………
………………………………………… it.

4 I meant to take the dog for a walk but I didn't have time.
had
If I had ………………………………………………
………………………… taken the dog for a walk.

5 Those birds are so noisy that they get on my nerves.
much
Those birds make ………………………………………
………………………………… they get on my nerves.

6 They should warn people that the animals are dangerous; then they wouldn't go near them.
If
………………………………………… that the animals are dangerous, they wouldn't go near them.

7 I don't know how you can stand that dog barking all the time.
put
I don't know how ………………………………………
that dog barking all the time.

8   The dog has gone mad and will have to be destroyed.
rid
We will have to ....
.... because it has gone mad.

9   It's said that these monkeys are in danger of extinction.
be
These monkeys ....
in danger of extinction.

10 They bred this dog originally to protect sheep from wolves, they say.
said
This dog is ....
bred originally to protect sheep from wolves.

12 **A** *I wish, If only* **and alternatives**
(RS81)

Compare these sentences:

What a pity she **isn't** here!
I wish she **were/was** here.

What a pity we **can't** afford it!
I wish we **could** afford it.

Why don't you **do** as you're told?
I wish you **would do** as you're told.

What a pity he **won't/doesn't** take your advice!
If only he **would take** your advice.

It's a pity we **arrived** too late to say goodbye to her.
I wish we **hadn't arrived** too late to say goodbye to her.

You should have listened to your uncle. (Then this wouldn't have happened.)
I wish you'd listened to your uncle. (Then this wouldn't have happened.)

Rewrite the sentences below without changing the meaning, beginning with **I wish** or **If only**.

1   What a pity she's so busy! (I wish …)
2   What a pity they don't get on better! (I wish …)
3   It's a pity they didn't advertise the post more widely. (If only …)
4   You should have chosen the best candidate for the job. (I wish …)
5   Why don't they promote people on merit, not according to sex? (I wish …)

6   What a pity you can't see him making a fool of himself! (I wish …)
7   What a pity they won't accept that they make mistakes! (If only …)
8   You shouldn't have argued with him. It never does any good. (I wish …)
9   Why do you always interrupt me when I'm talking at the office meeting? (I wish …)
10 It's a pity they moved to the office outside the city. (I wish …)

B *still … not* **and** *not … yet* (RS67)

Compare these sentences:

They've been talking for an hour but they **haven't reached** a decision **yet**.
They've been talking for an hour but they **still haven't reached** a decision.

Rewrite the sentences below, making them more or less emphatic by using the word in brackets. Be careful of word order.

1   They haven't appointed a new manager yet. (still)
2   They've been trying to solve the problem for some time but they still haven't found the answer. (yet)
3   I've asked him several times to pay the bill but he hasn't paid it yet. (still)
4   He's been working here for two months, but he doesn't know his way round the office yet. (still)
5   You still don't understand what I'm talking about, do you? (yet)

C *in case* (RS32)

Compare these sentences:

I'm going to stay late at the office **because** the boss **may/might need** to dictate some letters.
I'm going to stay late at the office **in case** the boss **needs** to dictate some letters.

I put a note on his desk **because** I thought he **might forget** to ring her.
I put a note on his desk **in case he forgot** to ring her.

I also left a message on his answerphone **because** he **might not have gone** back to his office.

I also left a message on his answerphone **in case** he **hadn't gone** back to his office.

Rewrite the sentences below without changing the meaning, using **in case**.

1 I'm going to answer some more advertisements for jobs because I may not get the one I've applied for.
2 He wants someone to go with him because he may need help.
3 She always has some aspirin in her desk because someone may have a headache.
4 They invited several candidates to the interview because they thought they might not find the person they were looking for immediately.
5 I've left a copy of my letter on your desk because you might not have seen it.

D Phrasal verbs: *turn*

Replace the phrase in *italic* type, using a phrasal verb with **turn** in the correct form.

1 I was surprised when my old colleague *appeared unexpectedly* (.................) at the office party.
2 I didn't think I'd like the job at first, but it has *proved* (.................) to be more interesting than I expected.
3 I wouldn't *refuse* (.................) promotion if they offered it to me.
4 She's the managing director of a firm that *produces* (.................) ten thousand washing machines a day.
5 Don't worry about that file you lost. It's sure to *be found by chance* (.................) somewhere sooner or later.

Test 12

Complete the second sentence so that it has a similar meaning to the first sentence.

1 What a pity she didn't get the job!
   wish
   I ....
   the job.

2 It's so annoying that they play pop music all the time!
   wish
   I ....
   play pop music all the time!
3 'I wish I hadn't left school so early,' she said.
   regretted
   She ....
   school so early.
4 It's a pity she doesn't work here any more.
   still
   I wish .... here.
5 Take an umbrella with you because it may rain later.
   case
   Take an umbrella with you ....
   .... later.
6 I don't see why they prefer a man to do this job.
   rather
   I don't see why they ....
   .... to do this job.
7 'You should complain to the boss about it,' I told her.
   advised
   I ....
   to the boss about it.
8 'I'm sorry we didn't send you the goods on time,' he said.
   apologised
   He ....
   the goods on time.
9 Give yourself time to decide on the best course of action.
   work
   Give yourself time ....
   .... the best course of action.
10 The move to the new offices proved less difficult than we expected.
   turned
   The move to the new offices ....
   .... less difficult
   than we expected.

13 **A Purpose clauses and alternatives (RS55)**

Study Reference Section 55 and compare these sentences:

I take these medicines **to avoid catching/because I don't want to catch** cold.
I take these medicines **so as not to/in order not to catch** cold.

The doctor has told him to take more exercise **to avoid getting/if he doesn't want to get** fat.
The doctor has told him to take more exercise **so that he won't get** fat.

He bandaged the wound carefully **to prevent it from becoming/because he didn't want it to become** infected.
He bandaged the wound carefully **so that it wouldn't become** infected.

Rewrite the sentences below without changing the meaning, using the word(s) in brackets.

1 I do aerobics because I don't want to lose my youthful figure. (in order)
2 We've installed this system in the hospital to avoid keeping patients waiting. (so as)
3 The nurse reassured him to prevent him from being frightened. (so that)
4 I gave them my health record because I wanted them to know I was allergic to penicillin. (so that)
5 To avoid being recognised when he went into the hospital, the thief wore a white coat. (in order)
6 He wore a white coat because he didn't want anyone to recognise him. (so that)
7 You should reduce your work load if you don't want to suffer from stress. (so as)
8 You must take these tablets before meals to prevent your blood pressure from rising. (so that)

B *What* **and** *It's ... that* **(RS78)**

Compare these sentences:

It's one's state of mind **that** matters most in health.
What matters most in health **is** one's state of mind.

It's your latest research work **that** I'm interested in.
What I'm interested in **is** your latest research work.

Rewrite the sentences below without changing the meaning, beginning with the word in brackets.

1 It's my heart that's worrying me; my lungs are all right. (What …)
2 It was the sea air that cured her, not the pills she took. (What …)
3 What she needs is care and affection, rather than a stay in hospital. (It's …)
4 It's your co-operation that they require, not your money. (What …)
5 What convinced them that they should operate was the risk of the disease spreading. (It was …)

C Proportional comparison (RS3d6)

Compare these sentences:

As she learns **more**, she becomes **more** skilful.
The more she learns, **the more** skilful she becomes.

As she wins **more tournaments**, she plays more confidently.
The more tournaments she wins, **the more confidently** she plays.

Rewrite the sentences below without changing the meaning, beginning with the words given.

1 As the game went on, she played better. (The longer …)
2 As her opponent grew angrier, she became calmer. (The angrier …)
3 When her opponent served faster, she returned the ball harder. (The faster …)
4 If I win more matches, I earn more money. (The more …)
5 If I train more often, I feel fitter. (The more …)

D Phrasal Verbs (fall)

Replace the phrase in *italic* type, using a phrasal verb with **fall** in the correct form.

1 Attendance at sports events has *decreased* (……………) since they began to televise them.

2 They took his TV set away because he had *failed to keep up* (.................) with his monthly payments.

3 She had planned the match carefully with her coach and everything *resulted* (.................) according to plan.

4 She was always very friendly with her tennis partner so I'm surprised they've *quarrelled* (.................).

5 He applied for several jobs as a tennis coach but they all *came to nothing* (.................).

Test 13

Complete the second sentence so that it has a similar meaning to the first sentence. Use the word given and other words to complete each sentence. You must use between two and five words. **Do not change the word given**.

1 I left him a note because I wanted him to know where I was.
that
I left him a note so .... where I was.

2 If that's all that worries you, you can relax.
only
If that's .... worries you, you can relax.

3 It's his tone of voice that annoys me, not his criticism.
What
.... his tone of voice, not his criticism.

4 As he gets older, he becomes more irritable.
the
The .... irritable he becomes.

5 I spoke gently so that she wouldn't be alarmed.
as
I spoke gently so .... her.

6 'Why don't you take the day off?' she said to me.
suggested
She .... take the day off.

7 They haven't dealt with my complaint yet.
still
They .... my complaint.

8 I was worried that he might take offence.
case
I was worried .... offence.

9 It's very sad when friends quarrel and no longer speak to one another.
fall
It's very sad when friends .... and no longer speak to one another.

10 Don't go to a hotel; we can give you a bed for the night.
put
Don't go to a hotel; we can .... the night.

14 A *Unless* and *provided, providing, as long as, so long as* (RS54, 75)

Compare these sentences:

We'll do the repairs on Thursday, **unless** that's a bad day from your point of view.
We'll do the repairs on Thursday, **provided** that's **not** a bad day from your point of view.

Unless there **are some** complaints from the customers, we'll carry on doing things the same as we always have.
As long as there **are no** complaints from the customers, we'll carry on doing things the same as we always have.

Rewrite the sentences below without changing the meaning, using the word(s) in brackets.

1 Provided you don't hear from me by tomorrow evening, you can assume that the deal will go through. (Unless)

2 I'd like to ask you a question unless you're too busy at the moment. (as long as)

3 Unless the customers are dissatisfied, there's no reason for you to worry. (So long as)

4 I won't come to visit her again until tomorrow provided the situation doesn't change during the night. (unless)

5 Unless she wakes up suddenly, she should sleep until the morning. (Providing)

B *should(n't) have* + past participle and alternatives (RS64a, 64d)

Compare these sentences:

You **shouldn't have sold** it without asking me.
Why did you **sell** it without asking me?
It was wrong of you **to sell** it without asking me.

You **should have checked** it before you sold it **and then** she wouldn't have had any reason to complain.
If you **had checked** it before you sold it, she wouldn't have had any reason to complain.

Rewrite these sentences without changing the meaning, using a form with **should**.

1   It was wrong of the company to blame her for their mistake.
2   Why didn't you look where you were going? If you had, you wouldn't have dropped it.
3   If you'd paid attention to your work, the error wouldn't have occurred.
4   Why didn't you make sure that the door was locked? If you had, the thieves wouldn't have got in.
5   If you hadn't been so careless, you wouldn't have lost the money.

C *would rather* and *prefer*: 2 (RS83)

Compare these sentences:

I'd **rather** they **paid** in cash.
I'd **prefer** them **to pay** in cash.

I'd **rather** you **didn't make** personal calls from the office.
I'd **prefer** you **not to make** personal calls from the office.

Rewrite the sentences below without changing the meaning, using the word(s) in brackets.

1   I'd rather you didn't take the day off tomorrow. (prefer)
2   I'd prefer you to make sure we're at home before delivering the goods. ('d rather)
3   I'd rather they came on Monday. (prefer)
4   I'd prefer him not to have any reason for complaint. ('d rather)
5   I'd prefer her to write to me herself, instead of asking the lawyers to do it. ('d rather)

D Phrasal verbs *(see)*

Replace the phrase in *italic* type, using a phrasal verb with **see** in the correct form.

1   Just a moment! I'*ll go with you to the front door* (.......... you ....).
2   They were trying to cheat me and charge me extra but I *was not deceived by* (..................) their plan.
3   Would you *deal with* (..................) this customer, please?
4   They came to the station to *say goodbye to us* (.......... us ....).
5   I have just enough money to *last me* (.......... me ....) till the end of the month.

Test 14

Complete the second sentence so that it has a similar meaning to the first sentence.

1   It was wrong of them to interrupt her when she was speaking.
    shouldn't
    They .... when she was speaking.
2   I threatened to take him to court if he didn't replace it.
    or
    'Replace it .... to court!' I said.
3   Why didn't you tell me you were coming?
    should
    You .... you were coming.
4   You shouldn't have said that because it upset her.
    hadn't
    She wouldn't have got upset .... said that.
5   'You broke the window on purpose, didn't you?' he said to the boy.
    accused
    He accused .... the window on purpose.
6   I'd prefer you not to tell them about it.
    rather
    I'd .... tell them about it.

7   Jogging is good exercise provided you don't overdo it.
unless
Jogging is good exercise ....
.... overdo it.

8   This job needs doing before the customer complains.
should
This job ....
.... the customer complains.

9   The only other person I've told is my sister.
nobody
I've told ....
.... my sister.

10   We haven't received any complaints from the customers.
no
The customers ....
.... complaints.

15 **A   Inversion** (RS36)

Study the examples in Reference Section 36 and then rewrite the sentences below without changing the meaning, beginning with the word(s) given in brackets.

1   I have never seen such a beautiful island. (Never ...)

2   I didn't realise how beautiful it was until we lived there. (Not until ...)

3   You seldom have any cause to complain about the weather. (Seldom ...)

4   We had hardly arrived when people came to welcome us. (Hardly ...)

5   I only understood how much I had enjoyed my stay when we left. (Only ...)

B   *Had better (not)* (RS64b)

Compare these sentences:

It would be a good idea if you went home now.
You **had better go** home now.

It's getting late. It **wouldn't be wise/right for us to stop** for a drink.
It's getting late. We'd **better not stop** for a drink.

Rewrite the sentences below without changing the meaning, using **had better (not)**.

1   It would be helpful if you hurried, or we'll be late.

2   It wouldn't be a good idea if we turned up without telling them what time we're likely to get there.

3   It would be polite if we rang them once we're on our way.

4   It wouldn't be wise if we told them we're bringing the dog, though.

5   Perhaps it would be a good idea if we left it with my parents for the weekend.

C   Phrasal verbs *(carry)*

Replace the phrase in *italic* type, using a phrasal verb with **carry** in the correct form.

1   They've been *doing* (..................) research into the effect of the changing climate on the tribe's way of life.

2   She *continued* (..................) when the rest of us were ready to give up.

3   He's not really the leader of the expedition although he *behaves* (..................) as if he were.

4   They've *successfully concluded* (.................) their plan to retrain the islanders in spite of considerable opposition.

5   I got so *excited* (..................) when I saw the coast of Antarctica for the first time that I've never forgotten it.

D   Phrasal verbs *(hold)*

Replace the phrase in *italic* type, using a phrasal verb with **hold** in the correct form.

1   I hope the rain will *stay away* (..................) until after the picnic.

2   The army have captured most of the city but a few of the defenders are still *resisting* (..................).

3   I'm sorry I'm late. I was *delayed* (.................) in the heavy traffic.

4   *Wait at your end of the telephone* (..................) for a moment, please. I'm just putting you through.

5   The three armed men *stopped the mail van by force* (............... the mail van) and stole the money.

Test 15

Complete the second sentence so that it has a similar meaning to the first sentence. Use the word given and other words to complete each sentence. You must use between two and five words. **Do not change the word given**.

1   I haven't studied geography for a long time.
    since
    It's a long time ....
    .... geography.

2   It's thought that the settlers arrived 200 years ago.
    are
    The settlers ....
    .... 200 years ago.

3   It wouldn't be a good idea to mention that here.
    better
    You ....
    mention that here.

4   They're very hospitable, despite their great poverty.
    although
    They're very hospitable, ...
    .... poor.

5   I've never been to this part of the world before.
    time
    It's the .... ever been to this part of the world.

6   It's such a pity that they have cut all those trees down!
    wish
    I ....
    all those trees down.

7   The islanders have not adapted to modern life until now.
    until
    Not ....
    adapted to modern life.

8   The islanders have nearly all adapted to modern life.
    Hardly
    ....
    have failed to adapt to modern life.

9   She continued working normally although she felt ill.
    carried
    She ....
    normally although she felt ill.

10 'Won't you please come in?' I said to her.
    invited
    I ....
    come in.

In one section of the Cambridge First Certificate examination you may be asked to correct errors in a text. Some lines of the text are correct but others contain an additional word that should not be there. The unnecessary word is in many cases a common error in students' written work and is often the result of differences in form between their first language and English. The preliminary exercises here are meant to point out the main sources of such errors. When you do

an exercise, you should think about the equivalent structure in your own language because the errors that will be most difficult for you to recognise in English are the ones you are most likely to make yourself.

When you have done the preliminary exercises, you can attempt the fifteen test passages, which imitate the form of this section of the Use of English paper.

Preliminary exercises

A   Repeating the subject or the object

In each of these sentences there is a word that should not be there. The writer has repeated a subject or an object incorrectly. Underline the word that is wrong. When you know that you have chosen the correct answer, cross it out and then read the sentence to yourself again, as in this example:

(Read:) My uncle he is a bookseller.
(Underline:) My uncle he is a bookseller.
(Cross out:) My uncle ~~he~~ is a bookseller.
(Read again:) My uncle is a bookseller.

1   My friend John he lives over there.
2   He gave me it this book.
3   I remember it that it is very interesting.
4   Don't worry about the money because I will pay you back it.
5   All the presents I gave her she sold them.

Before continuing, look at Reference Section 58 and then find the word that is wrong in these examples:

6   The man who has just come in he is my uncle.
7   Everything that you can see on the table it is mine.
8   A girl whose name it was Sarah sat next to me.
9   The reason why I asked you about her it is that I was at school with her.
10   The other girl's name was Eugenia, which it is not a common name in England.

B   Use and omission of the definite article (*the*)

In many languages the definite article (**the**) is used where it is not used in English. Study Reference Section 70b and 70c and make a note of any differences you find between the usage in English and your own language. In the following exercises, cross out **the** when it is not correct in English, but note that in some cases it is correct.

1 1   Is this the John's book?
2   I wanted a dress like the Judith's.
3   I'm very fond of the Beatles' music, especially the John Lennon's songs.
4   The books on the table are yours, I think, but those are the mine.
5   My children are friends of the Helen's but they don't go to the same school as the hers.

2 1   Helen and I were at the school together when we were children.
2   My children are at the home watching the TV.
3   Are you here on the holiday or on the business?
4   The lift is out of the order, but they're coming to repair it in the afternoon.
5   He goes to the work by the train every day and always leaves the house in the good time to catch it.

3 1   I love playing the tennis but I'm not very fond of the swimming.
2   My sister plays the piano but I'm not very interested in the music.

3 My father and mother used to play the cards every week but I don't approve of the gambling.

4 I always have the breakfast at the eight o'clock before I go to the station to catch the train.

5 Her favourite subjects at the school are the English, the geography and the art.

4 1 If I don't see you the next week, I'll ring you at the beginning of the November.

2 I haven't heard from the other members of the family since the last winter but I got a card from the Jane the last Tuesday.

3 The most people I know don't like the getting up early.

4 I'm glad we've been able to solve the most of the problems I told you about.

5 According to the radio this morning, the heavy storms the last night caused the floods in the different parts of the country but in the most cases the damage was not serious.

5 1 There is a proverb that says that the honesty is the best policy in the life.

2 The life a hundred years ago was very different from the life today because the things happen more quickly now and so the modern life is full of the stress.

3 The life of the villagers who lived here a hundred years ago was much quieter than the life led by their descendants who live in the village today.

4 What I have learnt from the life is that the people have to respect the other people's opinions.

5 That's the only way we will ever have the peace in the world.

C Mass nouns in English

If a noun is countable in your own language but not in English you may write **a(an)** in front of it by mistake. Study Reference Section 41 (3) and check whether the words listed there are countable in your own language. Another cause of difficulty is that in some cases words describing a pair in English like **trousers, scissors** may be countable in your own language. In the exercise below cross out **a(an)** if you think the word is not countable in English, but note in some cases it is correct.

1 He was sacked from the firm for causing a damage to an equipment.

2 What an extraordinary behaviour! That boy's going to get into a trouble if he isn't more careful!

3 When we have such a hot weather I never know whether to put on a trousers or a shorts.

4 If I get a better job I'm going to buy a new furniture for the flat.

5 You should see a doctor to get a medical advice. Those tablets you are taking could do you a harm.

6 It was cold so she decided to wear a tights and a jeans instead of a stockings and a skirt.

7 We had a good weather on holiday until the last day when there was a great storm. I woke up in the middle of the night and heard a thunder in the distance.

8 A news that has just reached us with an information about the crime committed last night indicates that the police have discovered a new evidence that may lead to the arrest of the criminal.

D The infinitive without *to*

Study Reference Section 35a and 48c for examples of the infinitive being used without **to**. Then cross **to** out in the sentences below in every case where it is wrong. Note that in some cases it is correct.

1 I can't to understand this yet but I hope I will be able to before long.

2 My secretary let you to come in but she forgot to tell me so I didn't to know you were here. You must to forgive me.

3 When they first let me to get up after my operation I realised that I could stand up but could only to walk with a stick.

4 When I saw the light to go on suddenly in the house opposite it made me to wonder if something was wrong but I wasn't sure if I should to get up to find out.

5 If you hear someone to make a noise downstairs you need not to go down to investigate. My father doesn't usually to sleep very well and often gets up to work at night. He ought to see a doctor about his insomnia but I can't make him to do it.

E *Enough* and *too*

Study Reference Section 20 and 74, paying attention to the use of **of** after **enough** and the word order used with it and to the use of **too, too much** and **too many**. Then read the sentences below and cross out any words that should not be there.

1 He eats too much bread and too many cakes and that's why he's too much fat.
2 There isn't enough of room here for the children to play enough happily.
3 I told her she hadn't bought enough of food for the party but she was too much busy to listen.
4 I don't like him enough to want to go out with him. He's too much pleased with himself and makes too many silly remarks.
5 His trouble is that he spends too much money on himself and doesn't save enough of his salary. He's too much selfish to have enough of money left for his family.

F Verbs without prepositions

Some verbs take a direct object in English but the equivalent may take a preposition in your own language; for example, He **entered** the room (NOT *entered in the room*). Look at the sentences below and cross out the prepositions that are wrong. Note that not all of them are wrong. Make a note of any verbs where a preposition is used with the equivalent verb in your own language, but not used in English.

1 a What time does the train arrive at the station?
  b What time does the train reach to the station?
2 a He came towards me with a paper in his hand.
  b He approached towards me with a paper in his hand.
3 a Why didn't you answer to her question?
  b Why didn't you reply to her question?
4 a I'm in a hurry. I'm very short of time today.
  b She's always in a hurry. She lacks of the time to relax.

5 a She asked me for the time.
  b She asked me for some money.
6 a We argued about the problem for a long time.
  b We discussed about the problem for a long time.
7 a They have paid for the work he did.
  b They have paid for the money to him.
8 a I called to her several times last week but she didn't answer the phone.
  b I called out to her but she was too far away to hear me.
9 a He always listened to his parents' advice.
  b He always obeyed to his parents.
10 a I'll expect for you about half-past eight.
   b I'll wait for you on the corner.
   c But I won't wait for you for all night.

G Reflexive verbs

Study Reference Section 57d and compare the list of verbs given there with the equivalent verbs in your own language. Take particular note of those that are used without a reflexive pronoun in English. In the sentences below cross out the reflexive pronoun (**myself, themselves** etc.) where it is not required.

1 I shaved myself in a hurry this morning and cut myself.
2 I blame myself for getting myself lost and I must apologise for myself arriving late.
3 If you feel yourself tired, you should go to bed early.
4 Remember yourself to look where you're going or you may fall down and hurt yourself.
5 The children woke themselves up early this morning and got themselves very excited. They're enjoying themselves so much at the seaside and today it may be warm enough for us to bathe ourselves in the sea.

H Double-object verbs

Study Reference Section 77b. Pay careful attention to the word order and the use or omission of **to**, indicating the indirect object. In each case below, cross out the whole of the sentence that is incorrect.

1 a I've given to her the money.
  b I've given the money to her.
2 a Can you lend to me five pounds?
  b Can you lend five pounds to a poor man?
3 a I told to the children a story.
  b I told the story to the children.
4 a I've written a letter to her about it.
  b I've written to her a letter about it.
5 a I could never refuse to an old friend a helping hand.
  b I could never refuse a helping hand to an old friend.

I Tenses of the verb

Some mistakes made by including an extra word are really due to misunderstanding of the use of tenses. To avoid the most common errors of this kind, study Reference Section 69, paying special attention to b (present perfect and past); d (past and past perfect); f 6 (tenses in future time clauses) and also look at 24d (**for** and **ago**) and 16 (tenses used in conditional sentences). Cross out the part of the verb form that is incorrect in the sentences below.

1 I have met her three weeks ago at a party and if I will see her this weekend I will ask her to go out with me.
2 I had lost when I played against her before but if I would play her again I may win.
3 I must make a phone call before I will leave because after I will arrive home it will be too late.
4 If you would pay me back the money you owe me, I won't bother you any more.
5 If I paid you, you would have had to give me a receipt.
6 They have phoned me yesterday to ask me if I would like to go with them when they will go on an excursion next weekend.

J *ask, say, tell* etc.

These verbs cause special problems. Study Reference Section 59 and 62 and then cross out the whole of the sentence that is incorrect in each case below.

1 a 'You're late!' I said to him.
  b 'You're late!' I told to him.
2 a 'Ask her to come in.'
  b 'Ask to her to come in.'
3 a 'Can you tell to me the time, please?'
  b 'Can you tell me the time, please?'
4 a 'Tell them not to make so much noise.'
  b 'Tell them that not to make so much noise.'
5 a She said that she had not seen the film.
  b She said me that she had not seen the film.
6 a I asked him how that he had done it.
  b I asked him how he had done it.
7 a I wondered that what she was doing.
  b I wondered what she was doing.
8 a I wonder why do people behave like that.
  b I wonder why people behave like that.
9 a Ask me no questions and I'll tell you no lies.
  b Ask to me no questions and I'll tell to you no lies.
10 a 'I don't understand what do girls see in him,' she said to me.
   b 'I don't understand what girls see in him,' she told me.

K Numbers, proportions etc.

There may be differences between the expressions used for numbers in English and those of your own language. In each sentence below there is an extra word that is not correct in English. Cross it out.

1 I have a brother and three of sisters.
2 My sisters are older than me but my brother is only three years.
3 The time is five minutes to four hours.
4 She lives quite near me, only half of a kilometre away.
5 There were three hundred of people at her wedding.
6 He is so short that he is only the half the size of his opponent.

7 I've told you a hundred of times to pay attention to what I say.
8 The bank are paying the seven per cent interest on the loan.
9 He offered to sell it to me for the half the original price.
10 The crowd numbered sixty thousand of people and there were thousands of people outside without tickets.

L Adjectives, adverbs and comparative forms

Study Reference Sections 3 and 4 and then correct the sentences below. In each sentence cross out the word that is not correct.

1 She's several years more older than me.
2 I'm not as old as is John.
3 A little and old woman opened the door.
4 She plays more better than I do.
5 Henry is not very much like to his sisters.
6 She bought a same hat like mine.
7 She was wearing the same kind of clothes as did her sister.
8 What a lovely and sunny day!
9 Don't stay too long in the sun because it is more stronger than yesterday.
10 She runs much more faster than I do.

M *what*

Study Reference Section 58a and 78 and then correct the sentences below. In each sentence cross out the word that is not correct.

1 I don't know what is you're talking about.
2 Have you seen the lovely presents what he gave me?
3 What I need at this moment it is a cool drink.
4 He complains about everything what I do.
5 The main problem what we have to deal with is pollution.
6 All what I asked you to do was to be patient.
7 No matter what that you say about her, I still like her.
8 What 'Murphy's Law' says is that everything that can go wrong it will go wrong.

N Purpose clauses

Study Reference Section 55 and then correct the sentences below. In each sentence cross out the word that is not correct.

1 I hope you haven't come here for getting money.
2 I borrowed your pen for to do my homework.
3 I brought a book with me so as that I would have something to pass the time.
4 He came in very quietly, for not making a sound.
5 I've put aside some money in order for to save for my old age.

O *that*

In many cases, the equivalent to a phrase in English in your own language may require a word you could translate by **that**. In the sentences below, cross out **that** in all the sentences where it is not correct, but note that in some cases it is correct. Then compare it with the equivalent in your own language.

1 It's at least a year since that I saw her.
2 The only thing that worries him is his health.
3 As far as that I know, she still lives there.
4 Though that she was tired, she went on working.
5 No matter what that they say, don't take any notice.
6 I'd like to borrow your typewriter, as long as that you don't mind.
7 He hadn't met her before so that he did not recognise her.
8 If only that I knew the answer!
9 It's obvious that they're in love with each other.
10 I'd rather that you asked her yourself.

Tests

Test 1

Read the text below and look carefully at each line. Some of the lines are correct, and some have a word which should not be there. If a line is correct, put a tick (✓) by the number at the end of the line. If a line has a word that should **not** be there, write the word in the space provided. There are two examples at the beginning (**0** and **00**)

My little brother

I belong to quite a large family because I have	0	........✓........
three brothers and four of sisters. I love them	00	........of........
all but perhaps the one I love most is my little	1	....
brother George. George is seven years, so he is	2	....
six years more younger than me. My mother says my	3	....
little brother he is unique and I agree that he	4	....
is not very much like to me or the other boys in	5	....
the family. The reason why my mother says this it	6	....
is because he has a terrible temper; of course	7	....
all of children lose their tempers at times, but	8	....
the George's temper is really terrible. When he	9	....
is angry, we cannot do anything with him. He is	10	....
as bad-tempered as is my elder sister, Charlotte.	11	....
I always remember an argument my mother once had	12	....
with her because Charlotte wanted a same dress	13	....
like hers. But Charlotte and George are different	14	....
because Charlotte is always bad-tempered but	15	....
George is usually a happy and little boy.	16	....

Test 2

Read the text below and look carefully at each line. Some of the lines are correct, and some have a word which should not be there. If a line is correct, put a tick (✓) by the number at the end of the line. If a line has a word that should **not** be there, write the word in the space provided.

My study

As you know, that I work at home so when we moved	1	....
into this new flat I wanted a study where I could	2	....
work enough comfortably. In the old flat almost	3	....
all the rooms were too much small. Apart from	4	....
that, the flat was rented, so we could not throw	5	....
out a furniture we did not like, or put in all	6	....
the bookshelves I needed for my books. So when we	7	....
came here I decided – and Jenny was agreed with	8	....
me – that I would take this room at the back of	9	....

the house and make it my study. I enjoy to work | 10 | ....
but I like to see the light to come through the | 11 | ....
windows. Now, as you enter into this room, you | 12 | ....
get light on two sides because outside of the | 13 | ....
windows is the terrace, and there are bookshelves | 14 | ....
along the other walls so I have enough of space | 15 | ....
for all my books. | 16 | ....

Test 3

Shopping in the West End

It's a long time since that I went shopping in | 1 | ....
the West End so when Monica asked me if I would | 2 | ....
like to go with her, I said: 'Yes, I would like.' | 3 | ....
She was going to buy a tennis shirt for her | 4 | ....
husband and a shorts to go with it, and then to | 5 | ....
look for something for herself. 'I would rather | 6 | ....
that someone came with me,' she said, 'because I | 7 | ....
have bought some things for John a few weeks ago | 8 | ....
and I am sure that I paid too much. I always feel | 9 | ....
myself a fool when that sort of thing happens.' | 10 | ....
We went to London by the train and then took the | 11 | ....
underground to the West End. We soon found John's | 12 | ....
tennis clothes and Monica saw a tennis dress for | 13 | ....
herself. But when she asked for the price she was | 14 | ....
surprised: 'I can't to pay that much,' she said. | 15 | ....
She seemed be very disappointed so I told her I | 16 | ....
would pay the half the cost if she really wanted | 17 | ....
it. 'It can be your birthday present,' I said. | 18 | ....

Test 4

Letter to an old school friend

I was pleased indeed to get your letter the other | 1 | ....
day. These days I don't often hear from anyone | 2 | ....
who was at the school with us. I wrote to Paula | 3 | ....
the last Christmas at the last address I had for | 4 | ....
her but she didn't to answer. Perhaps she has | 5 | ....
moved since she last wrote to me. But the friend | 6 | ....
I really miss is Angela. I had lost touch with | 7 | ....
her some time ago after a silly quarrel. Because | 8 | ....
she was late for a lunch date with me so I | 9 | ....
started eating before she arrived, and she was | 10 | ....
very annoyed: 'You've never been punctual,' I said | 11 | ....
'but I'm very busy. We said one o'clock and now | 12 | ....
it's ten to two hours.' 'And you've always lacked | 13 | ....
of good manners,' she said, and she just walked | 14 | ....

out of the restaurant and I was too much proud to	15 ....
run after her. I've thought of that incident a	16 ....
hundred of times. How childish we were! Just like	17 ....
two kids at primary school!	18 ....

Test 5

Manoj

Manoj is a typical representative of the Indian	1 ....
merchant class who they were driven out of Kenya	2 ....
in the 1960s and came to England. He was popular	3 ....
at school because he was friendly and pleasant to	4 ....
talk to him but he was already making a profit	5 ....
from things what he brought from his father's	6 ....
shops and sold them to his classmates. His	7 ....
father assumed Manoj would join the family	8 ....
business but the boy wanted a shop of his own.	9 ....
'Lend to me the money, Father,' he said, 'and I	10 ....
will pay you back it after a year.' 'But my son,'	11 ....
his father argued, 'you know everything what I	12 ....
own it is yours. You can run one of my shops. The	13 ....
manager who is there now he is no good.' 'No,'	14 ....
Manoj said, 'give me a chance by myself. The shop	15 ....
where he works at is too small.' By now Manoj has	16 ....
repaid the loan and opened another shop	17 ....
in his own name.	18 ....

Test 6

The excursion this weekend

The Ramblers Club I belong to are going on an	1 ....
excursion this weekend and if I will have enough	2 ....
money, I'll go with them. They've given to us an	3 ....
information sheet about the excursion and it	4 ....
seems quite interesting. I'm not sure how much	5 ....
far we will have to walk but I feel myself very	6 ....
fit at the moment and it will finish beside the	7 ....
sea so we may be able to bathe ourselves when we	8 ....
are tired. The most people are going to the	9 ....
meeting place by the train but Jack is giving me	10 ....
a lift in his car. I'll ring you after I shall	11 ....
arrive back on Sunday to tell you all about it. I	12 ....
imagine you will have returned from your parents'	13 ....
before I will get home, but if you haven't, I'll	14 ....
ring you the next week some time.	15 ....

Test 7

A car accident

I had a few days' holiday in March and Ruth and I	1 ....
discussed about the alternatives. 'How's the	2 ....
weather like for skiing?' she said. She was so	3 ....
keen that we decided to go to Glenmore; it seemed	4 ....
as a good place to stay and although I wasn't	5 ....
looking forward to driving because the roads were	6 ....
icy, I thought: 'Why to argue? It'll probably be	7 ....
all right.' Ruth was used to like driving but she	8 ....
hasn't driven since her cousin was died in a car	9 ....
crash last year, so I was at the wheel. All went	10 ....
well until we were only about two miles far from	11 ....
our destination and then the car skidded and we	12 ....
went off the road. Ruth gave a cry of pain. 'Oh!	13 ....
I think I've got broken my arm!' she said. Just	14 ....
then a car stopped near us, and the driver came	15 ....
to help. 'I live only half of a mile from here,'	16 ....
she said. 'I'll go straight to home and ring for	17 ....
a doctor.' Luckily Ruth's arm was only bruised	18 ....
but we couldn't do any skiing.	19 ....

Test 8

Why Cathy was late

It is very worrying for parents to wait for all	1 ....
evening for a child to come back to home. Last	2 ....
weekend Cathy insisted on her going on an	3 ....
excursion with a party from school. She said us	4 ....
that the bus would get back by 7.30 and we agreed	5 ....
to pick her up at 7.30. By nine o'clock everyone	6 ....
waiting was worried because of the children had	7 ....
not returned and no one had explained the delay	8 ....
but then a teacher rang up to the school to say	9 ....
they were on their way. We were very relieved to	10 ....
catch sight of Cathy in her anorak and a bright	11 ....
red jeans as she got down from the bus. She was	12 ....
bursting to tell us about her adventure. She and	13 ....
other three girls with her had got lost. 'But I	14 ....
told to them to keep calm,' she said, 'and gave	15 ....
them some chocolate to eat it, and we climbed a	16 ....
hill so the teachers could see us. But we had to	17 ....
call out for ages before someone saw my jeans.'	18 ....

Test 9

My new telephone number

I was annoyed when I picked it up the telephone	1	....
and found it was out of the order. But before I	2	....
had time to ring the company and ask to them what	3	....
was wrong my brother rang me. I wondered that how	4	....
he had been able to ring; it seemed I could	5	....
receive calls but not to make them. 'Why didn't	6	....
you tell me you had changed your number?' Bob	7	....
asked. I asked him how that he knew I had because	8	....
I didn't and he said there was a recorded message	9	....
informing people. Then I remembered myself taking	10	....
a call from the bank about a telephone bill for a	11	....
different number from the mine and telling them	12	....
that not to pay it. 'What a mess!' I said to Bob.	13	....
'They've changed the number and told everyone	14	....
except me. But after all, people don't usually	15	....
ring to themselves. That's why I didn't know.'	16	....

Test 10

The Shakespeare mystery

There is a mystery about the authorship of	1	....
Shakespeare's plays, which it is not who wrote	2	....
them but why do people think someone else	3	....
wrote them. No one has suggested this until about	4	....
a hundred years ago when a woman whose name it	5	....
happened to be Bacon argued that the plays were	6	....
written by Sir Francis Bacon, the Shakespeare's	7	....
contemporary. Her idea was that Bacon, who was a	8	....
political figure, paid to Shakespeare, an actor,	9	....
to say everyone he had written them because at	10	....
that time the theatre was not respectable. The	11	....
explanation for such theories is simple; they are	12	....
prompted by the snobbery. Most of the other	13	....
candidates have been aristocrats or men like	14	....
Marlowe, who educated at Cambridge University.	15	....
Yet anyone who knows the plays well understands	16	....
that they must have been written by a	17	....
professional actor for the other actors.	18	....

Test 11

A puppy for Tina

We had a dog at home when I was a small child. I	1 ....
remember it that it had a sweet nature but	2 ....
despite of being fond of dogs I have never had	3 ....
one of my own. No matter what that people say,	4 ....
dogs require such a constant attention that I did	5 ....
not think I could spare the time. But the other	6 ....
day Tina saw a puppy in a pet shop with a so	7 ....
beautiful expression on its face and she will	8 ....
not be happy until we give it to her to keep it.	9 ....
Although we intend to buy it for her, but we want	10 ....
to make sure she understands that she must be	11 ....
responsible for it. 'If we bought it, you would	12 ....
have had to look after it,' we told her. 'If	13 ....
animals are belong to you, you must take care of	14 ....
them.' 'Of course,' Tina said. 'But if you would	15 ....
get the puppy you wouldn't need to do anything.	16 ....
Except buy its food.' she added.	17 ....

Test 12

Succeeding in a man's world

Far more of women are employed nowadays so for	1 ....
most of them work has become one of the facts of	2 ....
the life. Of course their husbands and fathers	3 ....
have usually gone out to the work every day, too,	4 ....
but without their responsibilities in the home.	5 ....
In the past women ambitious to succeed in	6 ....
business were advised that there was no need for	7 ....
to act like men. But the latest school of thought	8 ....
argues that employing feminine charm it is not	9 ....
enough. Few women, however, are willing to pay	10 ....
the price that copying successful businessmen	11 ....
usually involves: the getting home late and	12 ....
hardly ever seeing the children. 'If only that I	13 ....
could work in a woman's world, this wouldn't	14 ....
happen,' is the complaint what I hear from many	15 ....
tired women executives. If you want to avoid so	16 ....
long, inconvenient hours, start your own business	17 ....
and make them your own rules for your employees.	18 ....

Test 13

Sheila's boss

Sheila was very unhappy at the work so she asked   1   ....
Joan, the senior secretary at her office, for an   2   ....
advice. They went to a café for having a coffee.   3   ....
'What I need it is a bit of encouragement, I   4   ....
suppose,' Sheila said. 'I just don't know how to   5   ....
deal with Mr Sargent. I took the job here for to   6   ....
improve my skills as well as for the extra money   7   ....
but nothing what I do seems to be right. No   8   ....
matter what that it is, he finds something to   9   ....
complain about.' 'Don't get upset!' Joan said.   10   ....
'Sargent complains for the sake of it. As long   11   ....
as that you're doing your best, there's nothing   12   ....
for you to worry about. Provided you do all what   13   ....
you're asked to do, no one will mind. Anyway,   14   ....
Sargent's retiring next month, so why to worry?'   15   ....

Test 14

Dragon lost in the post

The Post Office is often blamed for the things   1   ....
getting lost. In most the cases the reason is   2   ....
that the parcel was wrongly addressed. This is   3   ....
what has happened in the case of the dragon that   4   ....
Wagner ordered for the first performance of his   5   ....
opera *Siegfried*, at Bayreuth in Germany. The   6   ....
dragon which was made in London and should have   7   ....
been sent in the good time, well before the first   8   ....
performance, but it was too much long to go into   9   ....
one parcel and had to be sent in sections. When   10   ....
the first night arrived, all what Wagner needed   11   ....
had appeared except for the long neck. Deciding   12   ....
that the half a dragon was better than none,   13   ....
Wagner had the head stuck to the body but this   14   ....
made the dragon be so short that when Siegfried   15   ....
killed it the audience laughed. Years later   16   ....
Wagner was told that the neck, which it had never   17   ....
appeared, had been sent to Beirut in the Lebanon.   18   ....

Test 15

Reviving Deadwood

Deadwood, South Dakota, has earned its reputation	1 ....
as a dangerous place known for the gambling and	2 ....
violence in 1876, when Wild Bill Hickok, one of	3 ....
the America's most famous gunfighters, was shot	4 ....
there while he was playing the cards. The town,	5 ....
with a population of only about two thousand of	6 ....
people, was gradually declining until a few years	7 ....
ago, when some casinos were opened. Though the	8 ....
casinos brought a welcome business to the town,	9 ....
but there was considerable opposition from the	10 ....
inhabitants. The casinos wanted to buy the store	11 ....
where it is said the bullet that killed Bill	12 ....
Hickok was bought at, but the owner refused to	13 ....
sell, no matter what that they offered. She hung	14 ....
a sign outside which said: 'This building is not	15 ....
for sale. Don't even to think about asking.'	16 ....

In one section of the Cambridge First Certificate Use of English paper you are asked to complete a paragraph, supplying words derived from a root word that is given to you, like this:

According to many (1) .... SCIENCE sports can be very (2) .... in VALUE training people to overcome their ...

In the first case, you are expected to see that the word that is missing is a noun, it is plural, and if it is derived from **science**, it must be **scientists**. In the second case the word that is missing is an adjective derived from **value**, so it is **valuable**.

You will find 15 tests of this kind at the end of this section of the book. Before you attempt them, however, it will be useful for you to learn the best technique for dealing with this kind of question, and at the same time to expand your vocabulary by referring to the appendices at the back of the book.

The best way to learn new vocabulary is to meet it in context in the course of your reading, but while you probably know the root words that are given in most cases – **friend**, for example – you may not have seen the abstract noun, **friendship**, or the adjective, which looks like an adverb, **friendly** or the negative form, **unfriendly**.

The root words may be verbs, nouns or adjectives, but many of them belong to related families. For instance, from the adjective root, **sweet**, we can derive the verb **sweeten**, the noun **sweetness** and the adverb **sweetly**. The preliminary exercises here are meant to draw your attention to the commonest families of related words in English, where the forms have the same beginnings or endings, and also to the exceptions, which are the ones most likely to appear in an examination!

Preliminary exercises

A   Adjective root: verb *-en*, noun *-ness*

Study Appendix 5:1 on page 121. A number of common adjectives act as roots for verbs and nouns. In these cases, the verb ending **-en** has the meaning of increasing the quality of the adjective, the noun indicates the state. So the state of being **black** is **blackness** and to make something **blacker** is to **blacken**.

Most of these combinations are consistent but pay special attention to those that are irregular (shown in different type in the Appendix). For instance, the noun derived from **strong** is NOT *strongness* but **strength** and to make something **stronger** is to **strengthen** (NOT *strongen*) it.

Without looking at the Appendix, make nouns derived from these adjectives, but do not assume that all of them will be regular and if you think you know a correct form that is irregular, put it down: **bright, dark, deep, fresh, light, long, mad, quiet, weak, wide**.

Check the Appendix to see if any are irregular. Did you know which they were?

Now form verbs in the same way from the following: **fat, fresh, hard, long, ripe, sharp, soft, straight, thick, white**.
Only one in this list is irregular. Which is it?

1   In completing the exercises that follow, you must decide on the function of the word in the sentence and whether it is affirmative or negative. Look at these examples.

a   These days many people use saccharin to *sweeten* their tea.
(SWEET)

b   Putting saccharin in the tea has *sweetened* it.   (SWEET)

c   Putting saccharin in the tea makes it *sweeter*: it has a *sweetening* effect.
(SWEET, SWEET)

d   She sang so *sweetly* that everyone was impressed.   (SWEET)

e   She had the *sweetest* singing voice I've ever heard.   (SWEET)

2 Complete the following sentences with appropriate words, derived from the root word supplied.

1 The sky .... and filled with black clouds. (DARK)

2 December 21st is one of the .... days of the year because there are very few hours of sunlight. (DARK)

3 He thinks it is a sign of .... to admit that he is wrong but I would .... change my view if I thought it would do any good. (WEAK, GLAD)

4 The .... of the spring flowers .... her heart. (FRESH, GLAD)

5 At first they were surprised by the .... of the resistance to their plan but now it seems to be .... (STRONG, WEAK)

6 He should go on a diet because he's got much .... and the kind of food he is fond of is very .... (FAT, FAT)

7 You can't expect me to sit here .... when I know someone is deliberately .... my character. (QUIET, BLACK)

8 The only way to produce a square room would be to .... the front wall and .... the side wall so that the .... and the .... would be exactly the same. (SHORT, LONG, LONG, WIDE)

9 'What a lovely day!' she said ...., but the .... noise from the street outside, where the workmen were .... the road, prevented me from hearing any more. (BRIGHT, DEAF, WIDE)

B   Noun root: adjective *-ful*, *-less*

Adjectives ending in **-ful** and **-less** are formed from a large number of common nouns. In general, those ending in **-ful** indicate that the person or thing shows or has that quality, so a **beautiful** person is one who has beauty, a **merciful** person shows mercy, a **hopeful** person is a person 'with hope.' In the same way, the **-less** ending indicates that the person or thing lacks or does not show the quality, or is 'without' it – a **merciless** person shows no mercy, a **hopeless** situation is one without hope of a solution.

Study Appendix 5:2 on page 122. Note the variations from the regular pattern, and the difference between such words as **helpless** and **unhelpful**. Then complete the sentences below with an appropriate adjective form or adverb, using the noun root given. Consider whether the adjective required is affirmative or negative, whether the correct form is **merciful** or **merciless**, for example.

1 I'd like to live in a nice .... spot in the country, a .... old village where nothing changes. (PEACE, SLEEP)

2 I don't know if we're going there for our holiday yet – it's still .... – so it's .... arguing about what to do when we get there. (DOUBT, POINT)

3 The room was .... designed and .... decorated. (BEAUTY, TASTE)

4 She moves so .... about the tennis court that it is a pity she makes so many .... mistakes. (GRACE, CARE)

5 I was lost in a strange city and felt .... because I could not speak the language; when I finally found someone who spoke English and asked her the way, she was .... 'I don't know,' she said, and walked away. (HELP, HELP)

6 He was very upset to discover that the painting he thought was .... was only a copy and almost .... (VALUE, WORTH)

7 I was very .... to her for her .... advice when I was young. When I was leading an .... existence, she put me on the road to a .... career. (GRATITUDE, THOUGHT, AIM, SUCCESS)

8 When I was a child and suffered .... hours at the dentist's, I always wondered why dentists were so .... Why couldn't they be honest and say: 'This is going to hurt!' (PAIN, TRUTH)

C Common negative prefixes

You have already seen how the negative of many adjectives in English is formed either with the prefix **un-** (**unhelpful**) or with the suffix **-less** (**helpless**).

Other common prefixes with negative force are **dis-**, **mis-** and **in-**. The prefix **mis-** usually indicates something done wrongly or badly, so children who **misbehave** behave badly.

Negative forms beginning with **in-** are subject to some variations, depending on the first letter of the root word. If it begins with **l, m** or **r**, the letter is usually doubled, (not legal = **illegal**, not moral = **immoral** and not regular = **irregular**). If the root word begins with **p**, the negative prefix will usually be **im-** (not proper = **improper**).

Complete the following sentences with appropriate words, derived from the root word supplied. In all cases the word will begin with one of the negative prefixes indicated above. Before you complete the sentence, decide whether the word you require is a noun, a verb, an adjective or an adverb.

1   On the whole I like living in the country but it has some .... (ADVANTAGE)

2   If you answered the first question ...., look again at the instructions. (CORRECT)

3   I'm sorry if I gave you the wrong information. I didn't mean to .... you. (LEAD)

4   What you're saying doesn't make sense. It's completely .... (LOGIC)

5   The driver responsible for the accident was .... from driving for ten years. (QUALIFY)

6   Everyone at the hospital was very efficient, but there was nothing friendly about them – it was all very .... (PERSON)

7   If you find a word spelt wrongly in this book it's a .... (PRINT)

8   There was some .... between them about the best treatment to give the patient. (AGREE)

9   I didn't mean to insult you. I think you've .... what I said. (UNDERSTAND)

10 His poetry is ....; it will never die. (MORTAL)

11 He said my advice was .... and had nothing to do with the case. (RELEVANT)

12 I was very .... that I couldn't come to your wedding. (APPOINT)

13 I thought he was rather unpleasant when I first met him, but I realise that I .... him; actually, he's quite nice. (JUDGE)

14 As soon as they heard of the climbers' .... in the fog, they organised a search party. (APPEAR)

15 When he suddenly appeared with so much money we wondered if he had acquired it .... (HONEST)

D Verb root: adjective -*able*, -*ible*

A large number of verbs that take an object form adjectives with the ending **-able** or with the variations indicated below. The meaning is normally equivalent to 'can be + past participle' so a proposal that 'can be accepted' is **acceptable**. When the adjective is applied to a person it sometimes has the additional meaning of 'willing to + infinitive'. An **adaptable** machine is one that can be adapted for use in different conditions; an **adaptable** person is one who can work in different conditions, and is probably willing to do so.

Note the following variations in form:

a   forms are sometimes made with the ending **-ible** (**sensible, responsible**);

b   Most forms derived from verbs ending in **-e** drop the **e** so that something that can be argued is **arguable**, something that can be imagined is **imaginable**;

c   forms derived from verbs ending in **-mit** are made with **-missible** (for example, **admit – admissible**);

d   forms derived from verbs ending in **-ate** are made without the **t**, so someone who can be educated is **educable**;

e   a few other irregular forms, such as **applicable** from **apply** and **soluble** from **solve**;

f negative forms are usually made with the prefix **un-**; a proposal that cannot be accepted is **unacceptable**. Some, however, are made with other common negative prefixes like **in-** and the variations **il-, im-, ir-** that you have seen in Exercise C. Something that cannot be compared, normally because it is superior to everything else of its kind, is **incomparable**; something that cannot be moved is **immovable**.

1 Study Appendix 5:3 on page 123 and then form adjectives ending in **-able** or **-ible**, derived from the following verbs: **allow, enjoy, manage, notice, divide, sense, permit, communicate, operate, explain, practise, remember**.

Now make negative adjectives ending in **-able** or **-ible** derived from the following verbs: **employ, believe, govern, describe, solve, imitate, pass, respond, explain, practise**.

2 In the exercise that follows replace the word or phrase in *italic* type with an appropriate adjective form derived from the verb given in brackets. Change the word order to put the adjective in front of the noun where necessary. Note that in all these cases the meaning is not exactly 'can (not) be + past participle'.

1 If anything goes wrong, you will be held *responsible*. (account)
2 For some reason *that I cannot explain* I left all my luggage on the station platform. (account)
3 I've never met such an *unpleasant* person. (agree)
4 She always wears clothes *that are no longer in fashion*. (fashion)
5 We'll go sailing if the weather is *in our favour*. (favour)
6 They are people *whose behaviour is accepted by society*. (respect)
7 She is a person *with common sense*. (sense)
8 He hit his head on the wall and fell to the ground *unconscious*. (sense)
9 He's behaved in a completely *careless manner*. (respond)
10 The plan they have suggested is *impossible to put into practice*. (practise)

11 The painting is *worth a lot of money*. (value)
12 The painting is *worth so much money that its value cannot be estimated*. (value)

E Participles used as adjectives

Present participles, like **exciting** and past participles, like **excited**, can be used as adjectives. The past participle forms indicate how people feel, the present participle forms describe what causes the feeling. Compare:

The **exciting** game kept the crowd on their feet. At the end of the game, the **excited** crowd ran onto the field.
(The game was **exciting** because it filled the crowd with excitement; the crowd were **excited** because of the game.)

a Present or past participle

Complete the sentences with a participle derived from the verb given in brackets. There are two sentences for each verb.

1 a The success of the film is .... No one expected it.
  b I'm .... the film has been so successful. (SURPRISE)
2 a The .... travellers were resting after their journey.
  b You need a rest after such a .... journey. (TIRE)
3 a It was such an .... book that I couldn't put it down until I had finished it.
  b Anyone .... in attending the lectures should fill in the form provided. (INTEREST)
4 a 'Stop making that awful noise!' he said in an .... voice.
  b He has an .... voice. It's very sharp and unpleasant to listen to. (IRRITATE)
5 a They shouldn't show horror films with .... scenes in them at times when children are watching TV.
  b Sarah was looking at the TV with a .... expression, horrified by the images on the screen. (FRIGHTEN)

b Present participle combinations

Some present participle-noun combinations define the purpose of a thing, so a **walking stick** is a stick people use to help them walk, **running shoes** are special shoes they use for running (not shoes that run!).

Others define people or things actively. A **working group** is a group of people chosen to work on a project, for example; **running water** is water that runs, either because we turn on a tap or naturally, in a river.

1 Produce noun combinations that mean the following:

1 a room where people live
....

2 a pool where people can swim
....

3 a machine used to wash clothes
....

4 a basket used when people go shopping
....

5 soap used when shaving ....

2 Now, link the participles in box **A** below with nouns in box **B** to make common expressions in English, as in the example that has been done for you:

A	advertising developing dividing greetings helping leading losing managing opening performing surrounding

B	agency animals article card countries director hand line side speech villages

I don't like going to the circus very much because I'm not fond of watching <u>performing animals</u> doing tricks.

1 He's one of those unfortunate people who always seems to pick the .... in any argument.

2 There are times when the .... between what is right and wrong is very difficult to define.

3 I hadn't heard from her for a few months but she sent me a .... the other day to say she had been made sales representative for Fairton and the ....

4 The .... in the newspaper today says that it is the responsibility of people in the richer nations to lend a .... to those in the .... of the Third World.

5 In his .... at the convention, the .... of the .... began by saying that he was pleased to report increased business during the past year.

c Past participle combinations

Most combinations with the past participle have a passive sense; a **detached house** is one that is detached from those near it, **dyed hair** is hair that has been dyed a different colour. There are some exceptions with an active sense; a **qualified teacher** has passed an examination. Link the participles in box **A** below with nouns in box **B** to make common expressions in English, as in the example that has been done for you:

A	broken buried detached elected fitted lost packed prescribed revised satisfied used

B	book cars carpets cause customers edition heart house lunch representative treasure

As a Member of Parliament, she is an <u>elected representative</u> of the people.

1 If you go out for the day, the hotel will supply you with a ....

2 R L Stevenson's most famous novel is about pirates looking for .... on a desert island.

3 It's a .... with .... in every room.

4 The page numbers in my copy of the .... are different from yours; perhaps you have a ....

5 She died of a .... when she realised that her country's independence was a ....

6 He's like most salesmen selling ....; he's more interested in a quick profit than in ....

F Verb root: noun endings *-ion*, *-or*; adjective ending *-ive*

A number of verbs form nouns usually ending in **-ion**, some of which have personal nouns ending in **-or**; they also form adjectives ending in **-ive**. There are some irregular forms, but a person who **possesses** things, for example, has **possessions**, he is the **possessor** of the things he owns, and if he is strongly attached to them he is called **possessive**.

Study Appendix 5:4 on page 124, paying special attention to any forms that are irregular. Complete the sentences below with an appropriate noun or adjective derived from the verb root given. Read the sentence carefully to decide whether the adjective is affirmative or negative.

1 She's a very .... girl with a vivid .... (ATTRACT, IMAGINE)

2 Your work on the .... desk of the hotel has been most .... so as a token of our .... we're going to promote you.
(RECEIVE, IMPRESS, APPRECIATE)

3 The .... moment in the war came when the President gave the general .... to attack.
(DECIDE, PERMIT)

4 My .... of this student is that she has not been paying .... in class and her attitude has been rather .... but I am sure she will respond to .... criticism.
(IMPRESS, ATTEND, CO-OPERATE, CONSTRUCT)

5 Some people think he is a great .... but I've always thought his range of .... very limited, probably the .... of a rather ...., selfish personality.
(ACT, EXPRESS, REFLECT, SENSE)

6 On top of being very ...., the latest sales campaign has been .... in .... with the previous one.
(SPEND, EFFECT, COMPARE)

G Verb root: noun endings *-nce*, *-nt*, adjective ending *-nt*; adjective ending *-nt*, noun ending *-nce*.

A number of verbs form nouns usually ending in **-ance** or **-ence**. Some of them also form nouns describing people, which usually end in **-ant** or **-ent**, and adjectives which usually end in the same way. For example, the relationship between things that **correspond** or the letters people write to each other are called **correspondence**; someone who writes letters regularly to another person is a **correspondent**; and the adjective derived is also **correspondent**.

Study Appendix 5:5 on page 125, paying special attention to any forms that are irregular.

1 Complete the sentences below with an appropriate noun or adjective derived from the verb root given. Read the sentence carefully to decide whether the adjective is affirmative or negative.

1 In spite of her .... self-...................., she is really rather a shy person. (APPEAR, CONFIDE)

2 From the outside the house has a very attractive .... but we'll need to spend a lot of money on .... because it is rather old.
(APPEAR, MAINTAIN)

3 We have a good candidate for the post of administrative .... with a good .... from her previous employer.
(ASSIST, REFER)

4 The first .... of the ballet last night was a great success. It was a .... to see such beautiful dancing. (PERFORM, PLEASE)

5 She is the oldest .... of the village, and is said to be a .... of the original lord of the manor, but she doesn't regard that as being of any ....
(INHABIT, DESCEND, SIGNIFY)

2 A number of adjectives ending in **-nt** relate to nouns ending in **-nce**. Study Appendix 5:5 on page 125 and then complete the sentences below with an appropriate noun or a negative adjective formed from the root given.

1 .... of the law is not considered proof of ....
(IGNORANT, INNOCENT)

2 Anyone who argues that the increase in crimes of .... in the United States is not connected to people being able to buy guns is either very .... or deliberately ignoring the ....
(VIOLENT, INTELLIGENT, EVIDENT)

3 Of course it's .... that the school is such a long .... from their house, but that doesn't justify the .... of the child's .... from class.
(CONVENIENT, DISTANT, FREQUENT, ABSENT)

H Verb root: noun endings -*ment*, -*er*; adjective ending -*ing*

A number of nouns ending in **-ment** derive from verbs, and there are sometimes personal nouns ending in **-er** or **-or** also related to the same root. In most cases adjectives forming part of this family of words end in **-ing** (also see Exercise **Eb**). The noun **government** derives from **govern**, and someone put in charge of a province, for example, may be called the **governor**. Schools may have a Board of **Governors**, which is the **governing** body (the group of people responsible for it).

Study Appendix 5:6 on page 126 and then complete the sentences below with appropriate nouns or adjectives derived from the verb root given.

1 The children were very .... that they could not go on the picnic but perhaps they will be able to go tomorrow if there's an .... in the weather.
(APPOINT, IMPROVE)

2 I suppose some people regard that sort of film as a form of .... but I find it .... to look at.
(ENTERTAIN, EMBARRASS)

3 The forest disappeared because of the constant .... of the early .... from one area to another.
(MOVE, SETTLE)

4 She read the .... in the newspaper with mounting .... The job was just what she was looking for so she rang for an ....
(ADVERTISE, EXCITE, APPOINT)

5 On his .... the .... director received a large .... in cash as well as his pension.
(RETIRE, MANAGE, PAY)

I Noun root: nouns ending in -*ship*, -*hood*

Abstract nouns can be made from the names of groups of people by adding **-ship** or **-hood**. Generally, these words indicate a state or condition of being, so **manhood** and **womanhood** mean the state or condition of being a man or a woman. Words ending in **-ship**, especially those ending in **-manship**, may imply a skill as well as a condition, so **craftsmanship** indicates the skill of being a good craftsman, or making something well.

Make nouns of this kind from the roots given in the box. Check with a dictionary if necessary. Then choose an appropriate one to use in the sentences below.

champion   child   father   mother
owner   relation   scholar   sponsor
workman

1 Her parents have encouraged her throughout her .... and now she has won a .... to study abroad.

2 The football .... this year is taking place with the .... of one of the big companies.

3 When a couple have a child, their new roles of .... and .... are bound to change the .... between them.

4 This old firm of furniture manufacturers, famous for the superb .... of their products, has been sold and is now under new ....

J Nouns relating to subjects of study, personal nouns and adjectives derived from them

The words relating to subjects of study have various endings, as have the names of people qualified in them. The adjectives derived almost always end in **-ical** or **-ic**. So a student of **chemistry** may qualify as a **chemist**, and the adjective derived is **chemical**; a student of **mathematics** may become a **mathematician** and the adjective derived is **mathematical**. Study Appendix 5:7 on page 127, and note in particular any differences that exist where there are two adjectives derived (between, for example, **economic** and **economical**, **historic** and **historical**).

Now, without looking at the Appendix, name the expert you would consult in these situations and the kind of knowledge the expert possesses, as in this example:

You want to know something about the past of the place you live in. (*a historian, historical*)

1 Your car has broken down.
2 You don't know the rules of your own language.
3 You don't know the rules of a foreign language.
4 You want your portrait painted.
5 You want your photograph taken.
6 You think you need to take some medicine.
7 You have to buy some medicine.
8 You find difficulty in understanding the country's finances.
9 You need to install electrical equipment.
10 You don't know who to vote for in an election.

K Common adjective endings derived from nouns

Among the commonest adjective endings in English are **-y, -al** and **-ous**. You can see a list of common adjectives of each type in Appendix 5:8 on page 128. While there are no absolute rules for derivation, the following advice will help you:

a almost all adjectives relating to weather and conditions produced by it derive from the noun and end in **-y,** so on a rainy day the fields may be **muddy**.

b most other adjectives ending in **-y** derive in the same way from very common feelings: **hunger, thirst, sleep** etc. produce **hungry, thirsty, sleepy**.

c adjectives ending in **-al** are often derived from nouns ending in **-ion, -nce** and **-ent** (**educational, influential, continental**).

d it is difficult to relate adjectives ending in **-ous** to any particular noun ending. Study Appendix 5 and pay particular attention to those that derive from nouns ending like those in Note **c** above, where you might expect an **-al** ending, like **ambitious** from **ambition**.

Without looking at the Appendix, complete the sentences below with appropriate adjectives, derived from the noun given in brackets. Read the sentence carefully and decide whether the adjective is affirmative or negative.

1 The ground was .... after a cold night and the .... conditions near the river were an .... risk to motorists. (FROST, MIST, ADDITION)
2 His skill in .... matters had made him a .... man, but he was deeply .... and gave most of his money away to charity. (FINANCE, WEALTH, RELIGION)
3 It's a mainly .... area of the city, where .... people like lawyers and doctors are quite .... (RESIDENCE, PROFESSION, NUMBER)
4 The man waiting outside my house had a .... look on his face that made me ....; I wondered if he had some .... purpose in mind or if it was just his .... expression. (GUILT, SUSPICION, CRIME, NATURE)
5 I had .... reasons for coming here; I wanted to get away from the .... polluted atmosphere of the city and the sea air here is .... (PERSON, HEALTH, BENEFIT)

L Less predictable derivations

It is not always possible to derive words from a given root according to the groups of words described in the previous exercises. Many words do not form part of a 'family' of related words with similar endings. This exercise draws attention to some less predictable derivations. In each case, complete the sentences with appropriate words derived from the root given.

1 He takes part in so many spare-time .... that he's always busy.
(ACT)

2 You should obtain professional .... before buying the house.
(ADVISE)

3 You cannot make alterations to your house without the .... of the local council. (APPROVE)

4 His .... was delayed because of the late .... of the aircraft.
(FLY, ARRIVE)

5 She made a .... to the ticket .... about the bad .... of the children on the train.
(COMPLAIN, INSPECT, BEHAVE)

6 If he had had a .... he would have picked a different .... to defend him. (CHOOSE, LAW)

7 As it was, only his .... in .... enabled him to face the .... with any confidence.
(BELIEVE, JUST, TRY)

8 If it had not been for your medical ...., the patient would have .... to ....
(KNOW, BLOOD, DIE)

9 The postman is at the door with a .... He needs your .... on the .... and there's an .... sum to pay for the ....
(PACK, SIGN, RECEIVE, ADDITION, POST)

10 Judging from the .... I read in the newspapers, the play was a .... but the audience greeted it with roars of ....
(CRITIC, FAIL, LAUGH)

11 I didn't feel .... about her .... when she left the firm but now I miss the .... of her .... in the office.
(STRONG, DEPART, WARM, PERSON)

12 There is no .... between the .... standards of the .... in a .... district like this and the .... of the people in the district ....
(COMPARE, LIFE, INHABIT, WEALTH, POOR, NEAR)

13 His .... and his fine .... hair made him very .... to girls but I always thought his fits of .... if anyone paid more .... to someone else made him rather a .... child.
(HIGH, GOLD, ATTRACT, JEALOUS, ATTEND, SPOIL)

14 The pearl .... her father gave her was the most .... she had ever received from him and she took great .... in wearing it.
(NECK, BEAUTY, GIVE, PROUD)

15 There's no .... in measuring the .... and .... of the lake but we would need to take .... at different points to calculate the maximum ....
(DIFFICULT, LONG, BROAD, MEASURE, DEEP)

16 After the .... of the expedition's food supplies, I had doubts about our .... but .... the .... at that time of year is heavy so we weren't ....
(LOSE, SURVIVE, FORTUNE, RAIN, THIRST)

17 I was so tired that I .... a sigh of .... when my house came in .... and I realised the long journey was over.
(BREATH, RELIEVE, SEE)

18 He claims this .... of herbs and vegetable protein builds up his .... but the only .... that I can see is that he has put on ....
(MIX, STRONG, NOTICE, DIFFERENT, WEIGH)

Tests

Test 1

Use the word given in capitals at the end of each line to form a word that fits in the space in the same line. There is an example at the beginning (**0**). Write your words in the spaces provided.

1 How I became a writer

Throughout my (0) ...*childhood*.... I wanted to be a writer   CHILD
when I grew up but I lacked (1) .... in myself. I   CONFIDENT
knew I had the technical (2) .... and even the   ABLE
(3) .... and encouragement of my parents but I was   APPROVE
afraid that I had a serious (4) .... that would be   WEAK
difficult to overcome, not enough (5) .... What   IMAGINE
changed everything was my first (6) .... with   MEET
Eric. I had always had a great (7) .... for his   ADMIRE
novels, and the (8) .... he gave me that day, at   ADVISE
the (9) .... of my writing career, was of great   BEGIN
(10) .... He just said: 'Think of the characters   IMPORTANT
and then let them tell the story.'

2 Selling our house

I have just put our house on (1) .... because we   SELL
are moving out of the (2) .... and going to live   NEIGHBOUR
elsewhere. We have put an (3) .... in the local   ADVERTISE
newspaper and hope that we will be (4) .... enough   LUCK
to sell it quickly. The house is a new (5) ....   BUILD
and so the (6) .... costs are not very high, and   MAINTAIN
it has plenty of (7) .... space, which many people   STORE
look for these days. The only (8) .... is that   ADVANTAGE
people are short of money and this (9) .... our   LESS
chance of selling quickly. The agent's (10) ....   RECOMMEND
is to accept the first reasonable offer we get.

3 Moving to the country

I have spent most of my (1) .... in cities so
I'm still not sure if I made the right (2) ....
in moving to the village. The people are (3) ....
enough but I find the lack of (4) .... a little
boring. The only (5) .... here are the ones you
expect to find in a (6) .... farming community –
agricultural shows and so on. Still, I (7) ....
the fresh air, and a friend has just opened a
(8) .... shop in a small town not very far away.
I already do my (9) .... there and if I see her
quite often I may be able to enjoy the (10) ....
of town and country.

LIVE
DECIDE
FRIEND
ENTERTAIN
ACT
TYPE
BREATH

GIVE
SHOP
MIX

4 A weekend course

Veronica is on a (1) .... course this weekend in
Devon. She got the (2) .... a few days ago and
accepted immediately. The course is for (3) ....
people from different (4) .... backgrounds, such
as (5) .... and economists, and there are a number
of (6) .... representing different disciplines.
The idea in itself is (7) .... – they're going to
discuss a series of (8) .... to improve the use of
resources in society – but the (9) .... of the
matter is that once the (10) .... get involved,
they'll turn everything round to suit themselves.

RESIDENT
INVITE
PROFESSION
EDUCATION
LAW
SCIENCE
ATTRACT
PROPOSE
TRUE
POLITICS

5 My first job interview

I left university with good academic (1) .... but
writing out my first (2) .... for a job was very
difficult. I was not very (3) .... so I could not
see myself as a successful businessman: I was
looking for something quieter, (4) .... related to
my studies, but there was little (5) .... in my
field. Still, I had to earn my (6) .... somehow.
So I applied for the post of (7) .... to the press
officer of a company. As I stood at the (8) ....
desk before the interview I knew I had nothing to
recommend me but a reasonably pleasant (9) ....
and a good (10) .... from my tutor at university.

QUALIFY
APPLY
AMBITION

PREFER
CHOOSE
LIFE
ASSIST
RECEIVE

APPEAR
REFER

6 Commercialising sport

An old newspaper I have in front of me shows two women tennis stars of the 1930s, (1) .... dressed in the most (2) .... clothes before playing in an (3) .... match for charity. In those days, the players were amateurs who expected no (4) .... reward beyond their expenses during the (5) .... Nowadays sport is so commercialised that children of twelve apply to firms for (6) .... The stars earn more by giving companies (7) .... to use their names in (8) .... than they do from playing. But it is (9) .... to regret the past, when only players rich enough to devote themselves to (10) .... could afford to play.

BEAUTY
FASHION
EXHIBIT
FINANCE
COMPETE

SPONSOR
PERMIT
PUBLISH
POINT
PLEASE

7 An island holiday

We were tired of going on (1) .... tours and were looking for (2) .... places the tourists hadn't discovered. The travel agent suggested a (3) .... island. 'It's very quiet,' he said. 'The (4) .... still follow their (5) .... way of life. They're well known for their kindness to (6) .... and their cooking. You must try all the local (7) ....' This paradise seemed (8) .... in the 1990s but he was right, and we were deeply (9) .... of his advice. Apart from that, we had (10) .... weather, so we enjoyed ourselves enormously.

PACK
SPOIL
PEACE
HABIT
TRADITION
VISIT
SPECIAL
BELIEVE
APPRECIATE
GLORY

8 Lost in the fog

The landlord of the inn said it was too (1) .... to go out that morning. 'You'd be (2) .... to take the car out on the moor,' he said. '(3) .... is very bad.' He gave us a vivid (4) .... of what had happened to some guests whose car had broken down in the fog. '(5) .... they didn't listen to me and they'd made no (6) .... They had no food or water. We found their car without too much (7) .... when the fog cleared but by then the four (8) .... were practically dying of (9) .... and thirst. Even then their (10) .... was due to luck. Sometimes the fog doesn't lift for days.'

FOG
FOOL
VISIBLE
DESCRIBE

FORTUNATE
PREPARE
DIFFICULT
OCCUPY
HUNGRY
SURVIVE

9   A Gothic folly

Ever since my (1) .... in the village I had been
fascinated by a lonely tower on the (2) .... hill
that dominated the (3) .... for miles around. It
was like an old church tower but what (4) ....
(5) .... could it have, standing there alone? When
I climbed the hill one evening, the (6) .... it
made was more frightening as the sky (7) I
told the village teacher I imagined ghosts watching
me. 'It's not so (8) ....,' she said. 'It was built
by someone who liked reading (9) .... novels about
the Middle Ages. But (10) ...., I think it's ugly.
It spoils the view.'

ARRIVE
NEAR
LAND
RELIGION
SIGN
IMPRESS
DARK

MYSTERY
ROMANCE
PERSON

10   A novel for children

Pauline Walker's new novel, *Out of* (1) ....,
describes the (2) .... that develops between a
lonely old woman, whose only (3) .... is to look
after the garden at the (4) ...., and a poor boy.
Ms Walker is (5) .... convincing in conveying the
boy's initial (6) .... of the old woman's motives
and his inability to understand her (7) .... But
kindness wins, even overcoming the (8) .... of the
boy's lazy, rather (9) .... mother. Children in
the 10–14 age group will enjoy this (10) ....
moving story.

INNOCENT
FRIEND
OCCUPY
VICAR
REMARK
SUSPECT
GENEROUS
JEALOUS
PLEASE
WONDER

11   Saving a rare species of monkey

One of the victims of the (1) .... of the Atlantic
forest in Brazil is the (2) .... lion tamarin, a
species of monkey in danger of (3) .... Ecologists
became (4) .... aware of the tamarin's situation
when this once (5) .... species was reduced to a
few hundred. They tried to reverse the (6) ....
process by breeding them in zoos. Their re-(7) ....
into the forest has been difficult because the first
generation are not very (8) .... Their children
do better, but are also under (9) .... They need
(10) .... from hunters eager to capture and sell them.

APPEAR
GOLD
EXTINCT
PAIN
NUMBER
DISASTER
INTRODUCE

ADAPT
THREATEN
PROTECT

12 Why Julie missed out

When Julie did not get the (1) .... she had been
hoping for, she was very (2) .... 'I can't prove
there's been any (3) .... against me because I'm
a woman,' she said. 'There isn't any real (4) ....
of that. So I can't make a formal (5) .... But if
they'd paid more (6) .... to my real working
(7) .... here and not been so concerned with
questions of (8) .... , I'm sure I'd have got it.'
I agreed it was unfair and (9) .... 'The real
trouble is,' I said, 'that you're (10) .... and
like to go your own way, and they don't like that.'

PROMOTE
APPOINT
DISCRIMINATE
EVIDENT
COMPLAIN
ATTEND
ACHIEVE
PERSON
LOGIC
DEPEND

13 Have we really made progress?

One of the (1) .... of modern life most frequently
heard today is that the (2) .... in living
standards has been (3) .... technical and so not
really as (4) .... as people imagine. It seems
(5) .... to me to go to the other extreme and say
these advances have been (6) .... and the progress
we have made is more (7) .... than real. However,
it is clear that (8) .... proposals to avoid waste
are welcome. The (9) .... approach is for us to
use the world's resources in future more (10) ....
than we have been doing.

CRITIC
IMPROVE
ESSENCE
BENEFIT
REASON
WORTH
APPEAR
CONSTRUCT
SENSE
CARE

14 Misleading advice

It amazes me, as a (1) .... living abroad, that I
am often asked the way. By now I can (2) .... give
a (3) .... answer but I still recall with
(4) .... an occasion when I cheerfully sent a man
in the wrong (5) .... A few moments after his
(6) .... I realised my mistake but by then he was
out of (7) .... I burst out laughing as I imagined
him disappearing into the far (8) .... but almost
immediately my (9) .... died on my lips as I saw
him coming towards me. (10) .... I had time to go
into a shop before he noticed me.

FOREIGN
GENERAL
SATISFY
EMBARRASS
DIRECT
DEPART
SEE
DISTANT
LAUGH
LUCK

15 **The Neanderthals**

The generally accepted (1) .... theory is that we are the (2) .... of human beings who first came to Europe 40,000 years ago. It seems (3) .... that our arrival (4) .... coincided with the extinction of the Neanderthals already (5) .... there. Were our ancestors responsible for their extinction? The (6) .... findings, however, suggest a different cause. (7) .... found on Neanderthal remains point to violent (8) .... but there are no signs of human tools being used. Apparently, Neanderthals did not adapt very well to new (9) .... or live as long as our ancestors, who were (10) .... to migrate and learn from contact with others.

SCIENCE
DESCEND
SUSPECT
PRACTICE
SETTLE

LATE
INJURE
DIE

SURROUND
WILL

General revision

1 Adjectives

The exercises that follow practise the forms and usage indicated in Reference Section 3.

A Position

Correct the sentences given below. They are **all** wrong.

1 She's the actress most famous in my country.
2 She's a pretty and little girl.
3 She fell in love with a tall and dark and handsome stranger.
4 She has taller grown since I saw her last.
5 A short and fat man with long and dark hair was the only person other in the room.

B Order

Put the adjectives in brackets in the space in each sentence in the most natural order.

1 He's a .... boy. (little, strong)
2 The .... children in the race will get a prize. (three, first)
3 He was a .... man with .... eyes. (young, tall) (brown, big, round)
4 I don't use my .... racket any more. (old, tennis, wooden)
5 He's very proud of his .... car. (Japanese, new, lovely)

C Comparison

Complete the sentences with **one** appropriate word.

1 She's not as old as Mary but she's making better progress .... her sister because she's .... interested in studying.

2 I was in the same class .... Susan at school and she was already one of the .... intelligent girls I had ever met.
3 I think I'm .... good a player .... he is but he's .... determined to win .... I am.
4 .... longer we waited there, the .... irritable he became.
5 Our team is not .... as strong .... theirs because they've spent .... more money on new players .... we have.

2 Adverbs

The exercises that follow practise the forms and usage indicated in Reference Section 4.

A Word order, adverbs of frequency

Complete the sentences, putting the adverbs in brackets in the most appropriate position in the sentence, as in the example.

The trains from London are on time but the bus to the village is late. (usually, often)
The trains from London are **usually** on time but the bus to the village is **often** late.

1 I have much time for lunch so I have a big breakfast. (never, always)
2 Do you have the television on so loud? Haven't you thought of its effect on the neighbours? (always, ever)
3 I've been fond of dogs but I've wanted the bother of looking after one. (always, never)
4 I'll forget her kindness to me when I first joined the firm. She stopped her own work to help me even though she had been given lots of other things to do. (never, always, often)
5 I've been told that I look like my father but I can see any resemblance between us. (sometimes, never)
6 Have you wondered why I didn't answer your letters while you were in America? (ever, always)

7 I know the rent must be paid at the end of the month but I may have paid it a few days later during the year. (normally, occasionally)

8 If I hadn't been careful with money, we would have been able to save enough to buy this house. (always, never)

9 I don't think I've seen Robert without his dog; they go everywhere together. (ever, always)

10 She has said that she left her home town because she could have got such a good job there as here but she must have felt homesick from time to time. (always, never, surely)

B Adverbs of manner, place and time

Put the adverbs and adverbial expressions in brackets in the most appropriate order in the sentence, as in the example.

She sat down. (as soon as she came in, in an armchair, quietly)

As soon as she came in she sat down quietly in an armchair.

1 I played tennis (this morning, very well)

2 He usually has lunch (on Sundays, in a restaurant)

3 I went (in a hurry, out of the room)

4 She smiled (when she saw me, happily)

5 They met (yesterday, by chance, in the street)

6 He spoke to his guests (at dinner, last night, very rudely)

7 I heard them reading out the results (on the radio, a few minutes ago, excitedly)

8 The train arrived (half an hour late, this morning, at the station)

9 I've been working (at the office, hard, all day)

10 He jumped (with an alarmed expression on his face, as soon as the accident occurred, out of the car)

3 Conditional sentences

The exercise that follows practises the forms and usage indicated in Reference Section 16. Put the verbs in brackets into the most appropriate form and tense.

1 If I (have) any news tomorrow, I'll let you know.

2 I wouldn't do that if I (be) you.

3 Give her my love when you (see) her next.

4 If I (not) enjoy the job, I wouldn't stay here.

5 It would have been a pleasant day out if it (not rain).

6 I (not recognise) him if he hadn't told me his name.

7 If he (save) money while he was working, he'd be better off now he's retired.

8 I understand how the machine works now, but what am I supposed to do if something (go) wrong?

9 I'd help you if I (understand) your problem but I can't do anything unless you (tell) me the truth.

10 Provided nothing unusual (happen) they should be home by half past ten.

4 Gerund, infinitive and participle

The exercises that follow practise the forms and usage indicated in Reference Sections 26, 35 and 48b and c

A Gerund or infinitive

Complete the sentences with the correct form of the verbs given in brackets.

1 He was out of breath after (run) all the way home.

2 I enjoy (listen) to good music.

3 Would you like (come) to the concert with me?

4 I expected the doctor (tell) me what (do).

5 I'm sorry (have) kept you waiting. I stopped (get) some petrol on my way.

6 I'm surprised (see) you here. I don't remember (have) seen you here before.

7 He's been trying (pass) this examination for years and so he can't help (feel) nervous before (take) it.

8 If you don't know how (operate) the machine, I advise you (ask) the company (send) someone (teach) you.

9 I warned them not (let) him (make) a speech, because once he starts (talk) in public no one knows how (stop) him.

10 I meant (reply) to your letter last week but I delayed (write) until I had more definite news (give) you.

11 I promised (send) you information about the excursion but in the end I forgot (do) so. However, I have pleasure in (enclose) details of the next one and I look forward to (see) you there.

12 It's very kind of her (invite) me (spend) the weekend at her country house but I don't think I could (face) (make) another long journey so soon after (arrive) home from abroad.

13 If you've finished (do) the job I asked you (do) you can (go) home but before (leave), would you mind (lock) up the office?

14 I've got used to (travel) to work every day by underground so I don't mind (make) the journey but I'd much rather (work) nearer home and avoid (have) (get) up early every morning.

15 – They shouldn't (let) people (have) the television on so loud. I'm considering (call) the police to protest.
    – I object to people (make) so much noise myself but there's no point in (do) that. The police won't want (interfere).

B Gerund or participle

Compare these sentences:

Saving money is more difficult than **spending** it.
Saving a pound a week, **he managed** to get enough to buy the record player. (**he** = subject of the participle clause)

Write an appropriate subject for the participle clause in **one** of each of the pairs of sentences below.

1a Working all morning in the garden had made him hungry.
 b Working all morning in the garden managed to tidy it up.

2a Having breakfast outdoors soon saw the flies buzzing round the table.
 b Having breakfast outdoors attracted the flies to the table.

3a Bathing in the sea every day soon restored him to health.
 b Bathing in the sea every day soon felt better.

4a Concentrating on his work didn't notice the time passing.

 b Concentrating on his work enabled him to forget his troubles.

5a Deciding what to do proved more difficult than she had imagined.
 b Deciding what to do no longer felt depressed.

5 Modals

The exercises that follow practise the forms and usage indicated in Reference Sections 2, 14, 29, 42, 43, 44, 64. In each case, complete the sentence with an appropriate expression, using a modal form and the verb in brackets, as in the examples:

I'm sure I've got her address somewhere but I <u>can't find</u> it at the moment. (find)
You <u>must stop</u> at the traffic lights if the light is red. (stop)

A Ability and capacity (*can, could, be able to* and negative forms)

Use forms of **can** or **could** unless forms of **be able to** are the only correct ones.

1 He .... in the match yesterday because he had a bad cold. (play)

2 He hurt his leg in a game three months ago and he .... since then. (play)

3 He's afraid to go by boat because he .... (swim)

4 I .... a bicycle when I was five years old. (ride)

5 When fire broke out on the ground floor, the people in the upstairs flat .... the staircase but the firemen .... them down by using a ladder. (use, get)

6 The first idea we had that there was a fire was when my little daughter asked me if I .... something burning. (smell)

7 If you're going to the station tomorrow I .... you a lift in my car. (give)

8 If you changed the dates of your holiday, we .... together. (go)

9 What a pity I didn't know you were coming! I .... you at the station. (meet)

10 It's nice .... dinner outdoors on fine summer evenings. (have)

B Possibility and impossibility (*may, might, can, could* and negative forms)

1 The sun's coming out. It .... a fine day, after all. (be)

2 I suppose it .... later on, but I don't really think so, do you? (rain)

3 We usually have fine weather at this time of year although it .... heavily at times. (rain)

4 I'm not sure where she is at the moment. She .... lunch in the canteen downstairs. (have)

5 I wonder where she is. She .... out to post a letter. If so, she'll be back soon. (go)

6 I don't know where she is at the moment but I'm sure she .... very far. She's left her handbag on her desk. (go)

7 I don't want to sell the house but if they offered a lot of money I .... my mind. (change)

8 Don't use that sharp knife to spread butter on your bread. You .... yourself. (cut)

9 You shouldn't have used that sharp knife to spread butter on your bread. You .... your finger off. (cut)

10 They say anyone .... a murder but we know she .... this one because she was in Australia when it happened. (commit, commit)

C Deduction (*may, might, must, can, could* and negative forms)

1 – Oh, look, there's a man with a lot of photographers round him. It .... someone famous. (be)
– And there's a woman with him. She .... his wife or his girl friend, because they're taking pictures of her, too. (be)
– She .... She looks old enough to be his mother. (be)
– Yes, well, she .... be his wife, then. She .... his mother, for all I know. (be, be)

2 – Oh, dear, I can't remember where I put my car keys.
– Have you looked in your handbag? You .... them there. (put)
– No, I've looked.
– How about on the table in the dining room? You .... them there when you came in. (leave)
– No. I suppose I .... them into the kitchen with the shopping, though I don't usually do that. No, no, they're not there, either. (take)
– Well, I can't imagine what you .... with them. (do)
– I know! I had my arms full with the shopping, and I remember closing the car door with my foot. I .... them in the lock in the car. (leave)

D Obligation and no obligation (*must, have to, need* and negative forms)

Use forms of **must** and **need** whenever possible.

1 You .... so much. You'll make yourself ill. (worry)

2 You .... about the bill. I've already paid it. (worry)

3 I .... to bed early this evening because I have a lot of work to do tomorrow. (go)

4 I .... up early tomorrow because I'm not going to work. (get)

5 I promised her I would post her letter so I .... (forget)

6 I'm going to the post office and you can come with me if you like but you .... if you don't feel like it. (come)

7 There were no buses at the airport so we .... a taxi. (take)

8 We .... a taxi at the airport because John met us with his car. (take)

9 The doctor told me I .... any housework until I felt better. (do)

10 You .... all that housework by yourself. I would have helped you if you had asked me. (do)

E Advice, complaint, blame, regret (*should, had better* and negative forms)

Use forms of **had better** when it is possible.

1 You .... more care of your health. You're not as young as you were. (take)

2 You don't look well. You .... to work today. (go)

3 You .... any notice of what he says. He doesn't really mean any harm. (take)

4 What you say is very interesting. I .... a note of it. (make)

5 I was silly to go out in the rain like that. I .... your advice. If I had, I wouldn't be in bed with this awful cold. (take)

6 They .... a young girl of ten in charge of the children. It was very foolish of them. (leave)

7 I think I must have lost my passport. I .... to the Consulate to report it. I .... in the back pocket of my trousers. It must have fallen out. (go, leave)

8 They .... clearly on the bottle that these medicines .... out of reach of children. Of course I .... Jackie get his hands on it, but he did. He looks all right but I .... the doctor to make sure. (indicate, be kept, let, call)

6 Tenses of the verb

The exercises that follow practise the forms and usage indicated in Reference Section 69. You should also consult Reference Sections 8a and 77a. In all cases put the verbs in brackets into the most appropriate tense and put adverbs in the correct position.

A Present or timeless time

1 What (mean) you? I (not know) what you (talk) about.

2 He never (see) visitors when he (work). At present he (finish) work on his novel so I (think) you'd better come back another day.

3a What (think) of this picture? It (look) very ugly to me but I (not pretend) to know much about art.

 b What (think) you about? You (smile) but I (not see) anything funny in what I (say).

4 I (not understand) the mentality of our neighbours. They (make) unkind remarks about our children being noisy but whenever they (have) a party they always (play) dance music till three in the morning.

5 The play of *Macbeth* (begin) with three witches. They (wait) for Macbeth to come back from the battle he (fight).

B Present perfect and past tenses

1 I (not have) time to read your article yet.

2 I (work) so hard all day that I feel exhausted.

3 I only (speak) to him two or three times since Christmas.

4 They (plan) to move house for a long time.

5 I first (meet) her several years ago and since then we (come across) each other a few times on odd occasions.

6 I (try) to contact you all this morning but each time I (ring) they (say) you (go) out.

7 In those days they (live) in a big house near the park but it's a long time since they (sell) it and (move) away.

8 He (ran) up to me, (shake) hands and (smile): 'What (do) you since I last (see) you?' he (say).

9 While I (talk) to him he (look) nervously over his shoulder, and when I (ask) him what the matter was, he (tell) me he (think) someone (catch) the same train and (follow) him.

10 Until he (see) the advertisement for this job, he never (think) of coming to work in the city because he (spend) all his life in the country but now that he (move), he is very happy here.

11 I (wait) all afternoon for her to call but when she finally (ring) at about seven, it (take) me by surprise. She (talk) cheerfully at the other end of the line and all the time I (ask) myself: 'How am I going to explain to her that things (change) since I (ask) her to marry me?'

C Tenses in future time

Although in many cases alternatives are grammatically possible, use what you think is the most commonly used tense.

1 I (go) on holiday tomorrow. I (put) my alarm clock on because my flight (leave) at 8.00.

2 – What (do) she when she (retire)? (Be not) she bored if she (stay) at home all day?
– I'm sure she (find) plenty to do. Besides, she still (do) a little part-time work at home.

3 – Look at those black clouds! It (pour) down in a few minutes' time.
– Well, when it (do), we (get) wet unless we (find) somewhere to shelter. I haven't brought an umbrella.

4 – Would you mind giving her a message as soon as she (arrive)?
– No, I (make) a note if you (dictate) it to me.
– It's this: 'Don't bother to come this evening unless you really (feel) like it, but if you (want) to, give me a ring beforehand and we (wait) for you at the station.'

5 We (take) the children for a picnic this weekend if the weather (stay) fine. We (drive) out into the country, and when we (find) a nice spot, we (stop) for lunch.

6 Well, while you and the children (have) your picnic, I probably (work). If I (not finish) this article by Sunday night, it (be) too late to post it.

7 We were hoping to move into our new house next weekend, but the men say they (not finish) decorating it by then.

8 When the workmen finally (complete) work on this bridge, they (build) it for eighteen months, and they say it (take) twenty years to repay the cost of it.

Miscellaneous

7 *as*, *like* and *such as*

Before attempting this exercise, study Reference Sections 10 and 39. Complete the sentences with **as**, **like** or **such as**. Use **such as** in all cases where it is possible.

1a She's acting .... my secretary while Joan's on holiday.

 b Stop acting .... an idiot and pay attention!

1c Every actor would like to go on the stage .... Hamlet.

 d She's sung with .... famous tenors .... Placido Domingo and Luciano Pavarotti.

2 He's had some experience .... managing director of a company but that doesn't give him the right to behave .... a dictator.

3 He's lost his temper and he's screaming for his secretary .... a spoilt child .... usual.

4 When you've worked with really good bosses .... Mr Smith and Miss Jones, you wonder how anyone can put up with a rude man .... that.

5a He works hard, ... me, but not .... hard .... he says.

 b He works hard, ... we all do, and we all feel.................. having a rest from time to time. But none of us works anything .... the long hours they worked in my father's time.

6 – Why's Dad dressed .... that, Mum?
– We're going to a fancy dress ball, and he's going .... a Roman senator.
– He looks more .... a ghost in that old white sheet.

8   *some, any, no* and similar words

Before attempting this exercise, study Reference Sections 9, 46 and 66. Complete the sentences with **some, any, no** or words derived from them – **someone, anyone, no one, something, anything, nothing, somewhere, anywhere, nowhere**.

1   a   Their car's broken down. They look as if they need .... help.
     b   I don't mind stopping to help you. It's .... trouble.
     c   .... help you can give us will be very welcome.

2   a   I think there's .... at the door. I can hear them knocking.
     b   I opened the door but there was .... there.
     c   .... who says that is a fool.

3   a   I'd like .... to eat. I feel hungry.
     b   – What would you like for dinner?
         – Oh, ... special. .... will do.

4   – I'd like to move away from here but we've .... else to go.
     – Yes, I'd like to live .... else, too. .... would be better than this.

5   .... can say that the company ignores complaints from customers. .... complaint that arrives on my desk is looked at carefully and we always do .... about it, even if there is .... more we can do than answer the letter and explain why .... further action can be taken.

9   *either, or, neither, nor*

Before attempting this exercise, study Reference Sections 18 and 45. Complete the sentences with **either, or, neither** or **nor**.

1   We cannot get on together so you will have to choose between us. .... he goes .... I go.

2   – Would you rather come on Monday or Wednesday?
     – I don't mind. .... day would be all right for me.

3   a   I didn't enjoy the meal very much.
         – .... did I.
     b   – I didn't enjoy the meal very much.
         – I didn't, ...

4   a   .... of us is strong enough to carry those cases. They're too heavy.
     b   They're quite light. .... of us could carry them.

5   a   .... John .... Edward will be home for lunch.
     b   John won't be home for lunch, and .... will Edward.
     c   John won't be home for lunch, and Edward won't, ...

6   a   I don't dislike her .... hate her.
     b   I .... dislike her .... hate her.
     c   I don't dislike her and I don't hate her, ...

10   Exclamations

Before attempting these exercises, study Reference Sections 22 and 60.

A   Direct exclamation

Make appropriate exclamations from the information given, as in these examples.

They were very kind to us.
How *kind they were to us!*

You're wearing a very pretty dress.
What a *pretty dress you're wearing!*

1   She's very calm under pressure.
2   He drives very fast.
3   That's utter nonsense.
4   It's a great pity they couldn't come.
5   They're very friendly people.
6   We've had really terrible weather.
7   She works very hard.
8   That's a delightful idea.
9   It's been a very tiring day.
10 They were very happy to see you.

B Indirect exclamation

Sometimes we use exclamations of this kind in indirect speech. Convert the following exclamations to an indirect form, using the phrase given in brackets, as in the example.

How lucky we were! (You'll never believe)
You'll never believe how lucky we were.

1   What a mess the house was in! (You can't imagine)
2   How generous they were! (I'll never forget)
3   How quickly they get the job done! (It's extraordinary)
4   What beautiful cakes she made! (I'll always remember)
5   What rubbish people are willing to eat and drink. (It's amazing)

C Indirect exclamation and *so/such*

Compare these sentences:

We had **such a** lovely day at the beach. (You can't imagine)
You can't imagine **what a** lovely day we had at the beach.
The water was **so** warm. (It was extraordinary)
It was extraordinary **how** warm the water was.

Convert the sentences below into indirect exclamations in the same way, using the phrases given in brackets. Be careful of word order.

1   We had such a terrible journey. (I'm not going to tell you)
2   There was so much traffic on the road. (You'll never believe)
3   But the children were so cheerful all the time. (But the amazing thing was)
4   We had to stop so many times. (I can't remember)
5   It was such a nuisance not being able to get out. (But it's easy for you to imagine)
6   I felt so relieved when we finally got home. (Just think to yourself)

11 *few, a few, little, a little*

Before attempting this exercise, study Reference Section 23. Complete the sentences with **few, a few, little** or **a little**.

1   There's very .... demand for the bus service nowadays, but that may be because there are very .... buses.
2   We've had quite good weather this morning, ... drops of rain but .... sunshine, too.
3a   It's interesting that most people come to the doctor's surgery on Monday mornings but .... come on Friday evenings.
  b   There are .... people outside waiting to see you, Doctor.
4   She has very .... to live on so if her aunt left her .... money in her will it would at least make things a bit easier for her.

12 *for, since, during, ago*

Before attempting this exercise, study Reference Sections 5 and 24. Complete the sentences with **for, since, during** or **ago**.

1a   I've been waiting here .... half an hour, ... eight o'clock.
  b   I got here half an hour ...., at eight o'clock, and I've been waiting here .... then.
2a   I haven't played golf .... several years.
  b   I last played golf several years ...., in 1984.
  c   I haven't played golf .... I was at school.
3a   He lived here a long time ...., from 1930 to 1937.
  b   He lived here .... seven years, from 1930 to 1937.
4a   I heard several planes fly over the house .... the night.
  b   We can give you a bed .... the night. There's no need to go to a hotel.

5 William Shakespeare was born over four
   hundred years ...., ...
   the reign of the first Queen Elizabeth. He
   worked in the theatre .... over
   20 years, from about 1588 to about 1613,
   and .... that time wrote 37 plays.

6 – I woke up .... the night and
   heard a strange noise outside my door. I
   haven't felt so frightened I
   was a child. It sounded like a ghost trying
   to get in.
   – It probably was a ghost, actually.
   Someone died in that room a hundred
   years .... That noise has been
   going on .... ages, ever
   .... we moved in, but we're used
   to it by now.

13 Question tags

Before attempting this exercise, study Reference
Section 56. Complete the sentences with an
appropriate question tag, as in the example.

It's a nice day.
It's a nice day, **isn't it?**

1   He lives near here.
2   He's getting quite old by now.
3   I didn't tell you what happened.
4   They've improved the village quite a lot.
5   You'll write to me.
6   I should take more care of my health.
7   They must have arrived by now.
8   I'm being rather a nuisance.
9   Don't let them get away.
10 Let's play cards.

14 Reflexive forms and alternatives

Before attempting this exercise, study Reference
Section 57. Then complete the sentences with the
most appropriate form of the verb given in
brackets in the correct tense. Note the variations
indicated by the examples.

I *enjoyed myself* at the party. (enjoy)
They *are getting married* next week. (marry)
I *got up* early this morning (get up)

1   I .... for what went wrong.
    (blame)

2 The children .... when the head
   walked in. (stand up)
3 I hadn't been to their house for so long
   that I took the wrong turning and
   .... (lose)
4 The children .... and I was afraid
   they might fall down and ....
   (excite, hurt)
5 – .... up or you'll miss the train.
   – I just .... up. I need time to
   .... and .... and
   .... (hurry, wake, wash, shave,
   dress)
6 Are you coming to .... in the sea
   or are you afraid of .... (bathe,
   wet)
7 When we first came here we ....
   if the children would find enough to do to
   .... but they soon .... to
   living in the country. (wonder, amuse,
   accustom)

15 *still, yet, already, no longer, not any more*

Before attempting this exercise, study Reference
Section 67. Then complete the sentences with **still,
yet, already, no longer** or **not any more**.

1a He was born in that house and he
    .... lives there.
 b He was born in that house but he
    .... lives there.
 c He was born in that house but he doesn't
    live there ....
2   I didn't need to write to her because I'd
    .... told her the news on the
    phone.
3a – Has the postman delivered the letters
    ....?
    – Yes, he's .... been. He came ten
    minutes ago.
 b – Has the postman delivered the letters
    ....?
    – No, he hasn't come .... He'll
    be here soon, I expect.
4a – Have you found those papers you were
    looking for ....?
    – No, I haven't found them ....
    I'm .... looking.

b – Have you found those papers you were looking for ....?
– No, I've been looking for ages but I .... haven't found them.
– Try looking in the drawer of the writing desk.
– I've .... looked there. I've looked everywhere.

5 – Is she .... married to that pop star?
– No, they're not together .... The marriage is .... over.
`– Are they .... divorced then?
– No, not .... The lawyers are .... arguing about the settlement.

16 Verb forms

Before attempting these exercises, study Reference Section 77.

A Verbs not usually found in continuous forms

Complete the passage, putting the verbs in brackets into the present simple or continuous tense.

1 I (hear) a knock at the door. Go and see who it is, will you, John. I (listen) to the radio.

2 I (not) know why you (watch) the TV from so close. I (see) it perfectly well from here.

3 – What (do) you with that spoon in your hand?
– I just (taste) the soup to see if it's ready. It (taste) very good.

4a What (try) to tell me? I (not understand).
 b What (mean) you? You (not speak) clearly.

5 – She (plan) to sell the house. What (think) you of that?
– Well, it (belong) to her. It (not matter) as much as you (think).

B Double-object verbs

Rewrite these sentences in the form shown, and then transform them into the passive, with a personal subject, as in the example.

Someone lent some money to him.
Someone **lent him** *some money.*
He was lent *some money.*

1 They awarded a medal to her for her courage.

2 They granted a scholarship to her to study.

3 Someone paid a sum of money to him for the information.

4 They showed the royal apartments to us.

5 Someone owed a lot of money to him.

6 They offered a free ticket to Australia to her.

7 Someone told the story to all the neighbours.

8 Someone handed a letter to him, requesting his attendance at court.

9 They guaranteed a pension to her when she retired from her job.

10 They promised a reward to anyone who gave them information.

C verb + object + *as*

All the sentences given below contain mistakes in the structure used after the verb in *italic* type. Correct them.

1 She *is regarded* to be the most efficient secretary in the office.

2 She *is considered* as the most efficient secretary in the office.

3 The leader of the gang *was known* as dangerous.

4 The leader of the gang *was known* for the King of the Underworld.

5 I *can't accept him* to be my boss.

6 She *described it* like the most beautiful house she had ever seen.

7 He was *expected* as arriving late.

8 I've never *thought of her* to be old.

9 You *seem* as very tired.

10 It was originally built to be a royal palace but now it *is used* to be a museum.

1 *a an*

An is used before a vowel sound: **an** elephant, **an** umbrella, **an** aeroplane; but not when **u** is pronounced like '**you**': **a use**ful book. It is also used before **h** when **h** is not pronounced: **an h**onest man.

When we mention something for the first time, we normally use **a/an**; when that thing is referred to again, we use the definite article **the**, because by now it is understood which one we mean:

A photographer took his photograph without permission. He got so angry that he broke **the photographer's** camera.

We also use **a/an** in numerical expressions (for example, in expressions of frequency or quantity):

She has classes three times **a** week.
Petrol costs about sixty pence **a** litre here.
(See also *the*, use and omission.)

2 *able*

1 **Be able to** is used instead of **can/could** in the infinitive and for tenses like the present perfect and past perfect where no form of **can/could** exists:
   I'd like **to be able to** play tennis more often but up to now I haven't been able to find the time.

2 **Will be able to** is used instead of **can** to indicate future ability:
   I can't speak English well yet, but I'll **be able to** when I finish the course.

3 **Was able to** is used instead of **could** to indicate the ability to do something on a particular occasion in the past (as distinct from general ability):
   Because he **could** swim, he **was able to reach** the shore when the ship sank.

3 Adjectives

a position

1 Adjectives generally come before the noun or as a complement after **be** and some other verbs (**look, seem, feel** etc.)
   She's a **pretty** girl. She **looks** very **pretty**.

2 When we use more than one adjective before a noun we do not usually write **and** between the adjectives. We use commas if the combination is not usual, but not if it is very common. Compare:
   He's a **nice little** man. (common)
   She's a **shy, secretive** woman. (not usual)
   We use **and** when the adjectives are a complement after **be, seem, feel**, etc.:
   He's **short and fat**./She seems **charming and intelligent**.
   With three adjectives, we usually put a comma after the first: We were **cold, wet and tired**.

b order

In normal usage, we prefer to put some adjectives before others: He's a **nice little** man (NOT *little nice*). The rule is that general adjectives like **nice** or **pretty** come before more precise ones. Note these examples:

a I've read the **first hundred** pages. (ordinal – cardinal)

b An **intelligent young** man (mental ability – age)

c A **large round** ball (size – shape)

d A **green cotton** dress (colour – material)

e A **German car** factory (nationality/origin – purpose)

c nouns as adjectives/possessive *'s/of*

We can often use nouns as adjectives: **tennis racket, pencil case**. But we use the possessive **'s** form for people: **my sister's racket** – and for expressions referring to a period or point of time: It cost me a **month's salary**.

The **of** structure is used with inanimate nouns, in expressions like: **the door of the house, the title of the book**. (see Genitive)

d compound adjectives

Compound adjectives are sometimes made with an adjective and a noun plus an **-ed** ending. The meaning is usually **with** or **having**:
He's a **red-haired, broad-shouldered** man. (He's a man **with red hair** and **broad shoulders**.)

e comparison of adjectives

1 We can use **as ... as** and **not as/so ... as** with adjectives for comparison:
   He's **as tall as** Mary but **not as/so intelligent** as she is.

2 We can use **more/less ... than** with some adjectives or the comparative form **-er ... than** with other adjectives.
   I'm **more interested** in the subject **than** Jane, but **less hard-working**. Really, I'm just **lazier than** she is.
   One-syllable adjectives and two-syllable adjectives ending in **-y** (and a few others) form the comparative with **-er**. The spelling changes from **y** to **-i** when **-er** is added (heavy-heav**ier**). Most two-syllable adjectives and all longer adjectives form the comparative with **more** (honest – **more** honest.)

3 If we want to emphasise the difference in a comparison, we use **far** or **much** with the adjective:
   She's **far/much more intelligent than** I am.
   With plural nouns after the adjective we use **far** or **many**:
   Far/Many more people came than we expected.
   We use **not nearly as/so ... as** to emphasise a negative difference:
   I'm **not nearly as/so intelligent as** she is.

4 The superlative form is made with **-est** or **most/least**. When we compare more than two people or things, we use the superlative, even when the number involved is not mentioned:
   She's **the nicest/the most agreeable** of the three sisters.
   She's **the brightest** student in the class but **the least interested** in the subject. (There are more than two students.)

5 There are a few irregular forms. Remember:

good	better	best
bad	worse	worst
little	less	least
much/many	more	most
far	farther/further	farthest/furthest

The **further/furthest** forms are both used for distance, but we say **further information** (= additional).
The irregular forms **elder, eldest** exist for **old** but are only used for members of the family; my **elder brother**.

6 When we want to say that two things happen together or at the same rate, we use two comparative forms with **the**:
   The older I get, **the more impatient** I become.

4 Adverbs

a position

1 Adverbs generally come at the beginning or end of a sentence or before the main verb, but not between the verb and the object:
   He plays tennis **well**. (NOT *He plays **well** tennis*.)

2 Most adverb phrases go at the beginning or the end of a sentence:
   A few days ago he came to see me./He came to see me **a few days ago**. (NOT *He **a few days ago** came to see me*.)

3 **Also** usually goes before the verb but **too** and **as well** go at the end:
   He **also** speaks French. He speaks French **too/as well**.

b position: adverbs of frequency and indefinite time

1 Adverbs of frequency like **always** and **often** and other single-word adverbs of indefinite time like **recently**, generally go before the main verb but after forms of **be**:
   Margaret **is never** late; Jane **never comes** late, either.

2 They usually go between an auxiliary and the main verb or after the first auxiliary if there are two or more:
   I **have never seen** such a good film.
   She **must sometimes have wondered** if she had made the right decision.

3 Adverbs of definite time, like **yesterday**, cannot come before the main verb. They usually come at the end:
   Did you see Jack **yesterday**?

c order: manner, place, time

1 Adverbs and adverbial phrases of manner (how), place (where) and time (when) usually follow that order:
   She worked **hard** (how) **in the garden** (where) **all morning** (when).

2 If the adverbial phrase of time is long, or we want to emphasise it, we may put it at the beginning, before the subject:
   After a long morning's work (when), she rested **peacefully** (how) **in an armchair** (where).

3 With verbs of movement, we usually put place before manner:
   He came **into the office** (where) **in a bad temper** (how) **a few minutes ago** (when).

d   comparison of adverbs

The comparative forms of adverbs are usually made with **more/less**; the superlative (not commonly used) with **(the) most/(the) least**. Exceptions include some irregular adverbs and those made with **-er, -est**.

well	**better**	**(the) best**
badly	**worse**	**(the) worst**
little	**less**	**(the) least**
much	**more**	**(the) most**
fast	**faster**	**(the) fastest**
hard	**harder**	**(the) hardest**

I play tennis **better** than my brothers, but John runs **the fastest** of all of us.
I work **harder** than my boss, but I earn **less**.

5   *ago*

1   **Ago** indicates when something happened in the past, looking back from the present. It is always used with the past simple:
They **moved** here **five years ago**.

2   But when measured back from a point in the past, we use **before** or **earlier**, with the past perfect:
Their parents already lived here then; they had come a few months **before/earlier**.

6   *all*

a   form

1   With a personal pronoun, we can use the form **We all** or **All of us** (subject), **us all** or **all of us** (object):
We all/All of us went to the concert.
Michael had given **us all/all of us** free tickets.

2   We do not usually use **all** as the subject of a negative verb:
Not all our friends came to the party. (NOT *All our friends didn't come …*) Note that **not all** means 'Some of them came', not 'None of them came'.

b   position

All with the subject form of the personal pronoun (we, you or they) goes in the same position as an adverb of frequency (see **Adverbs b**):
We **were all** hungry./We **all felt** hungry./They **have all arrived**. But: **All of us** were hungry/**felt** hungry./**All of them have arrived**.

c   *all* and *every*

1   **All** takes a plural noun and verb and is followed by **the** when it refers to a group. **Every** has a singular noun and verb without **the**:
All the students love her./**Every student loves** her.

2   We do not usually use **all** for general statements where we can say **everyone/everybody** or **everything**:
Everyone is in favour of the idea. (NOT *All the people are …*)
Everything has gone wrong. (NOT *All the things have …*)

d   *all* and *(the) whole*

1   The meaning of **all** and **(the) whole** is the same but the word order is different:
I have lived in this town **all my life/my whole life**.

2   **The whole** is more often used with singular nouns, and cannot be used with plural forms:
The whole house needs cleaning./**All the rooms** need cleaning. (NOT *The whole rooms …*)

7   *although*

a   *although* and *though*

Although and **though** are used in concession clauses, but **though** is less formal and can be used at the end of sentences:
(Al)though I am very fond of her, she sometimes irritates me.
I'm very fond of her. She sometimes irritates me, **though**.
Even though (NOT *Even although*) is a stronger form.
I'm going to ask Mum, **even though** I know she'll say no.

b   *although* and *in spite of/despite*

Although is used in a clause, followed by a verb in the indicative; **in spite of/despite** are followed by a noun or gerund:
Although it was raining, they went on playing.
In spite of/Despite the rain, they went on playing.
Although he was injured, he went on playing.
In spite of/Despite being injured, he went on playing.

8   *always*

a   with continuous tenses

Always usually appears with simple tenses; when it appears with a continuous tense, it suggests 'more often than expected' and usually indicates a complaint or irritation:
They**'re always making** a noise. I wish they'd keep quiet.

b   *always* and *ever*

Always means 'at all times', **ever** means 'at any time'. **Always** is much more common in affirmative sentences. In questions the meaning is different:
I **always** walk to work.
Have you **always** lived in London? (all the time)
Have you **ever** lived abroad? (at any time in your life)

9   *any*

a   *any* and *some*

Any is used in questions and **not...any** in the negative as the equivalent to **some** in the affirmative; this is also true of **anyone, anything** and **someone, something**. (see *some*)

b   *any, anyone (anybody), anything*

Used in the affirmative to mean 'it doesn't matter which (person/thing)' or '(a person/thing) of whatever kind':
Any advice would be welcome.
Anyone (anybody) who believes that is a fool.
They cannot be used as a negative subject, like **no, none, no one (nobody), nothing**:
Nothing worries him. (NOT *Anything...*)

10   *as* and *like*

1 Use **as** to talk about someone's job, or a part played in a film or play:
She works **as a taxi driver**. He was wonderful **as Hamlet**.
We use **like** to make a comparison that is not real:
She can climb trees **like a monkey**.

2   In comparisons, **as** is followed by a clause, **like** by a noun or pronoun:
He lives outside the city **like me/as I do**.

3   **As** is also used in adverbial expressions like **as always, as usual, as on the previous occasion, as in Russia** etc.

11   *as if/as though*

Used to express real or imaginary comparisons. For imaginary comparisons, the past tense is used in present time, the past perfect in past time:
She looks **as if/as though** she knows what she's doing (= real comparison: She seems to know …)
It looks **as if/as though** the thieves climbed in through this window. (= real comparison: They seem to have climbed in …)
He behaves **as if/as though** he **was/were** God. (= imaginary comparison: He isn't.)
He looked **as if/as though** he **had seen** a ghost. (= imaginary comparison: He hadn't.)

12   *because/because of*

Because is followed by a clause, **because of** by a noun or pronoun:
We stopped playing **because it was raining**.
We stopped playing **because of the rain**.

13   *by*

a   as agent

In passive constructions, where an agent is needed, we use **by**:
This picture was painted **by** Rembrandt.

b   transport

We use **by** to indicate the means of transport:
I came **by road/by bus/by air/by plane**.
The exception is: **I walked/I came on foot**.

c   in time expressions

By means 'before and not later than':
I'll pay you **by the end of the month**. (At some time before the last day).
(To compare **at** the end of the month, **on** the 31st, see **Prepositions of time**.)

14   *can* and *could*

a   form

Can and **could** are auxiliary verbs, followed by an infinitive without **to**. They do not exist in all tenses. (See **able**)

b   ability

1   **Can** (negative **can't (cannot)**) is used in present time to mean: 'have the freedom or capacity to' or 'know how to':
I live by the sea so **I can go** swimming whenever I like.
She **can carry** cases weighing 40 kilos.
I can swim. I learnt when I was three years old.

2   In future time, we normally use **will be able to**. (See *able* **(2)**)

3 **Could** (negative **couldn't**) is used for general ability in the past and **couldn't** is used to talk about particular occasions:
I **could swim** when I was three years old.
I rang her several times but I **couldn't get through**.
But see *able* (3) for when we use **was able to**, and not **could**.

4 **Could** is used as an alternative for **would be able to** in the conditional tense:
If you met me at the station, we **could/would be able to** go together.

5 **Can** (**could** in past time) is commonly used with verbs of the senses:
I **can smell** something burning.
He shouted but I **couldn't hear** him.

6 **Could have** + past participle suggests that someone had the ability or knowledge but did not use it, or was prevented:
He **could have won** the game but he didn't try.
He **could have won** the game if he hadn't fallen down.

c   possibility
Can (**could** in the past) expresses general or theoretical possibility:
Anyone **can make** mistakes.
But in particular circumstances, referring to the present or future, we use **may**, **might** or **could**. (See *may/might*)

d   impossibility
Can't is used to indicate that something is impossible:
That **can't be** true. (See *must*)
When we make deductions about the past, we use **can't have** or **couldn't have** + past participle to say something was impossible.
Can't have suggests 'I'm sure it hasn't happened'; **couldn't have** suggests 'I'm sure it didn't happen'.
He's not here, but he **can't have gone** very far because he's left the key in the door.
She **couldn't have gone** to her mother's by car yesterday because the car was at the garage, being repaired.

e   permission
Can, could, may and **might** are all used in asking for permission.
May and **might** are more formal; **could** and **might** suggest that the speaker is not sure whether permission will be granted:
Can Sarah **stay** to dinner, Mum? (expecting 'Yes, of course she can.')
Could Sarah **stay** to dinner, Mum? Please! (expecting: 'Well, I don't know …')
In giving permission, we use **can** or **may** (**may** is more formal):
Yes, you **can/may** go, but be back by nine o'clock.

15   Cleft sentences
These are sentences used for emphasis, often in order to disagree with someone. The structure used is **It was … that** (who):
I didn't do it. **It was** John **that (who)** did it! (instead of: John did it.)
This structure can also be used to draw attention to things, times or places:
It was on Tuesday **that** the accident happened, not on Monday.

16   Conditional sentences

a   general
Conditional sentences are usually made with a clause using **if** (but see also **provided** and **unless**). The **if** clause can come before or after the main clause.
If I **can't come** to the meeting, I'll phone.
I'll phone if **I can't come** to the meeting.

b   present and future
We generally use the present tense for the condition and a future tense for the main clause, but note the alternative with the imperative:
If I see him tomorrow, I**'ll give** him your message.
If you **see** him tomorrow, **give** him my message.
Modals may also be used in the main clause:
If you **go** out, you **must put on** your coat. It's cold.

c   imaginary situations in present or future
We use the past tense for the condition and the conditional tense (**would** + infinitive) for the main clause. With the verb **be**, we usually use **were** for all persons:
If I **were (was)** rich, I**'d buy** a house by the sea.
If we **offered** you the job, **would** you **accept** it?

d   past situations
In talking about the past, we usually use the past perfect tense for the condition and the conditional perfect (**would have** + past participle) for the main clause:
If I**'d known** what was wrong, I **would have told** you.
But if the present situation is a direct result of an unfulfilled condition in the past, the main clause may be in the conditional tense:
If I**'d studied** more when I was at school, I **would have** a better job today.

e   permanent condition
If a condition is always true we use the present tense for both parts of the sentence:
If it **doesn't rain**, the rivers **dry up** and the animals **die** of thirst.

f   variations
1   As alternatives to **b** we can suggest that the possibility is not very likely:
If you **should see** him, **will you give** him my message? (please give him my message)
There is also a formal variation of this:
Should you see him, …
2   Alternatives to **c** are:
If we **were to offer** you the job, **would** you **accept** it?
Were we **to offer** you the job, …
These suggest that the offer is unlikely.
3   Alternatives to **d** are:
Had I known, I would have informed you.
This is more formal than: **If I had known …**

17   each

a   form
Each can be used with a singular noun:
Each office has a separate telephone line.
Each of is used with plural pronouns or nouns, but with a singular verb form:
Each of us/the secretaries has his/her own computer. (but NOT *Each of secretaries …* and NOT *Each of the secretaries have …*)

b   each and every
Each emphasises the individual, **every** the individual as a representative of a group:
Each student has a separate examination paper.
Every student got the first question right. (See also **all** *c*.)

c   each one, every one and everyone
Each one and **every one** mean a number of people/things counted separately, with the same emphasis as **each/every**:
There was nothing wrong with the letters. I examined **each one** personally. (one after the other)
Every one of our products is made by hand.
But **everyone** means **everybody** (see **all** *c*).

18   either

a   either … or
Either is used with **or** to indicate alternatives:
You can **either** go with them **or** stay at home with me.

b   either with noun or pronoun
Either with a noun or pronoun means 'one or the other' of two.
With a plural form we use **either of**.
Either day would suit me.
Either of you /the children can come with me.

c   not … either
Used as the negative equivalent of **too** or **also**.
(I didn't like the film much.) I **didn't** like it, **either.**
Compare: (I liked the film very much.) I liked it, **too.**
An alternative for negative agreement is:
Neither/Nor (did I).
(I didn't like the film much.) **Neither/Nor** did I.

19   else
Else means 'other', and is used with words combining the beginning **any-, every-, some-, no-** and the ending **-body, -one, -thing** or **-where**; also after most **wh-** question words, and with **little** and **much**:
Everyone else has gone home. ('all the others have …')
What else can I do? (= what other thing).
We've nearly finished. There isn't **much else** to be done.

20   enough
Enough goes after adjectives or adverbs but before nouns:
I'm not **strong enough** to carry those heavy weights.
He isn't **well enough** to go out.
Have we bought **enough food** for the party?
Enough of is used before a pronoun, possessive or determiners like **the, this,** etc.:
There isn't **enough of it** for everyone.
That's **enough of this** noise!

21 *ever*

a *ever* and *always*

Ever is only used to mean 'always' in the phrase **for ever**.

He told me he would love me **for ever**. (also one word: **forever**)

b *ever* and *never*

Ever is the opposite of **never**. It means 'at any time', whereas **never** means 'at no time.'

Have you **ever** been to Glasgow? No, I've **never** been there.

In negative sentences with **almost,** we prefer the form **hardly ever** to **almost never.**

I **hardly ever** go out at night.

22 Exclamations

We use **how** with adjectives, and with adjectives or adverbs + subject + verb:

How pretty! How pretty she is! How well she plays!

We use **what** with nouns, or adjectives and nouns, **what a/an** with singular, countable nouns:

What nonsense! What an interesting idea! What beautiful trees!

In indirect speech the word order does not change:

It was amazing **how well she played.**
You can't imagine **what an interesting idea** she had.

23 *few/a few*

a *few* and *a few*

Few suggests something negative; it means **not many** (more common in informal contexts). **A few** is more positive; it means 'some, but not many':

There were **very few** good speeches at the meeting. (= not very many)
The meeting wasn't very well attended but there were **a few** good speeches. (= some, but not many)

b (*a*) *few* and (*a*) *little*

Few and **a few** are used with countable nouns, **little** and **a little** with mass nouns:

There's **very little** to eat but I've bought **a little cheese** and **a few tomatoes.**

c *fewer* and *less*

Fewer is the comparative form used with countable nouns, **less** with mass nouns, though **less** is commonly used with countable nouns like people, too, in informal modern English.

There are **fewer** boys **than** girls in the class.
We've got **less** money **than** they have.

24 *for* (See also **purpose a**)

a *for* and *during*

During and **in** are used to refer to something that happened at a time within a period; **for** refers to the length of time:

I woke up **during/in** the night. (at some time in the period)
I booked into the hotel **for** the night. (the whole period)

b *for* and *since*

For and **since** are used with present perfect tenses to indicate the duration of time from the past until now; **for** refers to the total length of time, **since** refers to the time when it started. (The time when it started may sometimes be expressed by a phrase using the past tense.):

I've been living here **for several years/since 1990/since I was a child.**
I **haven't seen** her **for a long time/since last summer.**

When the main action took place in the past, past perfect tenses are used with **for** and **since**:

When they finally arrived, we had been waiting for them **for two hours/since half past seven**.

c *for* and *from*

For indicates duration so it can be used with any tense. We can refer to periods of time either by using **for** for the total time involved, or **from ... to** to show the beginning and end:

We stayed there **for six months/from March to September.**

d *for* and *ago*

We can count forwards for periods of time from the past until now, using the present perfect tense with **for** or **since** (see **b**). We can also count backwards from now, using the past tense with **ago** (see *ago*).

I've known her **for five years.**
I first **met** her **five years ago.**

25 Genitive

a possessive *'s* and *of*

We use the **'s** form for people, animals, and in some time expressions, but not usually for things. The plural is written with the apostrophe after the **s** (**s'**), unless it is irregular and does not end in **s**:

That's **Mary's** coat. That's the **teachers'** room.
Those are the **children's** clothes. I'm taking three **weeks'** holiday.

We can sometimes use nouns as adjectives in phrases like **tennis racket** (a racket for playing tennis) but the possessive must be made with **of** in expressions like: **the door of the house, the title of the book.**

b double genitive

We do not usually say **your friend** or **my father's friend** unless we have indicated the person we are talking about. We can either say **one of your/my father's friends** or use the double genitive:

a friend of yours or **a friend of my father's** (NOT *of your/of my father*).

We also use this construction with proper names:

I was reading **a novel of Jane Austen's** (or by Jane Austen, but NOT *of Jane Austen*).

26 Gerund

a general

The gerund is the term used for a verb form ending in **-ing** when it is used like a noun. It has the same form as the present participle:

I like **listening** to music and **reading.**

Possessive forms (**my, John's, my mother's**) are used with this form; in informal English, the object form of the personal pronoun or the noun (**me, John, my mother**) is often used instead:

Do you mind **my/me going** away without you?
Do you agree with **John's/John getting** married so young?

b preposition + gerund

A preposition is always followed by a gerund verb form:

Before going home, hand in your books to me.
Some verbs are formed with the preposition **to,** and so are followed by the gerund. The most common are:
amount to, be (get) accustomed to, be (get) used to, look forward to, object to

c gerund and present participle

The form is the same but there is a difference between the gerund (**-ing** form used like a noun) and participle (**-ing** form used like a verb). Compare:

Playing games is healthier than **watching** them on television. (gerund)
Playing football, he broke his leg. (or He broke his leg **playing** football.) (present participle = While he was playing …)

d gerund and infinitive (impersonal structure)

Stealing is wrong.
We prefer the gerund at the beginning of a sentence like this, the infinitive in an impersonal structure:
It is wrong **to** steal.

e gerund and infinitive after certain verbs

Some verbs are always followed by the gerund, others by the infinitive. These common verbs are followed by the gerund, together with verbs ending in a preposition, like **give up: avoid, consider, delay, deny, dislike, enjoy, escape, face, feel like, finish, forgive, can't help, imagine, involve, mention, mind, miss, practise, resist, risk, can't stand, suggest, understand.**

I **enjoy playing** tennis. I **can't help thinking** about it. The job **involves travelling** a lot.

In some cases, either a gerund or infinitive may be used, but there are usually differences in meaning or usage:

1   **advise, allow:** infinitive with a personal object, otherwise gerund:
I wouldn't **advise making (you to make)** a complaint.

2   **begin, start:** infinitive only in continuous tenses:
I **was beginning to enjoy** the party when my ex-boyfriend walked in. (NOT *I was beginning enjoying* …)

3   **go on:** the gerund means 'continue', the infinitive indicates a change of topic or action:
She **went on talking** on the phone for half an hour.
She first explained the problem and then **went on to talk** about possible solutions.

4   **like, hate, love, prefer:** we use the infinitive in the conditional – **would like to, would hate to** etc.
Like and **love** generally take the gerund to express general liking, the infinitive when referring to regular habits:
I **like getting up** late and **going to bed** early. (general liking)

I **like to lie in bed** on Sunday mornings when I don't have to go to work. (regular habit)
Hate and **prefer** usually take the gerund in general, the infinitive on particular occasions.
I hate **being late** for work. I **prefer to take** a taxi if I think I'm going to be late.

5 **remember, forget, regret**: infinitive with future reference, gerund with past reference:
Remember to buy some apples on your way home. (Don't forget.)
He **remembered buying** apples for a penny when he was young. (He had the memory)

6 **stop**: the gerund means 'leave off, give up', the infinitive is really an infinitive of purpose:
I've **stopped buying** petrol because I've sold my car.
He **stopped (in order) to buy** some petrol at the garage.

7 **try**: the infinitive means 'attempt, make an effort', the gerund means 'use a different method, experiment':
I've been **trying to open** this door for five minutes.
Try turning the key the other way.

27 *hardly*

a *hardly* and *hard*
Hard is an adjective: a **hard** surface (= not soft); a **hard question** (= difficult). **Hard** is also an irregular adverb: She works **hard**. (= a great deal, with effort).
Hardly means 'almost not'. It can be used to qualify a noun, verb or adjective. We prefer forms like **hardly anyone, hardly ever** to negative forms like **almost no one, almost never.**
I **hardly ever** go to his lectures.

b *hardly, scarcely, only just, no sooner*
Hardly and **scarcely** are used, usually with the past perfect tense, to suggest that one thing happened almost immediately after another:
I **had hardly/scarcely closed** the door when the telephone rang.
Alternative constructions are:
I **had only just closed** the door when the telephone rang.
I **had no sooner closed** the door than the telephone rang.

28 *have/get something done*

a obtaining a service
We use these structures when we mean that someone else did something for us that we could not or did not want to do, like cutting our hair:
I went to the hairdresser's **to have my hair cut.**
We usually use **get** when we want to suggest the effort of going:
You should **get your hair cut.** It looks untidy.

b obtaining something without wanting it
These structures can also be used when what happens is not arranged or wanted by us, like someone stealing something from us:
I **had my bag stolen** in the market.

Get may imply that we provoked what happened in some way:
If you speak rudely to girls, you may **get your face slapped.**

29 *have to* and *have got to*

a general
Both forms are used to express obligation.
Have got to is normally used for particular occasions, not in general.
She **has to get up** early every morning.
I've **got to go** now or I'll be late for work.
In future time, we can use **have got to** or **will have to** on a particular occasion.
I've **got to/'ll have to get up** early tomorrow morning. I'm going to the airport.
The past form is **had to/didn't have to** + infinitive.
I **had to stay** late at the office last night.

b *have to* and *must*
Both indicate obligation but **must** suggests the obligation is felt personally, either by the speaker or the person being spoken to. **Have to** suggests the obligation comes from outside.
I **must** remember to give you back that book I borrowed.
The rule is that you **have to** return library books after two weeks.
In the negative, **mustn't** means prohibition, **don't have to** means there is no obligation:
You **mustn't eat** that! It's dirty!
You **don't have to eat** that if you don't like it.
We often use **needn't** instead of **don't have to** (see *need* and *needn't*).
The past form of both **have to** and **must** for obligation is **had to**:
I **had to get** to the station early to catch the first train.
Past forms which indicate no obligation are **didn't have to, hadn't got to, didn't need to** and **needn't have.**

30 *how/what … like?*

Questions with **how** refer to people's health, things that change, or people's reactions:
How's your sister? (She's very well, thanks.)
How's your new job going? (Fine, thanks.)
We use **what … like** to ask for a description of someone or something, or for an opinion:
What's he **like**? (He's tall/He's very intelligent).
What was the film **like**? (It was rather long, and …)
We use **what … look like** specifically for a description of physical appearance:
What does she **look like**? (Well, she's tall, with long black hair, and …)

31 Imperative
The imperative has the same form as the infinitive and is usually used without a subject. The negative form is made with **do not (don't)**:
Go on! **Don't** wait for me!
(See also **Conditional sentences (b)** and **Reported Speech (c)**.)

32 *in case*
In case usually means 'because (something) may/might (happen).' It is not the same as **if**. Compare:
Take an umbrella **in case** it **rains**. (… because it may rain.)
Take an umbrella **if** it **rains**. (but not if it doesn't.)

In past time, **in case** is usually followed by a past tense:
I took out insurance **in case** I **had** an accident.
In case of is used in formal notices with the meaning of 'if there is …'
In case of fire, break the glass.

33 Indirect questions: word order
In indirect questions, the question uses the affirmative or negative, not interrogative form; the word order is always subject before verb. If the direct question has no question word, the indirect question comes after **if/whether**; if it has a question word, this word is repeated in the indirect question:
She wants to know **if/whether you are** English.
I wonder **where I will be** tomorrow.
Note the changes in form in the present and past simple tenses:
(Does he speak English?) Ask him **if/whether he speaks** English.
(What did he say?) I wonder **what he said**.
If the question word is already the subject in the direct question, the word order will not change unless the verb is **be**:
(What happened next?) Tell me **what happened** next.
(Who is she?) I wonder **who she is.**

34 Indirect speech: paraphrase
Some verbs can be used in indirect speech to indicate the way things are said and the purpose of what was said. In the table below, note the purpose of the verb from the example in direct speech, and the constructions possible with the verbs we can use instead of **say** and **tell** in indirect speech:

Purpose	Verb	Direct speech and paraphrase
accusation	accuse	'You stole it, didn't you?' I accused **him of stealing** it.
admission	admit	'Yes, I took it.' He admitted **that** he **had taken it.** He admitted **having taken** it.
advice	advise	'You should take more exercise.' She advised **him to take** more exercise. She advised **taking** more exercise.
agreement	agree	'I think you're right.' She agreed **with** me/the idea. 'All right. I'll help you.' She agreed **to help** me. 'That's the best method.' We agreed **that it was** the best method. We agreed **on** the best method.
apology	apologise	'I'm sorry I arrived late.' He apologised **for arriving** late.
complaint	complain	'You should have done the job better.' He complained **that they should have …** 'I wish he wouldn't do that.' She complained **to me about him.**

denial	deny	'I didn't steal it.' He denied **that he had stolen** it. He denied **having stolen** it.
invitation	invite	'Would you like to come to the party?' He invited **her (to come)** to the party.
offer	offer	'I'll help you, shall I?' She offered **to help me**.
refusal	refuse	'I won't do it.' He refused **to do** it.
regret	regret	'I wish I hadn't broken it.' She regretted **having broken** it. She regretted **that she had broken** it.
reminder	remind	'Don't forget to post it.' She reminded **him to post** it.
suggestion	suggest	'Why don't you go with her?' She suggested **that I should go** with her. 'Let's go for a walk!' She suggested **going** for a walk.
threat	threaten	'If you don't go away, I'll call the police.' He threatened **to call** the police if they didn't go away.
warning	warn	'Be careful. The roads are icy.' He warned **them to be** careful. He warned **them of/about** the icy roads. He warned them **that the** roads were icy.

35 Infinitive (See also Purpose b and d)

a form

The infinitive is generally formed with **to**:
We're hoping **to go** to Spain this year.
Verbs followed by the infinitive without **to** are:
– many auxiliary verbs (**can, must,** etc.)
– **make** (only in the active)
– **let** (which has no passive)
– **help** (with or without **to** in the active)
– verbs of the senses (**see, feel,** etc.)
(see **Participle c.**)
You **can't be** serious.
Make him **do** it again. (He **was made to do** it again).
We **let** her **stay** up late. (She **was allowed to stay** up late).
You **can help (to) persuade** her to go.
I **saw** him **take** the money.
The negative infinitive is made by putting **not** before **to**:
I advised her **not to sell** the house. (NOT *to not sell*)
The perfect infinitive is made with **to have** + past participle:
I'm sorry **to have kept** you waiting.

b infinitive after verb

Many verbs are followed by the infinitive with **to**.
Among the most common are:

agree, appear, arrange, ask, attempt, choose, decide, expect, happen, help, intend, learn, manage, offer, prepare, promise, refuse, seem, try, want.
For verbs followed by gerund and/or infinitive, see **Gerund (e)**.

c verb + object + infinitive

Many verbs take this construction:
I want you to pay careful attention to what I'm saying.
Among the most common are:
advise, allow, ask, expect, forbid, hate, invite, like, need, order, permit, persuade, prefer, remind, teach, tell, want, warn.

d adjective + infinitive

Some adjectives can be followed by the infinitive:
I was **surprised to see** her there.
When the infinitive is used with a preposition this can come at the end of the sentence:
A log fire is **nice to come home to**.
In sentences of this sort the object is not placed after the verb:
She's very **pleasant to talk to**. (NOT ... *talk to her*).

e question words + infinitive

We can use **how, what, who, where, when** and **whether** with the infinitive after verbs like **ask, tell, know,** and **understand**:
I don't know **where to go**.
Tell him **how to do** it.

36 Inversion

a after *neither, nor, so*

Inversion means that the verb comes before the subject (as in the question form). In short answers beginning with **neither, nor** and **so**, we invert the verb:
(I don't like him.) **Neither/Nor do I**. (Compare: **I don't, either**.)
(But I like her.) **So do I**. (Compare: **I do, too**.)

b after negative adverbial expressions

In formal style, writers sometimes begin sentences with negative adverbs or adverbial expressions like **Never** ... or **Under no circumstances ...**. In such cases, we invert the verb:
Not until the day afterwards **did he realise** that he could have been killed in the accident.
In most sentences, however, it is better to use the more normal order:
He **did not realise** that he could have been killed in the accident **until** the day afterwards
Note that **seldom, rarely, hardly ever** (= not (very) often) count as negative adverbial expressions.

c after *only*

We invert a sentence when it begins with **Not only ...**, but also when it begins with **Only** ... if *only* refers to an adverbial expression:
Only in literary texts do we normally **find** this word order.
Compare: We normally **find** this structure **only** in literary texts.
Inversion is not required when **only** qualifies a noun:
Only John knew the answer.

37 *it's*: impersonal subject

a *it's* + infinitive, *it's* + *that* clause

We prefer not to begin sentences with the infinitive or a **that** clause. Instead we use an impersonal subject, **it**:
She speaks very clearly. **It's** easy **to understand** her.
It's obvious **that** she had a good teacher.

b *it's* + adjective/noun + *for/that*

Some adjectives and nouns are followed by the infinitive construction after **for** and a noun or pronoun; others are followed by a **that** clause. The first group includes the adjectives: **boring, dangerous, difficult, easy, expensive, hard, healthy, necessary, usual, useful**:
It's dangerous (for young people) to ride motor-cycles unless they've passed a driving test.
Common adjectives that take a **that** clause are: **certain, clear, curious, likely, lucky, obvious, probable, surprising, true**:
It's obvious that they've never seen anything like it before.

c *it's* and *there is/are*

There is/are indicates the existence of something. (see *there is/are*). Compare these sentences with the examples above in **b**:
There are a lot of **accidents** involving young people riding motor-cycles.
There is nothing like that in their country.

38 *let's*

Let's (let us) is used to make suggestions. It is followed by the infinitive without **to**. It is a more positive form than **Shall we?**
Let's go out! It's too nice to stay indoors.

39 *like*

a *like* and such *as*

These can both be used to indicate an example:
Famous writers **like/such as** Agatha Christie have stayed at this hotel. (NOT *as*).
The word order can be varied with **such as**:
Such famous writers **as** Agatha Christie ...

b *like* and *kind, sort, type of ...*

We can indicate the kind of thing we mean by saying:
This/That kind/sort/type of car is the best in difficult conditions.
In the plural, however, we prefer to avoid choosing between combinations like 'Those kind/Those kinds' by using **like**, usually with the singular form:
Cars **like this/that** are the best in difficult conditions.
We can also use the structure:
Cars of **this/that kind/sort/type** are the best in difficult conditions.

40 *likely*

Likely is similar in meaning to **probable**:
Rain is **likely/probable** tonight.
But **likely** can be used in an infinitive structure:
It's **likely** to rain tonight (It will probably rain).

41 Mass (uncountable) nouns

These fall into three main groups:
1 Abstract nouns, usually uncountable in other languages, like **honesty, wisdom, knowledge,** etc.
2 Uncountable nouns relating to: materials, food: **wood, metal, meat, cheese,** etc.
subjects for study: **music, biology, French,** etc.
games and sports: **football, tennis,** etc.
Some words have more than one meaning, so **paper** (material) is uncountable, and one example of it is a **piece of paper** or a **sheet of paper; paper** meaning '**newspaper**' is countable.
3 Nouns that are uncountable in English but countable in some other languages. Check this list of uncountable nouns against the equivalent in your own language: **advice, applause, behaviour, commerce, damage, equipment, evidence, furniture, hair, harm, information, insurance, knowledge, lightning, luggage, money, news, nonsense, practice, progress, research, rubbish, scenery, thunder, travel, trouble, weather, work.**

42 *may* and *might*

May and **might** are auxiliary verbs, followed by the infinitive without **to.**

a possibility
When talking about possibility in particular circumstances, we normally use forms of **may** and **might,** though forms of **could** can also be used.
I don't know where she is. She **may be** in the garden.
I'm not sure what she's doing. She **may be cutting** the grass.
It looks cloudy. It **may rain** this evening.
Might is used instead of **may** in present and future time to suggest that the possibility is less likely:
It **might** rain later, but I doubt it. It's not cloudy.
May not/might not + infinitive, the negative forms, suggest 'perhaps ... not':
She **may not be** at home today. She said she was going out. (Perhaps she isn't ...)
Can't/couldn't indicate impossibility (see *can* and *could* c).
In conditional sentences, **might** + infinitive is used for the conditional tense:
If she **changed** her job, she **might earn** more money.
May have and **might have** + past participle are used for possibility in the past:
It's surprising that she hasn't rung you, but she **may not have received** your letter. (= perhaps she hasn't received/didn't receive ...)
Can't have/couldn't have + past participle indicate impossibility':
They **can't/couldn't have done** it. They weren't even there.

b permission
May and **might** can be used when asking for permission, but are more formal than **can/could.** (See *can* and *could* d).

43 *must*

a obligation
See *have to* and *have got to* b.

b deduction
Must can be used to indicate certainty based on logical reasons:
It's getting dark. It **must be** about eight o'clock.
In the negative, we use **can't** (see *can* and *could* c).
For deductions made with reference to the past we use **must have** + past participle; for the negative we use **can't have/couldn't have** + past participle (see *can* and *could* c).
The thieves **must have climbed** in through this broken window.

44 *need* and *needn't*

Need is an ordinary verb but in the question and negative forms also exists as a modal, followed by the infinitive without to.
Needn't indicates lack of obligation (see *have to* and *have got to* b), and **don't need to** is an alternative form. Questions can be formed with **Need I/Do I need to:**
Need I/Do I need to go to the meeting on Thursday?
You **needn't/don't need to come** if you don't want to.
The modal form is generally used for particular situations in the present and future, the ordinary verb for general necessity and advice in the future (close to **will have to** in meaning):
If you want to go abroad, you'**ll need to get** a passport.
In past time, **didn't need to** + infinitive means there was no obligation; **needn't have** + past participle means there was no obligation but the person did the action anyway, unnecessarily.
I **didn't need to meet** them at the station because they said they would get a taxi. (so I didn't go to the station)
You **needn't have got** a taxi. I would have met you at the station if you had told me when you were arriving. (but they **got** a taxi)

45 *neither/nor*

a neither
Neither is used with regard to two people or things as the negative equivalent of **both;** the verb following it is singular:
Neither brother **is** old enough to go to school.
With pronouns and nouns that are qualified we use the form **neither of:**
Neither of them/the brothers goes to school yet.

b neither/nor
Neither and **nor** can be used in short answers:
(I don't like him.) **Neither/Nor** do I. (Compare: I **don't either**).

c neither ... nor
They can be used together to join two negative ideas. In formal English, the verb should be written in the singular:
Neither Jane **nor** Mary **works** on Saturdays.
I **neither** agree with her **nor** disagree. I have no opinion.

46 *no, no one, none*

a *no* and *any*
No has the meaning 'not any' but it is the only correct form at the beginning of a sentence (see *any* (b)). **No** can be used with singular or plural nouns:
No argument(s) will convince them.

b *no* and *none of*
We use **none of** with pronouns and with an article or possessive in front of the noun:
None of his arguments convinced them.
None of the students like her.

c *none* and *no one*
No one (Nobody) means 'not any person'; it is the negative form of **someone,** and must be used at the beginning of a sentence:
No one came with her. She came alone.
(Compare: **None of her friends came** with her.

47 *other* and *another*

Another is used as an adjective with singular nouns, **other** with plural nouns:
Wait! There's **another man** coming.
Wait! There are some **other people** coming.
Another can mean 'one other' but is often used to mean 'one or more additional' before a number or **few:**
I'd like **another cup/two cups** of tea, please.
It also means 'a different'
He'd be happier doing **another job.**
(Compare: He had three **other jobs** before this one.)

48 Participle clauses

a adjectival
We can use the present participle, ending in **-ing,** and the past participle, ending in **-ed,** in clauses that are rather like relative clauses. The present participle is only used when the action is happening at the same time as the main verb:
The girl (= ... who is dancing ...) **dancing** with Jack is my sister.
The man (= ... who was injured ...) **injured** in the accident lives near me

b adverbial
Present, past and perfect (**having** + past participle) participles can all be used:
Looking up from my book, I saw a fly on the wall. (= When I looked ...)
Having spent several years in India, he was used to the way of life there. (= Because he had spent ...)
Built in the eighteenth century, the house is still in good condition. (= Although it was built ...)

c with verbs of the senses
After verbs like **see** and **hear** we can use an object and either the infinitive without **to** or the present participle. In general, the infinitive is used when talking about a completed action and the participle when we saw or heard only part of it. Compare:
I **saw** her **cross** the road and **go** into the shop. (completed actions)
I **saw** him **crossing** the road and then the car hit him. (part of an action)
In the passive, the infinitive is formed with **to:**
She **was seen to cross** the road and **go** into the shop.

49 Passive voice

The passive is formed by the verb **be** and the past participle of the main verb. The only continuous forms normally found are the present and past.

The passive can occur with an agent (**by …**) when we are interested in a thing but also want to mention the person responsible for it:
The house **was built by** my grandfather.
But we prefer to use active forms in such sentences where possible.
The passive is essential in such sentences when no agent is mentioned:
The house **was built** a hundred years ago.
Use this table for reference:

Tense	Sentence
present simple	The desk **is made** of wood.
present continuous	The road **is being repaired**.
future simple	The new building **will be opened** next year.
past simple	The holiday **was booked** in London.
past continuous	The luggage **was being loaded** into the car.
present perfect	The book **has been translated** into English.
past perfect	He **had been invited** to the party.
modal	This door **must have been left** open.
infinitive	Is she going **to be picked** for the team?

50 Phrases in apposition

One way of giving additional information about a person or thing is to use a phrase in apposition (instead of a relative clause with a relative pronoun and a form of **be**).
Mr Taylor, (who is) **the team manager**, said …
The cathedral, (which is) **the oldest building in the city,** was built …

51 Prepositional verbs and phrasal verbs

Many verbs in English are formed from the combination of a verb and either a preposition or an adverb particle. The meaning of most prepositional verbs is obvious from the combination (for example, **look at**), but not always, (**look after** = take care of). The meaning of a phrasal verb is usually not clear from the combination (**look up** (a word in a dictionary) = try to find the meaning of). Note all those you **come across** ((prepositional verb) = find by chance) and look up their meaning!
It is not always clear whether a verb is prepositional or phrasal, but there is a difference in word order. Prepositional verbs take the preposition before the noun or pronoun object:
Look at me. Look at the sky.
Look after the children/Look after them.
Phrasal verbs with an adverb particle take the particle either before or after a noun, and after a pronoun:
Look up the word./Look the word up in the dictionary.
Look it up in the dictionary. (NOT *Look up it*.)

52 Prepositions of place

a   *at, in, on*
At is used:
– for particular points: **at** the end of the road, **at** number 27.
– for places when we are concerned with their purpose or location, not their size or shape: **at** the station, **at** the supermarket.
She works **at the post office**. (Compare: She's **in the post office**, buying some stamps (= inside).)
– for places (small towns, villages etc.) the speaker does not consider very important or does not know very well: **at Melton Mowbray**, a town near Leicester. (Someone who lived there would probably say: I live **in Melton Mowbray**.)
In suggests:
– 'inside' or a situation with three dimensions: **in the kitchen, in the High Street** (but USA = **on Main Street**) because of the houses on both sides.
– a large area, like a country, province, city: **in New Zealand, in Kent, in Manchester**.
On suggests:
– a surface: **on the wall, on Earth, on a small island.**
– a line: **on the coast, on the river Thames, on the road, on the way to …, on the left-hand side of the street.**
Also note the following:
They're sailing **in** their boat **on** the lake.
She's swimming **in** the lake.
In the corner of the room (= inside) but **at/on the corner** of the street (= outside).
He's at the cinema (he's gone to see a film).
I'll meet you **at the cinema**. (outside, or near the door)
They aren't here. They must be **in the cinema**. (inside the building)
On the screen (surface), **on the radio, on TV.**

b   *into, onto, out of, off*
With verbs of movement, we generally use **into** and **onto**, though **in** and **on** are common:
He fell **into/in** the water.
He got **onto/on** his bicycle.
Out of indicates the opposite movement to **into** and **off** the opposite movement to **onto**. (See **in** and **on** in **a** above, for the idea of being 'inside' or 'on a surface'. Compare:
He took the knives and forks **out of** the drawer. (opposite of **into/in**)
We'll have to take the tyre **off** the wheel. (opposite of **onto/on**)

53 Prepositions of time
at, in, on
Use this list as a check:
– **at** for exact periods of time: **at five o'clock, at dinner time, at this moment.**
– **at** for festivals: **at Christmas, at Easter, at New Year.**
– others are: **at night** (but **during the day**), **at weekends, at present** (= now)
– **on** for days and dates: **on Monday, on June 10th, on Christmas Day** (compare **at** for the festive period), **on summer evenings, on Sunday morning, on Friday night**
– **in** for longer periods of time: **in August, in spring, in 1985, in the nineteenth century, in the Middle Ages, in the past, in the future** (compare **at present**)

– **in** for periods of time within which or at the end of which something may happen: **in the morning, in five minutes, in a week's time.**

54   *provided, providing, as long as, so long as*
These expressions are all strong forms of **if**; they mean 'if, but only if', and can be used in conditional sentences with the same tense combinations. The meaning is almost always the same as **if** but compare:
If you pay the cost of the postage in advance, we'll supply the goods. (The speaker assumes the customer will pay.)
Provided/Providing/As long as/So long as you pay the cost of the postage, we'll supply the goods. (The speaker is warning the customer that he will not supply the goods **unless** he pays). (See also **unless**).

55   Purpose

a   *for + gerund*
This construction is only used to define the general purpose of an object, answering the question: 'What is this for?', not in particular circumstances, answering the question: 'Why?' (What is it for?) A paper knife is used **for cutting** the pages of books.
(Why did you use it?) The pages of the book I bought hadn't been cut so I used a paper knife **to cut** them.
In answer to 'why' questions, **for** can only be used with a noun:
(Why has he gone to London?) He's gone to London **for a meeting** with his business partner.

b   *infinitive of purpose*
When there is no change of subject we usually express purpose by using the infinitive with **to**. In more formal sentences we may use **in order to** or **so as to** and these expressions often appear at the beginning of the sentence:
I'm just going out **to buy** some stamps.
In order to/So as to clarify the situation, the Prime Minister has invited the ambassador to meet him tomorrow.

c   *so as not to, in order not to*
In negative sentences purpose is expressed by **so as not to/in order not to**, not by the infinitive alone:
I must get up early tomorrow **so as not to/in order not to** miss my train. (NOT *not to miss*).

d   *infinitive with double-object verbs*
We can use the infinitive construction with double-object verbs even though the subject changes:
I've sent Mary to the baker's **to buy** some bread. (In this case, I have sent Mary but Mary is going to buy the bread).
(For double-object verbs see **Verbs (b)** and (**c**).)

e   *so that*
With other verbs we use a clause with **so that** when the subject changes:
I'll leave a note for you **so that you will know** where I'm likely to be. (compare: I'll leave a note **to tell you** where I'm likely to be.)

56 Question tags

a usage and form
These are common in spoken English, usually when the speaker expects someone to confirm a statement or agree:
It's a nice day, **isn't it?** (Yes, it is.)
The form is usually the question form of the statement – negative if the statement is affirmative, and affirmative if the statement is negative. If an auxiliary is used it is repeated:
You're tired, aren't you?
We can't go home yet, **can we?**
He's finished it, **hasn't he?**
If there is none, forms of **do** are used:
They enjoyed themselves at the party, **didn't they?**
Note the following exceptions:
I'm giving you a lot of trouble, **aren't I?**
Open the door, **will you?** (**would you/could you** are more polite)
Let's go now, **shall we?**

b affirmative question tags
We sometimes repeat the affirmative in a question tag if we are guessing and asking for reassurance:
It's all right, **is it?** (The speaker is not sure, and does not necessarily expect the answer 'yes'.)

57 Reflexive forms

a form
We use the reflexive pronouns **myself, yourself, himself, herself, itself, ourselves, yourselves, themselves** and **oneself** for actions where the same person is subject or object:
That knife is sharp. Be careful or you could **cut yourself.**

b reflexive pronouns and *each other/one another*
Note the difference between reflexive and reciprocal forms:
He's too selfish to fall in love. He only loves **himself.**
They fell in love with **each other/one another** at first sight. (He fell in love with her and she fell in love with him.)

c reflexive pronouns for emphasis
We sometimes use reflexive pronouns for emphasis:
I'm not going to do it for you. **Do** it **yourself!**

d reflexive verbs and verbs with reflexive sense
In many cases where a reflexive verb is used in other languages, we either use the construction **get** + past participle or there is no reflexive pronoun. Use these lists as a check, and compare them to the usage in your first language:
Reflexive verbs:
– connected with pain or danger:
burn, cut, defend, drown, hurt, kill, shoot (oneself);
– connected with behaviour or emotion: **amuse, behave, blame, control, deceive, enjoy, be (feel) ashamed of, be (feel) sorry for** (oneself);
– connected with speech: **contradict, express, say to, talk to, tell** (oneself);
– connected with thought: **consider, count, think** (oneself).

Get + participle:
– **get accustomed to, get confused, get dressed, get engaged, get excited, get lost, get married, get tired, get upset, get wet.**
No reflexive pronoun:
– **apologise (for), bathe, decide, fall asleep, find out, forget, get up, hide, hurry, join, move, remember, shave, sit down, stand up, wake up, wash, wonder, worry**

58 Relative clauses

a defining relative clauses
Defining relative clauses identify the person or thing being talked about; without them the sentence would not be clear:
A baker is a person **who makes bread.**
The relative pronoun (**who, which, that** etc.) is often left out when it refers to the object of the main clause, making the relative clause a 'contact clause'.
Jane is the girl (**whom/that**) he's going to marry. (**whom/that** refer to the girl)
In prepositional clauses, we usually avoid using pronouns, but in some cases the preposition can be put at the end of the contact clause:
She's the girl (**whom/that**) he's been going out **with.**

Use this table for reference:

Type	Subject pronoun	Object pronoun
person	*who/that*	_____/*that/whom*
thing	*that/which*	_____/*that/which*
possessive	*whose*	*whose*
prepositional		_____ + preposition
		preposition + *whom/which*

b non-defining relative clauses
These clauses are normally used in writing to link two related ideas together in one sentence. (In spoken English we normally use two sentences for this.) These clauses may appear between commas, or if the person or thing referred to is the object of the main clause, after a comma at the end:
Daphne du Maurier, **who wrote** *Rebecca*, lived in Cornwall.
Before that she had written *Jamaica Inn*, **which also takes place in Cornwall.**

Use this table for reference and compare it to the one for defining relative clauses in **a** above:

Type	Subject pronoun	Object pronoun
person	*who*	*whom*
thing	*which*	*which*
possessive	*whose*	*whose*
prepositional		preposition + *whom/which*

c sentence-relative clauses
In some cases a relative clause refers to the whole of the main clause:
Daphne du Maurier's grandfather was also a novelist, **which influenced her in her choice of career.**
There is always a comma before the relative pronoun and the pronoun is always **which.**
Compare:
Daphne du Maurier was influenced by her grandfather, **who** had also written a successful novel. (**who** refers only to 'grandfather'). (See also *where* (**relative adverb**).)

59 Reported speech

a statement
When we convert direct speech to reported speech and the introducing verb is in the past, the tense changes. Expressions of time and place also change unless the speaker is still in the same place on the same day (**here** is still **here,** and **today** is still **today**). Use the conversion table for reference and note that in all cases **told me** could replace **said:**

Direct	Reported
I'm **working** hard.	She said she **was working** …
I **travel** by train.	She said she **travelled** …
I'm **going** to change my job.	She said she **was going to** …
I'll **see** you on Sunday.	She said she **would see** …
I've never **seen** it before.	She said she **had** never **seen** …
I **spoke** to him on Monday.	She said she **had spoken** …
I **can run** faster than him.	She said she **could run** …
The train **may arrive** late.	She said the train **might arrive** …
I **must go** to the doctor.	She said she **had to go** …
(with general future meaning)	She said she **would have to go** …

Other changes:

here	there
this	that
now	then
yesterday	the day before, the previous day
tomorrow	the day after, the next day, the following day
last week	the week before, the previous week
next week	the week after, the next week, the following week
ago	before

b questions
Note the word order of indirect questions (see **Indirect questions**). The tense changes in reported questions are the same as for statements (see table in **a** above).

Direct	Reported
Have you **seen** the film?	She asked me **if I had seen** …
Where does he live?	She asked me **where** he **lived** …

c orders and requests
These are made with the imperative in direct speech. In reported speech we use the object + infinitive after **tell** (for orders) and **ask** (for requests):

Direct	Reported
Don't worry.	She **told him not to worry.**
Please **keep** quiet!	She **asked them to keep** quiet.

When we do not reproduce the actual words used in direct speech we can paraphrase what was said by using other verbs (**offer, suggest,** etc.). (See **Indirect speech: paraphrase**).

60 Result clauses: *so, such, so much/many ... that*

So and **such** are used for emphasis:
I'**m so tired!** (Compare: **How tired** I **am!**)
It **was such a boring film.** (Compare: **What a boring film** it was!)
In phrases like these and in result clauses, we use **so** with adjectives, **such** with nouns, whether or not they are qualified by adjectives:
I was **so tired** when I got home **that** I went straight to bed.
It was **such a tiring journey that** I went straight to bed when I got home.
So much (with uncountable nouns) and **so many** (with countable nouns) are used in the same kind of clause:
There is **so much traffic** on the road today that it took me hours to get here.
There are **so many cars** on the road today **that** it took me hours to get here.

61 *the same ... as*

In making comparisons, we can say that two things are **the same**, or **the same as** one another (NOT *that* or *than*).
They work in **the same** office.
She works in **the same** office **as** her brother.

62 *say* and *tell*

Say means 'speak words'. It has no personal object. **Tell** usually means 'inform a person' and has a personal object. Compare:
'Hello,' I **said.** (This is not information.)
'I've just come back from Greece,' she **told me/said.**
Tell is also used with a few other expressions, not necessarily with a personal object or with the same meaning: **tell the truth, tell a lie, tell a story, tell the time** (understand the time indicated by a clock etc.), **tell the difference** (between two things/people).
See also **Reported speech a** and **c.**

63 *shall*

a in future time
Shall is used for the first person singular and plural of the future tenses, but **will** can also be used in almost all cases.
We **shall/will** be very happy to see you next week.

b *Shall I/we ...?*
Shall is the only form used in a question asking for advice or instructions, or making an offer or suggestion:
Shall I carry your case for you? It looks very heavy.
Shall we go to the cinema this evening?
As a suggestion, **shall we** is not as positive as **let's.**

64 *should*

a *should* and *ought to*
Should and **ought to** indicate obligation or advice. We prefer **ought to** if we are doubtful that the obligation will be met or the advice will be taken:
You've got a bad cough. You **should/ought to** see a doctor.
You **ought to** see a doctor, but I don't suppose you will.

The past forms are **should/ought to have** + past participle. They are used to express regret in the first person, blame or criticism in the second and third:
I **shouldn't have said** that to her. It was very unkind. (regret)
You **should have been** more careful. Then you wouldn't have broken it. (blame or criticism)

b *should* and *had better*
Had better is used with the infinitive without **to** to give advice on a particular occasion. It is also used in the first person to express 'It would be a good idea if I ...' In more general situations, we use **should.** The negative form is **had better not.**
It's cold. I'**d better put** the fire on. (a good idea)
It's snowing. You'**d better not go** out. (advice)
You **shouldn't go** out alone in snowy weather. (general advice).

c *should* in subordinate clauses
In British English, **should** indicates the subjunctive after verbs like **order, recommend, suggest:**
I **suggest** that you **should inquire** at the Consulate.
In American English the infinitive is generally used:
I **suggest** that you **inquire** at the Consulate.

d *should* and *would*
Should and **would** can both be used for the first person in the conditional tense, and as the past of **shall** for the first person in reported speech. But they have separate meanings and usage. (For **would** see **Conditional sentences c, d** and **f; I wish** and **if only b** and **c** and **Tenses e.**)
Where they are often seen in combination is where sentences of advice or regret/blame (see **should a**) are followed by conditional sentences:
They **shouldn't (should not) allow** motor cycles in the forest. If they kept them out, these fires **wouldn't (would not) start.**
You **should have taken** my advice. If you had, this **wouldn't (would not) have happened.**

65 *so*

a *so am I* etc.
So is used to indicate agreement by repeating the modal, or if there is no modal, using a form of **do.** The verb form is inverted:
I'm tired. **So am** I. (= I am, too.)
I **like** her. **So do** I. (= I do, too.)

b after certain verbs
So is used after certain verbs to avoid repetition of the whole phrase; the most common are **believe, expect, hope, imagine, suppose, think** and **be afraid:**
Do you think it will be fine tomorrow? I **hope so.**
In most cases, the negative can be formed either with **do** or by replacing **so** with **not:** (I **don't suppose so, I suppose not**). The second form is the only one possible with **hope** and **be afraid,** but the first sounds more natural with the rest.
(Has John hurt himself badly?) I **hope not.** (NOT I *don't hope so.*)
(Can I see him?) I'**m afraid not.** (NOT *I'm not afraid so.*)

66 *some*

a *some* and *any*
Some is used in the affirmative to indicate an indefinite number or quantity. In questions, we generally use **any** and in the negative **not ... any** or **no:**
I've bought **some bread/some apples.**
We use **some** in questions, however, when we expect or encourage the answer 'yes', so it is polite to say:
Would you like **some** tea?
Some, someone, something indicate a specific quantity, person or thing: **any, anyone, anything** in the affirmative mean 'of whatever kind' (see *any*):
Someone must know the answer (= at least one person in the group)
Anyone knows that. (= almost the same meaning as everyone...)

b *some* and *others*
Some is used with the stronger pronunciation /sʌm/ in balanced sentences contrasting with others:
Some people like his music; **others** can't stand it.

67 *still*

Still is frequently confused with **already, (not) yet** and **no longer (not ... any longer/any more).**
Still indicates continuity:
He was born in London and he **still** lives there.
It is most common in affirmative sentences but is also found in questions:
Is she **still** here? I thought she'd gone home.
In the negative it is a strong form of **not ... yet.** Note the emphatic word order:
We've been waiting for him for an hour but he **still hasn't** arrived. (Compare: He hasn't arrived **yet.**)
Already means that something has taken place:
You're late home. Everyone else has **already** had dinner.
Yet (almost always in questions or negatives) indicates that something has not started or finished:
Has the film started **yet?** (Yes, it's **already** started./No, it hasn't (started **yet**).)
In the negative form in a question, **yet** usually indicates surprise or annoyance and may be answered emphatically:
Haven't they finished **yet?** (No, they **still** haven't finished.)
No longer is the opposite of **still** because it indicates that continuity has ended:
They **no longer** come to visit us. (NOT *no more*)
Informally, it is more common to use the form:
They don't come to visit us **any more/any longer.**

68 *take* with time expressions

Note these three ways of expressing the duration of a journey:
It took me half an hour to get here by train.
I took half an hour to get here by train.
The train journey **took (me)** half an hour.

69 Tenses

a present tenses

The present simple tense is used for actions that occur repeatedly or at any time, often with adverbs of frequency like **always** and time expressions like **every day.** The question form and negative are formed with **do** as auxiliary:
She **lives** in the country but she **doesn't work** there.
Do you ever **wonder** what's going to happen in the future?
Everything **comes** to those who **wait,** so they **say.**
We do not normally use the present tenses in narrative except in describing what happens in books, films etc.:
Hamlet **takes** place in Denmark. When the play **begins,** the ghost of Hamlet's father **appears.**
The present simple tense can be used to refer to future time (see **f** below).
The present continuous tense is used for actions that are going on at present and for temporary situations. The tense is formed by the verb **be** + present participle:
Look! They**'re waving** at us!
What **is** she **doing** these days? She**'s writing** a novel.
The present continuous tense can be used to refer to future time. (see **f** below)

b present perfect and past tenses

The present perfect tenses are used:

1. to talk about actions or situations that began in the past and are still going on, sometimes with a time expression which refers to the present:
I**'ve been working** hard this year.

2. to talk about actions which have taken place repeatedly up to the present:
I**'ve seen** that film six times.

3. with **for, since** and expressions like **all my life:**
I**'ve lived** in the village for ten years, but my husband **has lived** here **all his life.**
They are not used with past time expressions, which always require a past tense. Compare:
I **haven't seen** her **recently/for a long time.**
I **saw** her **yesterday/three days ago.**
We use the present perfect for questions and answers referring to past events without a time reference, but the past must be used when a time is mentioned:
– **Have** you **seen** the film at the Palace?
– No, I **haven't.**/Yes, I **saw** it **on Saturday.**

c past simple and continuous

The past simple is used to refer to past actions in the order they occurred, but also for customary or continuing actions in past time:
He **spent** his childhood in London, and **did not move** to the country until he **got married** at the age of twenty-five.
The past continuous is used for continuing actions in past time in relation to a main action in the past simple.
He **met** his wife in the city; at that time he **was studying** at the university. (before and after he met her)
In everyday situations, we usually find these tenses in three combinations:

1. a sequence of completed actions (past simple):
She **came in, took off** her hat and coat, and **sat down.**

2. an action taking place before and possibly after a completed action (past continuous and simple):
I **was talking** to my father on the phone when she **came** in.

3. two actions continuing side by side in past time (past continuous):
While he **was talking** to me I **was looking** out of the window.

d past and past perfect tenses

We use the past perfect tenses when we are already talking about the past and want to refer to a previous time:
When he finally **arrived,** we **had been waiting** for him for over three hours.
Until he **met** her, he **had** never **been** in love.

e past and conditional tenses

We use the conditional tense (**would** + infinitive) in combination with the past when we refer forward in time in a narrative:
I **hoped** that she would soon feel better.
(Compare: I **hope** you **will** soon **feel** better.)

f tenses in future time

1 Present tenses

We use the present continuous tense with future time reference for a firm plan for the future. It is often used with verbs of movement, but not always:
They**'re having** a party next Saturday. Are you **going?**
We use the present simple tense with future time reference for fixed times such as timetables, which normally do not change:
We must get up early tomorrow. Our flight **leaves** at 8.30.

2 going to

Going to + infinitive is used for personal intention with regard to the future:
I**'m going to talk** to her about it next week.
It is used impersonally to talk about something happening in the future that seems inevitable:
Look at those clouds. It**'s going to rain.**

3 Future simple tense

This is formed with **will** (**shall** can be used in the first person) and is common in subordinate clauses:
I expect (that) I**'ll see** you at the weekend.
It is often used in the main clause of conditional sentences and future time clauses:
I**'ll send** you a card **when/if** I go to New York.
It is also the usual form for narrative in the future once the time has been established:
We're going to the country on Sunday. We**'ll meet** at Anne's house, then we**'ll go** by car …

4 Future continuous tense

This tense is formed with **will** (**shall** is possible in the first person) + **be** + present participle. It is mainly used for:
– continuous actions in future time:
I can't play tennis on Sunday. I**'ll be working** all day in the garden.
– in time clauses for actions taking place simultaneously with other actions:
While you**'re playing** tennis on Sunday, I**'ll be working** in the garden.

5 Future perfect tenses

These are used mainly to indicate that something will have been completed by a certain time in the future:
In a week's time, I**'ll have finished** this job.
Next July 10th, I**'ll have been married** for thirty years.
(Compare use of present perfect: I**'ve been married** for twenty-nine years now.)

6 Tenses in future time clauses

We use a present or present perfect tense after a time expression in future time clauses. The main clause may be formed with a future tense, **going to** or the imperative:
When he **arrives, I'll give** him your message.
By the time you **have finished** your first course, the rest of us **will be having** coffee.
Tell him what I said **as soon as** he **comes in.**
(For tense combinations used in conditional sentences and reported speech, see **Conditional sentences, Reported speech.**)

70 *the,* use and omission

The use of the definite article in English often differs from usage in other languages. Check each example against your own language.

a use

We use **the** when talking about:

1. weights and measures: Petrol is sold by **the** litre. (but: It's sixty pence **a litre.)**

2. musical instruments: She can play **the** violin.

3. groups or classes of people: **the** young, **the** blind (NOT *the youngs*) but the verb form is plural:
The young/Young people today **are** very different from my generation.

4. rivers, seas, oceans, mountain ranges (but not mountains or lakes): **the Thames, the Mediterranean, the Atlantic, the Alps.**

5. unique objects and points of the compass: **the world, the sun, the moon, the north. The moon** is **the earth's** moon, though there may be others. We say **travel north** (direction) but travel to **the north** (compass point, area).

b omission

We do not use **the** when speaking about the following:

1. games and sports: She plays **tennis** and goes **skiing.**

2. subjects of study: She studies **history** and **geography.**

3. languages: She can speak **English.** (Note that we talk about **the English** (the people as a group, as in **a** 3 above), but nationality has no article: I'm **English.)**

4. mountains: **Everest, Aconcagua.**

5. meals and clock times: She has **breakfast** at eight o'clock.

6. gerunds: She likes **getting up** early.

c use and omission

1. There are a number of common collocations where **the** is omitted unless we are referring to a particular place, already mentioned or understood:

He was injured in the accident and was taken **to hospital.**
I'm going to visit my sister **in the hospital.** (We know which one is meant). Use this list for reference:

in bed, (go) **to bed**
at church, in church (= inside)
in court, (take) **to court**
in dock
in harbour, (sail) **to harbour**
at home
in hospital, (go) **to hospital**
(go) **to market**
on paper
in prison, (go) **to prison**
at school, (go) **to school**
at sea, (go) **to sea**
at university, (go) **to university**
at work, (go) **to work**

2 In talking about species (of animals, for example) we can either use the plural or **the** with a singular noun. Generally we use the second form to discriminate between different types:
Elephants have long memories.
The African elephant is larger than **the Indian elephant.**

3 We use **the** when referring to something specific, not when we are talking in general terms; something specific includes something previously mentioned. Compare the following:
We want **peace,** not **war.**
The war in that distant country is still going on. (a specific war)
The is not used *unless* the noun is followed by a clause that modifies it; for example, a relative clause, or a phrase containing **of** that modifies it. Nouns modified by adjectives before them or prepositional phrases after them do not require **the:**
Life is hard.
Modern life is more complex than **life in the nineteenth century.**
The life that we lead today is more complex than **the life of our ancestors.**

71 there is/are
There is (plural **there are**) indicates the existence of something.
There can also be used in the same way with other tenses of **be,** with modals and in question tags:
There might be a letter for you when you get home, **mightn't there**?
It is/They are refer to something already mentioned:
There is a letter on the table. **It's** for you.

72 time: It's time …
Note the constructions used with this expression:
It's time (for us) to go home.(It's time + infinitive)
It's time we went home. (It's time + past simple)

73 time: It's the (first) time …
When we use an ordinal number (**first, second, last** etc.) in this construction, it is followed by the present perfect tense:
It's the first time I've visited the museum. (= I've never visited the museum before.)

In past time, the equivalent is to use the past perfect tense:
It was only **the second time** in his life that he **had been** away from home.

74 too, too much/many
Too is used before an adjective, **too much/too many** before a singular or plural noun, to mean 'more than is necessary, or good':
I'm **too tired** to do any more work.
He spends **too much money** on useless things.
If you feel ill, it's because you ate **too many hamburgers.**
Too much can also be used as an adverb:
He talks **too much.**

75 unless
Unless can usually be used to mean **if … not**, though in such cases it is really the opposite of **provided** or similar expressions (see **provided, providing, as long as, so long as**):
I'll come with you **unless** you **have** already **arranged** to go with someone else. (… **provided** you **haven't** …)
Unless cannot be used in sentences where the main clause is the result of the condition:
We'll be very disappointed **if** you **can't come.** (NOT *unless you can come.*)

76 used to
a used to and would
Used to, followed by the infinitive, refers to what habitually happened in the past in contrast to what happens now. The negative is either **used not to** or **did not use to. Used to** has no present form. For customary actions in the present, we use the present simple tense:
I **used to** live in London, but now I live in Bristol.
We usually prefer **would** + infinitive for repeated actions in past time in a context already established by a verb in the past simple tense or **used to.** It does not always indicate a contrast with present time but rather 'Whenever/Every time this happened …':
When I **was** a child, we **used to visit** my grandmother every Sunday. The whole family **would put on** their best clothes and we **would walk** to her house.

b used to and be used to
Be used to is a verb that can be used with all tenses of **be.** It means 'be accustomed to'. It is followed by a noun or a gerund.
I**'ve been used to (handling) animals** since I was a child so I don't think I'll have any trouble looking after these cats.

77 Verbs
a verbs not usually found in continuous forms
Certain verbs are almost never found in continuous forms. Use this list for reference:
– **hear, notice, recognise, see, smell, taste;**
– **believe, feel** (that), **think** (that);
– **know, mean, suppose, understand;**
– **forget, remember;**
– **care, dislike, hate, love, want, wish;**
– **appear** (= seem), **seem;**
– **belong to, consist of, contain, have** (= own, possess), **matter,**
– **refuse**

Compare:
What **do** you **think?** (What is your opinion?)
What **are** you **thinking** about? (What thoughts are in your mind?)

b double-object verbs
Some verbs can be followed by a direct and indirect object. Among the most common are: **award, bring, buy, cause, cost, give, grant, guarantee, hand, leave, lend, offer, owe, pass, pay, promise, read, refuse, send, show, teach, tell, throw, write.**
In general in active sentences we prefer the order:
I gave **him the book.**
But we may use the alternative order for emphasis:
I gave the **book to him** (not to her).

c double-object verbs: passive forms
In the passive, we can begin the sentence with a personal or impersonal subject. Generally we prefer the personal-subject construction, unless we are mainly interested in the thing rather than the person:
I **was given** a book.(personal subject)
The most beautiful present **was given to** my sister. (impersonal subject)

d verb + object + as
Some verbs have this construction:
I **regard her as** the most brilliant lawyer I know.
Here is a list of common verbs which can take this construction: **accept, behave, class, describe, know** (usually **be known**), **regard, see, think of, treat, use.**

78 what (the thing that)
What can be used as subject or object in noun clauses to mean 'the thing that':
What matters in this situation is to keep calm.
I did **what** I could to help him.
It is not used with an adjective or with phrases like **all, everything** etc.:
The only thing that matters is to keep calm.
All (that) he cares about is money.

79 where (relative adverb)
Where can appear in defining and non-defining relative clauses in place of a relative pronoun (see **Relative clauses**) with reference to a place, building etc. **Where** appears after a comma if the clause is non-defining:
That's the house **where I was born.** (defining) (NOT *born in*)
We are going to visit Stratford-on-Avon, **where** Shakespeare was born. (non-defining)

80 while
While is used in clauses of concession (see **although**) in balanced sentences. In sentences with **although** the main clause sounds stronger or more important, but **while** suggests they are of equal weight. Compare:
Although he says he didn't take it, I don't believe him. (The speaker is convinced that the man is lying.)
While some of my colleagues believe he is lying, others think that he's telling the truth. (The speaker is not taking sides.)

81 *I wish* and *If only*

We use these forms in a number of circumstances to say that we wish things were different or had been different. They can express desire in present, future or general time, complaint in present or general time, regret or blame in past time. The tenses of the verb used after them do not necessarily reflect time. The main uses and combinations are these:

a desire
The verb is followed by a verb in the past tense:
I wish I **were (was)** rich.
I wish she **felt** the same about me as I do about her.
I wish I **didn't have to go** to work tomorrow.

b complaint
The verb is followed by a verb in the conditional tense:
I wish you**'d pay** attention when I'm talking to you.
I wish they **wouldn't play** loud music at night.
If only is not used for complaint unless we feel more sorry than angry:
If only he**'d get** a steady job.

c regret and blame
The verb is followed by a verb in the past perfect tense:
I wish I **had had** the chance to go to university.
I wish you**'d been** more careful. Then you wouldn't have broken it. (See also *should* a.)
If only (but not **I wish**) can form part of a subordinate clause as a strong form of **if**:
If only I **could afford** to buy a house, I **would** be happy.
Compare:
I wish I could afford to buy a house. Then **I would** be happy.

82 *would like*

We use **would like** to express preference on a particular occasion, **like** or **prefer** in general terms. **Would like**, unlike **like** (see **Gerund e**) is always followed by the infinitive with **to**. It is polite in offers and invitations to use **would like**, not **want**:
I**'d like** to go to the cinema this evening. **Would** you **like to come** with me?
With a personal object we use the same construction; the meaning is the same as **want** but sounds more polite:
I**'d like you to help** me, if you don't mind.

83 *would rather*

We use **would rather** to express preference on particular occasions. General preference can be expressed by **prefer** or **would rather** but **would rather** suggests an imaginary particular occasion ('if you asked me', for example). **Would rather** is followed by the infinitive without **to**:
I**'d rather not go out** this evening. If you don't mind, I**'d** much **rather stay** at home and read a book.
To express preference about the actions of others, we use **would rather** + past tense to refer to present, future or general time:
I**'d rather** you **didn't** go out tonight. You've got a bad cold. I**'d rather** you **stayed** at home.

Appendix 1: Connectors and Modifiers

Expressing opinion in modern English depends to a considerable extent on the use of connecting words and phrases that help the reader or listener to understand. Such words or phrases can be used to show how an argument is organised, to prepare the reader for what is coming next or to convey the tone of what is being said.
Use this Appendix for reference when completing a writing task, especially one that requires you to express an opinion. Whenever you come across any of these phrases in this book or in your general reading, make a note of the phrase and see how it is being used.

A Developing an Argument

1 *Sequence*
When listing points of the same kind:

Point 1:   **In the first place, To begin with, To start with, First of all.**

Point 2:   **Secondly** (only if there are further points to come); **In addition to that** (as the second and final point); **Apart from that, What is more** (informal), **Moreover** (formal); **Besides** (a second point so important that it makes the first almost irrelevant).
Final point: **Finally, Lastly; Above all** (only if it is the most important).
Conclusion: **In conclusion, To sum up** (usually at the beginning of the last paragraph, not at the end of a list); **Taking everything into account, All things considered, All in all** (reaching a conclusion, whether or not all the points agree); **In brief, In short, In a word** (the last two are informal and only used if what is said is brief).

2 *Contrast*
This can be established by clauses with **but** or concession clauses with **although** etc. (see **Reference Section 7**). Connectors indicating that the point contradicts or limits the previous point(s) are:
However, Nevertheless, All the same, At the same time;
After all (an argument that has apparently not been considered);
In contrast (a direct contrast);
On the other hand (used for balance but also to indicate an alternative point of view).

3 *Balance*
This can be established by clauses with **while** (see **Reference Section 80**). In presenting arguments of equal strength **On the one hand** and **On the other hand** can be used.

4 *Examples*
For example, For instance.

B Establishing Facts

In fact, The fact of the matter is that ...; As a matter of fact (indicating that the hearer may be surprised).
At first sight, On the face of it (used in contrast to **In fact** to show the difference between appearance and fact).
In practice, used in contrast to **In theory** or **In principle** to establish what actually happens; **In**

effect, close to **In fact** and **In practice,** suggests 'for practical purposes'.

C Expressing Personal Opinion

In my opinion, In my view, To my mind, As I see it (informal).
Personally, For my part (contrasting the individual view with that of the majority).
As far as I'm concerned (informal) (= 'In so far as it affects me.')

D Modifying

1 *General statements*
Generally, In general, As a rule, As a general rule, On the whole, In the main, For the most part.

2 *Partly correct*
To some extent, To a certain extent, Up to a point.

3 *Limit of knowledge*
As far as I know, To the best of my knowledge;
For all I know. (informal) (suggests ignorance)

4 *Assigning responsibility*
According to ...
By all accounts (indicating responsibility lies with a number of people).

5 *Limited validity*
Under the circumstances, As it is, Things being as they are.

E Intensifying

1 *Obviously*
Clearly, Obviously, Of course, Needless to say, As everyone knows.

2 *Especially*
In particular, especially (Note that **especially** appears as a qualifying adverb, not at the beginning, like **Clearly**.)

F Rephrasing
In other words, That is to say.

G Referring to a subject or person
As regards ..., With regard to ..., In this connection, As far as ... is concerned.

H Terminating discussion
In any case, Anyway, At any rate. (The last two are more informal.)
They all suggest 'whatever happens, whatever the facts are' and imply that nothing else can be said or needs to be said.

Appendix 2: Distinguishing between similar words

The words practised in the lexical and structural exercises in Section 1 are listed here in alphabetical order so that you can refer back to them when revising. The numbers refer to unit and exercise, so **abandon** appears in Exercise 14B of Section 1.

Verbs
abandon 14B
accept 10A, 13A
accuse 14A
ache 13C
achieve 5A, 15A
admit 10A
advertise 12A
advise 12A
agree 1C, 10A
allow 13A
announce 12A
appoint 4A
approve 9A, 10A
arise 7A
arrive 3A
ask 6A
ask for 6A
attend 5B
avoid 15B
beat 15A
become 1A
bend 6C
blame 14A
borrow 2A
bring 12B
bring up 4B
can't stand 5C
carry 7B, 12B
charge 3B
check 11A
choose 4A
claim 6A
climb 6B
close 2B
complain 14A
cope 5A
consider 9D
continue 10C
control 11A
cost 3B
criticise 14A
cure 13B
damage 13C
demand 6A
deny 11B
develop 1A
discover 1B
dismiss 12C
do 12D, 12E
dress 7B
drip 7C

drive 6B
drop 7C
earn 15A
educate 4B
elect 4A
enjoy 3C
escape 15B
expect 5B
explain 10B
fall 7C
fetch 12B
find 1B
find out 1B
fit 1C
fold 6C
follow 10C
forget 14B
gain 15A
get 1A, 3A
get in (to) 6B
get on (to) 6B
get on with 1C
get to know 1B
get up 7A
give up 12C
glance 2C
grow 1A
grow up 1A
guard 2B
harm 13C
heal 13B
hope 5B
hurt 13C
ignore 14B
indicate 8B
injure 13C
insist 6A, 6D
instruct 4B
intend 8C
keep 2B, 10C
know 1B
lay 4C
learn 4B
leave 14B
lend 2A
let 13A, 14B
lie 4C
lift 7A
lock 2B
look 2C
look forward to 5B
lose 9A
make 12D, 12E
manage 5A
match 1C
matter 3C
mean 8C
meet 1B
memorise 9C
mend 13B
mind 3C
miss 9A
mount 6B
nod 8B
nominate 4A
notice 10B

owe 2A
pass 9A
pay 2A, 3B
pay for 2A
persist 6D
persuade 6D
pick 4A
plan 8C
pour 7C
prefer 3C
pretend 8C
prevent 15B
protest 14A
prove 9B
put away 2B
put on 7B
put up with 5C
raise 7A
reach 3A, 5A
realise 9D
recover 13B
refuse 11B
regard 2C, 9D
reject 11B
remain 10C
remark 8A, 10B
remember 9C
remind 9C
repair 13B
report 10B
resign 12C
resist 5C,11B
rest 10C
retire 12C
review 11A
revise 11A
ride 6B
rise 7A
rob 15C
say 8A
see 2C
shake 8B
shut 2B
sign 8B
sink 7C
solve 13B
speak 8A
spend 9A
spill 7C
stay 10C
steal 15C
stop 15B
study 4B
succeed 5A
suggest 6D
suit 1C
support 5C
take 12B
talk 8A
teach 4B
tell 8A
test 9B
think of 9D
threaten 12A
tolerate 5C
try 8C, 9B

try on 9B
try out 9B
urge 6D
wait 5B
warn 12A
waste 9A
watch 2C
wave 8B
wear 7B
win 15A
wind 6C
withdraw 12C
would like 3C
would rather 3C
wound 13C
wrap 6C

Nouns
absence 10E
accident 8E
action 14C
address 2D
advantage 11E
advertisement 3D
advice 3D
agenda 10D
announcement 3D
appearance 9E
article 10D
aspect 5F, 9E
attempt 8F
attention 11C
attitude 5F
audience 6E
autograph 9F
award 6G
band 6F
behalf 11E
behaviour 15D
benefit 11E
bill 3F
blame 14D
blow 8D
brand 11D
breed 11D
cabinet 12F
care 11C
career 5D
certificate 4E
chance 8E
character 1D
characteristic 1D
charge 14E
choice 10F
cloth 15E
clothes 15E
company 5E
complaint 14E
complexion 9E
conference 15F
cost 6G
costume 15E
count 3E
couple 1E
course 5D

crash 8D
crew 6F
cupboard 12F
custom 15D
damage 4G
degree 4E
demand 14E
diary 10D
direction 2D
disease 13F
double 1E
dress 15E
dresser 12F
dressing table 12F
duet 1E
duty 5D
effect 14C
election 10F
employment 5D
energy 13D
enterprise 5E
error 14D
event 14C
excursion 7D
expense 6G
experience 4E
expression 9E
extension 13E
extent 13E
fact 14C
factory 5E
fare 3F
fashion 15D
father 1F
fault 10E, 14D
fee 3F
field 2E
file 4D
fine 3F
firm 9F
flat 2E
flight 7D
floor 2E
force 13D
game 4F
gang 6F
ground 2E
group 6F
guilt 14D
habit 15D
harm 4G
hobby 4F
humour 1D
illness 13F
industry 5E
infection 13F
injury 4G
intention 2F, 8F
job 5D
journey 7D
knock 8D
lack 10E
lecture 15F
level 3E
licence 4E

limit 3E, 13E
loss 10E
luck 8E
make 11E
manner 15D
manufacture 5E
mark 9F
material 15E
matter 2F
meaning 2F
meeting 15F
mind 2F
mistake 14D
model 11D
mood 1D
move 4F
neighbour 1F
notice 3D, 11C
number 3E
occasion 8E
onlookers 6E
opinion 2F, 5F
opportunity 8E
outbreak 7E
outcome 7E
outdoor 7E
outfit 7E
outlet 7E
outline 9E
outlook 7E
output 7E
outskirts 7E
pain 4G
pair 1E
paper 10D
parent 1F
partner 1F
party 6F
pattern 11D
performance 15F
personality 1D
play 4F
point 13E
power 13D
practice 4F
price 6G
prize 6G
process 8F
procession 4D
product 5E
profit 11E
proof 8F
protection 7F
publicity 3D
qualification 4E
queue 4D
race 11D
rank 4D
rate 3E
recipe 11D
refuge 7F
relative 1F
remark 11C
respect 5F
reunion 15F
reward 6G
row 4D

sake 11E
scope 13E
selection 10F
shade 7F
sheet 10D
shelf 12F
shock 8D
shortage 10E
sickness 13F
sightseers 6E
sign 9F
signal 11C
signature 9F
site 2D
situation 2D
soil 2E
spectators 6E
sport 4F
staff 6F
strength 13D
stroke 8D
subject 9F
success 14C
taste 10F
team 6F
temper 1D
text 10D
tip 3F
travel 7D
trial 8F
trouble 14E
twin 1E
variety 10F
view 5F
viewers 6E
voyage 7D
wardrobe 12F
way 2D, 15D
word 5D
wound 4G

Adjectives
able 5G
alike 1G
along 2G
ashamed 14F
capable 5G
common 1G, 7G
confused 14F
crowded 3G
disappointed 14F
disgusted 14F
elder 14G
elderly 14G
embarrassed 14F
foreign 9G
former 14G
full 3G
ill 13G
infectious 13G
likely 1G
lonely 2G
odd 9G
older 14G
only 2G
ordinary 7G
plentiful 3G

plenty 3G
popular 7G
prior 14G
rare 9G
reliable 5G
responsible 5G
same 1G
scarce 9G
sensational 11F
sensible 11F
sensitive 11F
sentimental 11F
sick 13G
similar 1G
single 2G
strange 9G
unfit 13G
unhealthy 13G
unique 2G
vulgar 7G

Adverbs, abverbial phrases, conjunctions, connectors
actually 2H
ago 3H
although 11G
as 10G
as though 10G
beside 7H
besides 7H
as far as I am
concerned 13H
currently 2H
one day 9H
in those days 5H
despite 11G
during 3H, 8H
in effect 14H
even 15G
except 7H, 15G
to a certain extent 4H
on the face of it 14H
as a matter of fact 14H
in fact 14H
for 3H
in general 4H
generally speaking 4H
however 11G
immediately 2H
like 10G
in the main 4H
meanwhile 8H
to my mind 13H
at this moment 5H
nearby 7H
next to 7H
nowadays 5H
at once 9H
once and for all 9H
in my opinion 13H
up to a point 4H
at present 5H
presently 2H
provided 15G
as a rule 4H
all the same 13H
as I see it 13H

at first sight 14H
since 3H
in spite of 11G
such as 10G
suddenly 2H
though 10G
at one time 9H
at the same time 8H
for the time being 12G
from time to time 12G
in time 12G
on time 12G
once upon a time 9H
time after time 12G
unless 15G
whether 15G
while 3H, 8H
on the whole 4H

Appendix 3: *make* and *do*

In general, **do** relates to actions, so we **do work** or **do a job**. **Make** refers to creating or constructing, so we **make plans**, and a table may be **made of wood**. But this definition does not indicate which verb to choose in all circumstances. Use this list of common expressions with **make** and **do** for reference, but note that it does not include phrasal verbs like **make up for**.

Do
better
one's best
business
damage
one's duty
evil
an exercise
a favour
good
harm
homework
an injury
a job
justice to
a kindness
an operation
repairs
right
a service
wonders
work
worse
one's worst
wrong

Make
an appointment
arrangements
an attack on
the best of
certain of
a change
a complaint
a confession
a decision
a demand
a difference
a discovery
an effort
enquiries
an escape
an excuse
faces at
a fool of
friends with
fun of
a guess
haste
a journey
a mistake
money
the most of
a movement
an offer
peace with
a phone call
a profit
progress
a report on
a request
room for
a search for
a speech
a success of
sure of
a trip
trouble for
use of
a voyage
war on
way for
someone welcome
work (for others)

Appendix 4: Verbs taking prepositions

This list is not complete, and does not include phrasal verbs (**look after**, **give up**, etc.). It should be used for reference to check which prepositions commonly follow a number of verbs and also combinations of verb + adjective + preposition (**be absent from**) or verb + noun + preposition (**take an interest in**). In many cases, examples are given of typical usage, but these are not the only ones possible. We say **be absent from school** but we could also say **be absent from work**, **a meeting**, etc. Examples are given at the end where more than one preposition is found after a verb and there are different meanings. These verbs are marked (*).

Verbs taking prepositions
be absent from (school)
account for; take into account
accuse someone of (a crime); make an accusation against
be accustomed to
act on; take action on (a report)
adapt to (a situation)
add to (an amount)
admit to (an accusation) (a school)
advise someone on (health)
be afraid of
agree about, on, to, with (*)
aim at (a target)
be amazed at, by
amount to (a great deal)
be amused at, by
be angry with someone for ...
be annoyed with someone for ...
be anxious about someone; be anxious for (news)
apologise (to someone) for (a mistake)
appeal to someone for (help)
apply to someone for (a job); make an application for
appoint someone to (a job); make an appointment for
approve of (someone's action)
argue (with someone) about; have an argument with someone
arrest someone for (a crime); put someone under arrest
arrive at, in

be ashamed of
ask someone (a question) about; ask someone for (help)
be astonished at, by
attach to, be attached to
attend to, pay attention to
bargain with someone for
beg someone for (help)
believe in (ghosts)
belong to (the Government)
benefit from (advice)
bet (money) on, against
blame someone for; take the blame for
boast of, about (success)
be bored with (a subject)
borrow (money) from someone
be capable of
care about, for; take care of (*)
be certain about, of
change into, to (*)
charge someone for (service)
cheat someone out of (money)
choose between (A) and (B)
combine (beauty) with (talent)
comment on (the news)
communicate (news) to someone; communicate with (colleagues)
compare (A) with (B)
compensate (someone) for
compete against someone for
complain (to someone) of/about; make a complaint about
be composed of
concentrate on (work)
be concerned about, in, with (*)
confess (a crime) to someone
be confident of, about; have confidence in
congratulate someone on (success)
be conscious of
consent to, give consent to
consists in, of (*)
be content with
contrast (A) with (B)
contribute to; make a contribution to
be convenient to, for
convince someone of (facts)
co-operate with someone
cope with (problems)
count on someone for (help)
be critical of
be cruel to
cure someone of (disease)
deal with (problem)
decide on (policy)
depend on someone for (support)
die of (a disease)
differ from; make a difference to; be different from

be distant from

dream of (success); have a dream about someone/something

dress, be dressed in

be engaged in (business); to (a young man/woman)

be equal to

escape from (the enemy, prison)

exchange (pounds) for (pesetas)

excuse someone for (a mistake); make excuses for someone

experiment on, with; make an experiment on, with

explain (a subject) to someone

be familiar with

be famous for

feed (rabbits) on (lettuce)

be fond of

be free from, of (*)

be friendly with; make friends with

be frightened of

be full of

be generous (to someone) with (money)

be glad of

be good at (English)

be grateful (to someone) for (help)

be guilty of

head for (a destination)

hear about, of, from (*)

hope for (better things)

improve on (previous work); make improvements in

infect someone with

inform someone of

inquire into; make an inquiry into

insist on (knowing the truth)

be interested in; take an interest in

interfere in, with (*)

introduce someone to

invest in; make an investment in

be involved in

issue someone with (documents)

be jealous of

be keen on

be kind to

laugh at (joke)

lean against, on (wall)

leave to, with (*)

listen to (radio)

long for, have a longing for

be lucky at, in (*)

mean by (remark)

mistake someone for another

object to (proposal)

be occupied with

operate on (patient)

pay (someone) for (work)

persist in (believe)

point at, to (*)

be polite to

prepare for (visit)

present someone with

protect someone against

protest against (law)

be proud of, take pride in

provide (food) for someone; provide someone with (food)

punish someone for (behaviour)

quarrel with someone about

be ready for

reason with someone

release someone from (prison)

rely on someone (to act)

remind someone of (a relative)

replace with (another)

reply to (a letter)

report on (an event) to someone

rescue someone from (danger)

reserve (seat) for; make a reservation

resign from (job); be resigned to

be responsible for (work, children); be responsible to (boss)

result from, out of, in (*)

retire from (work)

reward someone for (work)

get rid of (old clothes)

rob of (money)

be rude to (customer)

be satisfied with

save from (disaster)

search (the woods) for someone

send for (a doctor)

separate (A) from (B)

shoot at (a target)

be short of

signal to someone

be similar to

smile at someone

be sorry about (action); be sorry for (someone)

spend (money) on

stare at someone

steal (money) from someone

succeed in (a career)

suffer from (a pain)

be suitable for

be superior to

supply (goods) to someone; supply someone with (goods)

be sure of

be surprised at, by

suspect someone of (a crime)

sympathise with someone about

talk to someone about (a subject)

give a talk on; have a talk to

thank someone for (help)

threaten someone with (law)

be tired of

transform (A) into (B)

translate (A) into (B)

treat someone for (a disease) with (medicine)

trouble about; take trouble over; make trouble for (*)

be unaware of

be used to

be useful to someone for (a purpose)

vote for (a candidate)

wait for (a bus)

worry about (problems)

Verbs with more than one preposition possible

agree (**with** someone) (**about/on** an action) **about** a subject; **agree to** an action

care about (= be concerned about) someone/something; **care for** (= like, look after) someone/something; **take care of** (= look after) someone/something

change into (other clothes); **change something into** (= transform); **change something to** (= alter)

be concerned about (= worried); **in** (= involved); **with** (= responsible for)

consist in (= be, in essence); **of** (= be composed of)

be free from (pain); **of** (tax (= not subject to))

hear about, of (= have information about); **from** (= receive news from)

interfere in (an action); **with** (what someone is doing)

leave (a decision, problem) **to** someone (= it became my responsibility); **leave** (a decision, problem) **with** someone (= asked me to take care of it)

be lucky at (cards); **in** (love)

point at (= indicating aggressively); **to** (= indicating)

result from (= was caused by); **in** (= caused)

trouble about (= care, worry); **take trouble over** (= be careful to do well); **make trouble for** (= cause)

Appendix 5: Word building

Note that these lists are not complete, but contain the most common examples of related words that students at First Certificate level might be expected to recognise. Words which do not follow the general pattern are in *italic* type. For an explanation of the relationship between roots and words derived from them, see the exercises referred to.

1 Adjective root: verb *-en*, noun *-ness* (Section 5, Exercise A)

adj root	verb *-en*	*rzeczownik* noun *-ness*
black	blacken	blackness *czerń, ciemność*
bright *jasny*	brighten	brightness [v] *jaskrawość, blask*
broad	broaden	*breadth*
dark	darken *ściemniać się*	darkness *ciemność*
deaf *głuchy*	deafen *ogłuszać*	deafness [v] *głuchota*
deep	deepen	*depth* *głęboki* adv deep - *głęboko* deeply
fat	fatten	fatness
flat *płaski*	flatten	flatness
fresh	freshen	freshness
glad	gladden	gladness
hard	harden	hardness
high	*heighten*	*height*
less	lessen	*lessening*
light	lighten	lightness
long	*lengthen*	*length*
loose	loosen	looseness
mad	madden	madness
quiet	quieten	quietness
red	redden	redness
ripe	ripen	ripeness
sad	sadden	sadness
sharp	sharpen	sharpness
short	shorten	shortness
soft	soften	softness
stiff	stiffen	stiffness
straight	straighten	straightness
strong	*strengthen*	*strength*
sweet	sweeten *słodzić*	sweetness *słodycz*
thick	thicken	thickness
tight	tighten	tightness
tough	toughen	toughness
weak	weaken	weakness
white	whiten	whiteness
wide *szeroki*	widen *poszerzać się*	*width* *szerokość*

2 Noun root: adjective (-ful, adjective (-less)
(Section 5, Exercise B)

In some cases, the true opposite to an adjective ending in **-ful** or **-less** is formed differently; in other cases, more than one opposite exists or the meaning of an adjective is no longer connected to that of the noun. These are marked with an asterisk (*) and you should study the notes that follow.

root	adjective (+)	adjective (-)
aim		aimless*
art	artful*	artless*
beauty	beautiful	
care	careful	careless
cheer*	cheerful	cheerless
colour	colourful	colourless
delight	delightful	
doubt	doubtful	doubtless*
end		endless
event	eventful*	
faith	faithful	faithless, *unfaithful*
fancy	fanciful	
fault	*faulty*	faultless
fear	fearful	fearless
fruit	fruitful	fruitless, *unfruitful*
grace	graceful	graceless, *ungraceful*
gratitude	grateful	
guilt	*guilty*	guiltless
harm	harmful	harmless
hate	hateful*	
heart		heartless
help	helpful	helpless, *unhelpful*
home		homeless
hope	hopeful	hopeless
humour	*humorous*	humourless
joy	joyful	joyless
law	lawful	lawless, *unlawful*
meaning	meaningful	meaningless
mercy	merciful	merciless
name		nameless
need	needful*	needless
pain	painful	painless
peace	peaceful	
plenty	plentiful*	
point		pointless
power	powerful	powerless
rest	restful	restless
sense	*sensible*	senseless*
shame	shameful*	shameless
shape		shapeless
skill	skilful	*unskilful*
sleep	*sleepy*	sleepless
spot	*spotted*	spotless
stain	*stained*	stainless
success	successful	*unsuccessful*
taste	tasteful*	tasteless
thanks	thankful	thankless
thought	thoughtful	thoughtless
truth	truthful	*untruthful*
use	useful	useless
value	*valuable*	valueless
waste	wasteful	
wonder	wonderful*	
worth		

NOTES:

aimless: usually, without an aim or purpose in life

artful/artless: not with ability in art (**artistic**) but clever in a tricky way/simple, without this cleverness

cheer: a shout of encouragement. **Cheerful/cheerless**: lively and happy/dull and miserable

doubtless (an adverb): probably; the adjective for 'not having doubt' is **undoubted**

eventful: full of important or interesting events

faithless is used more generally for not having faith; **unfaithful** for husbands/wives/lovers who are not loyal to their partner, but have sexual relationships with other people.

unfruitful is used for trees, crops, etc. without fruit; **fruitless**: unsuccessful, not having the result desired

ungraceful (the true opposite): without physical grace; **graceless**: bad-mannered

hateful is not really 'full of hate' but 'horrible, to be hated'

helpless: in need of help; **unhelpful**: not giving help

lawless (personal): without respect for the law; **unlawful** (action): against the law

needful/needless: **necessary** (especially) and **unnecessary** are more common

plentiful: abundant, in large quantities

senseless: (action) lacking in common sense, and so the opposite of **sensible**; (personal) unconscious, which is more common

shameful: bad, disgusting. A person who feels shame is **ashamed**

tasteful: in good taste aesthetically. Food that tastes good is **tasty**. **Tasteless** can mean without taste in both cases

wonderful: marvellous, not 'full of wonder'.

3 Verb root: adjective *-able*, *-ible*, negative forms
(Section 5, Exercise D)

The list below indicates the most commonly used adjectives of this kind. The meaning of those marked with an asterisk (*) cannot always be deduced from the verb root, and you should study the notes that follow.

root	adjective (+)	adjective (−)	NOTES:
accept	acceptable	unacceptable	**accountable** (personal): responsible (for); **unaccountable** (action); inexplicable, what cannot be accounted for
account	accountable*	unaccountable*	
adapt	adaptable		
admire	admirable		**agreeable**: pleasant; **disagreeable**: unpleasant
admit	*admissible*	*inadmissible*	
agree	*agreeable**	*disagreeable*	**unbelievable**: incredible, very surprising
apply	*applicable*	*inapplicable*	**comfort**: the verb means 'console' but the adjectives **comfortable/uncomfortable** (usually describing a thing, like furniture) mean 'not pleasantly satisfying'
argue	arguable	unarguable	
bear	bearable	unbearable	
believe	believable	unbelievable*	
comfort	comfortable*	uncomfortable*	
communicate	*communicable*	*incommunicable*	**considerable/inconsiderable**: (not) important enough to be considered
compare	comparable	*incomparable*	
consider	considerable*	*inconsiderable*	**indefensible**: (actions) unjustifiable; (place) that cannot be defended against an attack
cure	curable	*incurable*	
defend	*defensible*	*indefensible**	
depend	dependable		**fashion**: the verb now means 'make, shape', but the adjectives **fashionable/unfashionable** mean 'in/out of fashion'
desire	desirable	undesirable	
divide	divisible	*indivisible*	
educate	*educable*	*ineducable*	**inimitable**: usually, too good or brilliant to be imitated
employ	employable	unemployable	
enjoy	enjoyable		**manageable**: usually of objects that can be handled easily
excite	excitable		
explain	*explicable*	*inexplicable*	**passable**: (things) usually just acceptable; **impassable** refers to roads, rivers that cannot be used or crossed
fashion	fashionable*	unfashionable	
favour	favourable*	unfavourable	
forget	forgettable	unforgettable	**practicable**: that can be done in practice, as against in theory
govern	governable	ungovernable	
imagine	imaginable	unimaginable	**reasonable**: (person) sensible; (things, like prices) not too expensive. A person or action that is not subject to reason, or logic, is **irrational**
imitate	*imitable*	*inimitable**	
inhabit	*habitable*	uninhabitable	
manage	manageable*	unmanageable	
move	movable	immovable	**remarkable**: interesting enough for someone to make a remark about it
notice	noticeable		
pass	passable*	*impassable*	**respectable**: (personal) with behaviour acceptable to society; (thing) quite good
permit	*permissible*		
practise	*practicable*	*impracticable**	**responsible**: trustworthy; people are **responsible for** what they do (accountable for their actions) or for people in their care, like children; they are **responsible to** those above them, like employers (having a duty towards them)
prefer	preferable		
reason	reasonable*	unreasonable	
recognise	recognisable	unrecognisable	
remark	remarkable*	unremarkable	
remember	*memorable*		
respect	respectable*		**sensible**: having common sense; **insensible**: unconscious (physically) or unaware (mentally). A person who has/lacks feelings is **sensitive/insensitive**; an action that does not show common sense is **senseless**
respond	*responsible**	*irresponsible*	
sense	*sensible**	*insensible**	
solve	*soluble*	*insoluble*	
think		*unthinkable**	**unthinkable**: too absurd or horrible to be thought about
value	valuable	*invaluable**	**invaluable**: too valuable for its value to be calculated (compare **valueless**, which means 'without value')

4 Verb root: noun endings -ion, -or, adjective ending -ive
(Section 5, Exercise F)
Words given with an asterisk (*) have some variation in meaning from the root. For an explanation of the difference see the NOTES that follow.

root	noun	noun (person)	adjective (-/+)
act	action	actor*	(in)active
affect	*effect*		*(in)effective*
appreciate	appreciation		(un)appreciative
argue	*argument*		*argumentative*
attend	attention		(in)attentive
attract	attraction		(un)attractive
collect	collection	collector	collective*
communicate	communication	communicator	(un)communicative
compare	*comparison*		comparative*
compete	competition	competitor	competitive
conclude	conclusion		(in)conclusive
conserve	conservation		conservative*
construct	construction	constructor	constructive*
co-operate	co-operation		(un)co-operative*
decide	decision		(in)decisive
defend	*defence*	defender	defensive
describe	description		descriptive
expand	expansion		expansive*
explode	explosion		explosive
express	expression		expressive*
extend	extension*		extensive*
imagine	imagination		(un)imaginative
imitate	imitation	imitator	imitative
impress	impression		(un)impressive*
include	inclusion		inclusive
instruct	instruction	instructor	(un)instructive
invent	invention	inventor	inventive*
object	objection	objector	objective*
offend	*offence*	offender	(in)offensive
operate	operation	operator	(in)operative
permit	permission		permissive
possess	possession	possessor	possessive
prevent	prevention		preventive
produce	production	producer	(un)productive
protect	protection	protector	protective
receive	reception		(un)receptive*
reflect	reflection	reflector*	reflective*
represent	representation	*representative*	(un)representative
reproduce	reproduction		reproductive
select	selection	selector	selective
sense	sensation	sensor*	(in)sensitive*
spend	*expense*	spender	(in)expensive*

NOTES:

actor: only used for someone who acts in the cinema or theatre, etc.; the feminine is **actress**

collective: relating to a group acting together or owning something together

comparative: based on or judged by a comparison; grammatically, a form of adjective or adverb like **more**, **bigger**

conserve, conservation: preserve, preservation (often used in connection with ecology); **conservative**, usually political or social, favouring the established order, resistant to change

constructive: helping to develop, not usually related to buildings

co-operative: helpful, as well as done or owned by people working together

expansive: (personal), friendly, willing to talk

expressive: (of a face or words): full of feeling and meaning

extension: a part added (to a building); **extent** indicates size, area; **extensive**: considerable, or covering a large area

impressive: making an impression on others, admirable

inventive: having originality

objective: fair, not prejudiced

receptive: (personal) willing to listen, sympathetic

reflector: not a person but a surface that reflects light, *reflective* (personal) thoughtful

sensation: feeling or state of excitement (adjective: **sensational**: causing excitement); **sensor** is an apparatus to discover the presence of something; **sensitive** (personal): with deep feelings, easily hurt; (thing): fine, measuring exactly or showing reaction to a force or influence

expensive: costing a lot of money, requiring expense

5 Verb root: noun endings *-nce*, *-nt*; adjective ending *-nt*; noun ending *-nce*
(Section 5, Exercise G)

verb root	noun	noun (person)	adjective (-/+)
account	account	accountant	*(un)accountable*
(dis)appear	(dis)appearance		apparent
apply	*application*	applicant	*(un)applicable*
assist	assistance	assistant	
attend	attendance*	attendance	
confide	confidence	*confidant**	confident
correspond	correspondence	correspondent	correspondent
defend	*defence*	*defendant**	*defensive*
depend	(in)dependence	*dependant**	(in)dependent
descend	*descent**	descendant	descendant
differ	difference		(in)different*
exist	existence		existent
hinder	hindrance		
ignore	ignorance		ignorant
inhabit		inhabitant	*(un)inhabited*
insure	insurance	*insurer*	*insured*
interfere	interference		*interfering*
maintain	maintenance		
obey	*obedience*		*obedient*
occupy	*occupation*	occupant	
perform	performance	*performer*	*performing*
please	*pleasure*		(un)pleasant
refer	reference	*referee**	
resist	resistance		resistant
signify	*significance*		*(in)significant*

(b) root	noun
absent	absence
(in)convenient	(in)convenience
distant	distance
evident	evidence
(in)frequent	(in)frequency
(un)important	(un)importance
innocent	innocence
(un)intelligent	intelligence
(im)patient	(im)patience
present	presence
violent	violence

NOTES:

attendance: the number of people present. Compare paying **attention**
confidant: someone you can trust to confide in, with secrets
defendant: person accused in a trial
dependant: a member of the family (economically); **dependent** on someone else
descent: going down; also family origin
indifferent: (personal) not interested in, not caring about
referee: the judge in some sports; also someone who gives a reference for a job

6 Verb root: noun endings *-ment*, *-er*, adjective ending *-ing*
(Section 5 Exercise H)

root	noun	noun (person)	adjective (-/+)
achieve	achievement	achiever	
advertise	advertisement	advertiser	advertising
(dis)agree	(dis)agreement		*(dis)agreeable*
appoint	appointment		
arrange	arrangement		
astonish	astonishment		astonishing/ed
discourage	discouragement		discouraging
encourage	encouragement		encouraging
develop	development	developer	
employ	(un)employment	employer/ee*	*unemployed*
enjoy	enjoyment		
entertain	entertainment	entertainer	entertaining
embarrass	embarrassment		embarrassing/ed
excite	excitement		(un)exciting/ed
govern	government	governor	governing
improve	improvement		improving/ed
judge	judgement	*judge*	
manage	management	manager	managing
measure	measurement		measuring
move	movement		moving
pay	payment	*payee**	paying
punish	punishment		punishing
refresh	refreshment		refreshing
retire	retirement		retiring*
settle	settlement	settler	(un)settling/ed
treat	treatment		

NOTES:

employer: the **employer** employs the **employee**
payee: person to whom money should be paid
retiring: person who is retiring from work or shy, unwilling to come forward

7 Nouns relating to subjects to study, personal nouns and adjectives
(Section 5 Exercise J)

noun (subject)	noun (person)	adjective	NOTES:
analysis	analyst	analytical	**economic:** relating to economy or economics; **economical** making economy, saving money, not expensive
art	artist	*artistic*	
biology	biologist	biological	
chemistry	chemist	chemical	
economics	economist	*economic*, economical*	
electricity	*electrician*	*electric*, electrical*	**electric:** worked by or producing electricity; **electrical** is used more generally for people working in the field or in theory
geography	*geographer*	geographical	
geology	geologist	geological	
geometry		*geometric*, geometrical	**historic:** of historical importance, making history; **historical:** that took place in history
grammar	*grammarian*	grammatical	
history	*historian*	*historic*, historical*	
languages	linguist	*linguistic*	
logic	*logician*	logical	
mathematics	*mathematician*	mathematical	
machines	*mechanic*	mechanical	
medicine	*doctor*	medical	
music	*musician*	musical	
photography	*photographer*	*photographic*	
physics	physicist	physical	
psychology	psychologist	psychological	
science	scientist	*scientific*	

8 Common adjective endings (*-y*, *-al*, *-ous*) derived from nouns

noun	adjective	noun	adjective
addition	additional	profession	professional
(dis)advantage	(dis)advantageous	provision	provisional
ambition	ambitious	price	precious
anger	angry	rain	rainy
anxiety	anxious	religion	religious
artifice	artificial	residence	residential
benefit	beneficial	sensation	sensational
caution	cautious	sleep	sleepy
cloud	cloudy	stone	stony
commerce	commercial	storm	stormy
continent	continental	sun	sunny
crime	criminal	suspicion	suspicious
curiosity	curious	thirst	thirsty
danger	dangerous	tradition	traditional
disaster	disastrous	water	watery
emotion	emotional	wealth	wealthy
experiment	experimental	weight	weighty
fate	fatal		
finance	financial		
fog	foggy		
formality	formal		
frost	frosty		
fun	funny		
generosity	generous		
glory	glorious		
grass	grassy		
guilt	guilty		
happiness	happy		
health	healthy		
hill	hilly		
horizon	horizontal		
humour	humorous		
hunger	hungry		
ice	icy		
industry	industrial		
infection	infectious		
influence	influential		
instrument	instrumental		
intention	intentional		
luck	lucky		
mist	misty		
mountain	mountainous		
mud	muddy		
mystery	mysterious		
nation	national		
nature	natural		
nerves	nervous		
noise	noisy		
number	numerous		
occasion	occasional		
occupation	occupational		
origin	original		
ornament	ornamental		
person	personal		
poison	poisonous		